The Uffington White Horse in Oxfordshire is the oldest of a variety of figures carved out of English hillside turf to reveal underlying chalk or limestone.

110m [360 feet] long, it sits alongside the ancient Icknield Way and looks across the valley of the River Thames. It was carved by Celts over 2000 years ago beneath the Uffington Castle hill fort site close to small ceremonial-use hilltops.

The even older Waylands Smithylong barrow estimated at over 5000 years old is nearby.

Graceful, powerful and energetic, the White Horse continues to command attention and interest.

*

The Vale of White Horse is a local government district of Oxfordshire.

Quakers
in the
Vale of White Horse
and Pennsylvania

for Jean

James oldest and best friend
in loving memory of happy times.

All love —
Alan

Quakers
in the
Vale of White Horse
and Pennsylvania

Janet I Rothery

Quakers in the Vale of White Horse

CONTENTS

Page

ILLUSTRATIONS

Page

Colour photographs [circa 2000] and artwork by Janet Rothery except where acknowledged in the text.

ACKNOWLEDGEMENTS

I wish to thank everyone who has helped me to gather this material together. The Faringdon Friends helped me with information about the later years and shared their experiences. Witney Monthly Meeting allowed me to quote freely from the Quaker material in the Oxfordshire Archives and elsewhere. I wish to thank the staff of Friends House Library, of Woodbrooke Library, Charney Library, Abingdon Library, Oxford Library, Witney Library and Reading library. Also I am grateful for the information received from Haverford Library Pennsylvania. I thank the many other institutions that helped me with information and these I list under Sources at the end of the book.

I have tried to contact all copyright holders of quoted material to get their permission to do so, but there are one or two cases where this has not been possible and I shall be glad to remedy this situation if they can let me know. I am very grateful to be able to use material from the *Book of Discipline of Britain Yearly Meeting* other books and pamphlets that were published by central committees of the Society of Friends. In all cases I do give references either in notes at the end of chapters or in the Bibliography at the end of the book.

I would like to thank the Farrand Press for allowing me to quote from the book *George Fox 1624-1691 Our living contemporary.* Also I wish to thank Sessions of York for allowing me to quote from their book *Charlbury of our Childhood.* I wish to thank THE FRIEND for allowing me to use their 1952 cover picture. Also Palgrave Macmillan at Oliphant Publicity Saint Martin's Press for permitting the printing of the map on page 28 of Barry Reay's book 'The Quakers and the English Revolution' © Barry Reay et al.I am grateful for permission granted by Curlew Graphics 'Quakerism in Britain, a century of change 1885 - 1995' Alastair Heron.

There are so many individuals to thank. The late Jean Pocock who inherited The Farmhouse in Faringdon and had so much wonderful material to show me about the family and so many first hand stories to share. I wish to thank her family who also allowed me to look at family correspondence, pictures and other valuable material. So many people also helped in their different ways and I wish to thank them all: Jack Bungey, Mrs Milly Bryan, Mrs Church, Janie Cottis, David Saunderson, Robert Dyer, Rev John Lockey, Edward Milligan, Nancy Reeves, the late Sylvia Ross, Edward Thatcher of Oregon, Mrs Wickens, Karen Garvey (Oxfordshire Archives), William Sessions and his editors, and everyone else who helped in editing and in giving advice which I fear I did not always manage to follow.

I am especially grateful to my husband Alan who has tirelessly encouraged me to persevere and who has edited and dealt with the layout of the text and the scanning of the pictorial material. He has made it possible for me to complete the task.

                                          Janet Rothery
                                          [Louth, 2004]

INTRODUCTION

This is a story about a Quaker Community as it grew and flourished in the early periods of the movement. Also of how, later on, the strength fluctuated. Sometimes the meetings ticked over, and sometimes they disappeared altogether for one reason and another. Sometimes the Vale Quakers were at the forefront of national Quaker activity and witnessed at home and abroad. At other times it is hard to decide whether they were part of the Quaker movement at all. What does become clear is that there have been Dissenting groups in the area for at least four hundred years and a Quaker presence since the sixteen-fifties.

The Farmhouse in Faringdon where the Reynolds's lived. [Grade II listed late C16[th] early C17[th]. Timber framed, small portion remains in centre two bays; rest clad in limestone rubble. Addition of outer C18[th] staircase.]

I decided to write this book when 1 discovered that there was the possibility of following the Quaker experiences of the Reynolds family right through from the beginning of the seventeenth century up to the mid-twentieth century. One thing led to another and,.although I have done what I set out to do, I have also written the History of the Quaker movement itself in the Vale of White Horse. I have found this exercise of following up clues and trying to fill gaps, absolutely fascinating, and only wish that I had been trained to do historical research before I felt impelled to embark on it.

Sometimes I have failed to record the source of an item of information because I neglected to make a note of it at the time I recorded it. I hope that I have not taken material as my own that is not mine, certainly I have not knowingly done so. This is therefore not an academic piece, but a record of Quakers in the Vale in which material has been collected into some kind of a whole. Wherever possible I have noted the source either under the quotation or at the end of the chapter concerned. A bibliography is also included at the end.

The backbone of the story is based on archival evidence wherever possible and leaps of imagination elsewhere. I am indebted to the people still living in the Vale for the information and anecdote that colour the material. Also I offer thanks to the Quaker Historians, dead and alive, who have provided background and facts. Not least 1 have to thank the Members and Attenders of Faringdon Meeting who have helped me with comment and encouragement.

I am hopeful that as the manuscript is more widely read some of my leaps of imagination about the reasons for the Quaker movement passing through its various vicissitudes in the way it has done in the Vale of White Horse will be challenged or supported with more concrete information, so that we can arrive at a more complete story.

A final warning, or rather encouragement: do not assume that you have no Quaker ancestors because you have never heard of any, or because there is now no Quaker meeting in your family's village. Despite persecution, Quakers probably formed a much larger proportion of the population in the later 17th century than they do today. [1]

NOTES

[1.] COTTIS (Janie*), Quaker Records for Oxfordshire FamilyHistorians*
Journal of Oxfordshire Family History Society Vol. 5, No 7, p291,1991.

CHAPTER ONE

THE VALLEY BETWEEN

The spirit of man is the candle of the Lord. [Proverbs 20.27]

Blackthorn on the Downs looking across the Vale and the **River Ock**

This area was until 1974 part of the county of Berkshire, set between the high chalk downlands of the Neolithic White Horse Hills, the Lambourne Downs, in the south and the red sandstone, greenstone, ridge to the north, and to the Upper Thames valley beyond. The clay vale mainly drained by the river Ock is the area where the first Quaker yeoman farmers lived. The main markets were Faringdon and Wantage, with Stanford-in-the-Vale also, a local, smaller market centre. On the edge of the area was the County market town of Abingdon. The Downs were and are rich grain belts, also noted for sheep, wool and lamb. The red sandstone areas down to the Thames were and are well suited to the dairy industry, cheese and butter, which used to be shipped down the river to Oxford and London from

Radcott. Cheese was a taxable commodity and several thousand tons of it were transported to London annually. It was similar to Gloucester cheese but with local variations. A farm near Buscot produced `pineapple' cheese, so called because of the markings made by the mesh of nets in which it dried. At Stanford-in-the-Vale the local cheese was shaped like a hare and flavoured with sage.

Blossom near East Hanney

This is a beautiful place even today. The Vale is still quite well wooded, at least in some parts, and the Downs rise up blue and golden or silver as season and light dictate. The vernacular architecture varies according to the material at hand. This being a geological jigsaw so the buildings vary. Some houses are of local stone, some built of imported Cotswold stone. Others are heavily timbered with brick or wattle and daub. Brick works were scattered about so many buildings are brick. Most houses are a delightful mixture of materials.

Much of the valley parts around Stanford, Shellingford and Goosey are very wet being composed of Kimmeridge clay, in early days too sticky and weighty for ploughing with oxen or horses. So this valley floor area was mainly dairying, though wheat and vegetables were grown in large open fields near the settlements for subsistence. Marginal low lying land was for grazing and wild birds. This area was drained mainly by the farmers themselves in the eighteenth century, about the time when the North Wiltshire and Berkshire canal was constructed. Even today if we get heavy rain the valley is liable to flood. Often too, damp mists hang over the fields and trees and the Downs rise up above in undulating bumps and lines. It can all look very Chinese, on a misty morning, with the higher trees and hills floating out of the mist.

A thatched cottage in Uffington opposite the 'new' Meeting House suggests meeting house was originally thatched too.

Now the Vale is part of Oxfordshire, but it has always had this rather isolated feature. It is far from the county centres of Oxford, Gloucester, Reading and Salisbury and one can see why the Vale people could and did develop an independent character. This has had positive and negative results depending on the circumstances of the times - but certainly in my story it was one of the factors that perhaps enabled Nonconformism to flourish in the early days. Later when most Quakers were no longer farmers this was not the place for them to live and indeed they moved away. So Quakerisrn nearly died in the Vale.

Hiinton [I was told that the Hinton family were Wiltshire Quakers but I could not substantiate this.]

Nevertheless although a family could live in an isolated hamlet or farm and get away with doing their own thing, yet the little towns were busy. The east-west routes on the chalk and sandstone, and the north-south routes across the river Thames, a ford at Lechlade and the bridge at Radcott served to bring trade and new ideas into the area. The River Thames led to the Port of London and thence to Europe and the outside world. Gossip and stories of new ways could travel into the Vale via the traders and boatmen.

Christianity spread westward in the sixth century and Dorchester-on-Thames became one of the first Bishoprics. Its church was a Cathedral and smaller churches were built all around the area. Most of these are still in use today. In 849 Alfred was born in Wantage and succeeded his brother as King, thus ruling Wessex. In marrying into the ruling family of Mercia he virtually became King of all England. Later when the Normans came they took over much of the best Vale land and in fact even in the seventeenth century a few old families held most land and wielded most power.

A view of the Vale from the Downs

There are some large Estates even today - at Kingston Lisle, Buckland, Pewsey, Buscot, Coleshill and Faringdon to name a few. These flourished during the period of the Agrarian revolution, when land was enclosed. Some very fine large houses were built or extended at about this time. Nevertheless at some stage during the sixteenth and seventeenth centuries some land was sold and independence given to yeoman farmers, some of whom seem to have accumulated land and wealth in the latter part of the seventeenth century.

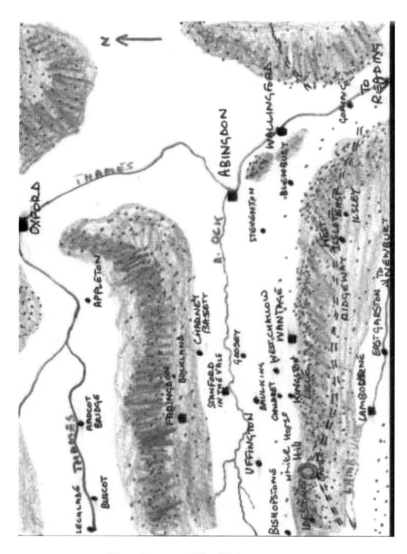

Sketch map – The Vale

Looking up to the Downs from near Uffington

I am a lamp to thee who beholdest Me;
I am a Mirror to thee who perceivest Me;
I am the Door to thee who knockest at Me;
I am a Way to thee a wayfarer

An early Christian hymn

Perhaps well-known and sung by all who attended Christian Churches in the Vale all those centuries ago, this little hymn has a most Quakerly tone to it. I think that the story of Quakerism has always been a mixture of the Quaker group intertwined with the background of the general culture within which it lives. This isthe best balance because it enables Quakers to be useful within their wider community and yet to remain faithful to their way. It is a balance that has through the ages not always been possible to fulfil either because the wider community was not tolerant or because the Quakers themselves did not see the need for it.

CHAPTER TWO

Part I: THE BEGINNINGS

'..I saw the infinite love of God. I saw also that there was an ocean of darkness anddeaths but an infinite ocean of light and love, which flowed over the ocean of darkness. And in that also I saw the infinite love of God; and I had great openings.' [George Fox]

One wonders how it came about that there were enough Quakers in Faringdon, Uffington, West Challow and Blewbury to build four meeting houses, probably even before the Toleration Act of 1689. Quakerism wasn't a movement or sect before 1652. We shall never quite know the answer because it happened in response to so many influences. First the groups gathered in their own homes and in barns to worship as Quakers and by the 1660's they had become the Vale Monthly Meeting with local regular Meetings for worship and business. Soon after, they procured land and money and built their Meeting Houses.

The Lollards had arrived in England from the continent in the fourteenth century and being closely linked to the highly mobile cloth and wool trade they were strongest in the Thames valley, the Chilterns, East Anglia, Kent, Bristol, London. Some of the themes of Lollardism anticipate those of Protestant radicals, such as Quakers. They were hostile to the magic and ceremony of the Roman Catholic Church. They rejected sacramental or priestly intermediaries saying that God was in direct relationship with his worshipper. They taught that holy bread and holy water had no special properties, and that Christ's physical body was not present at the altar. They did think that Christ's Spirit was a living light and strength, available to all who were ready to accept it. They felt certain that God alone could forgive and remit sins and that all the tradition around Confession through priests and the payments communicants could give for forgiveness was false and not of the teaching of Christ.

From at least the fifteenth century the Bible had come to the English people translated into English. At last the literate could read it and grasp the richness of meaning for themselves. The Wyclif Bible was the first, probably circulating in English ecclesiastical circles from the early fourteenth century. Parts of it were possibly coming into use in free thinking homes by the fifteenth century and certainly in the sixteenth century. The Tyndale Bible, using Erasmus as an authority, was printed and was passed around and used by nonconformists widely from 1534, especially the later Great Bible that Coverdale brought out. So it is certain that, in the hamlets of the Vale, horizons of theological interest were widened and for some the priest was no longer the fountain of all knowledge. Education became important to the farmers andCraftsmen. They wanted to read *The Good Book* for themselves and so itinerant tutors travelled round and later stayed in better-off homes, and children were taught to read and write and listened to their elders discussing the Bible and its wider meanings. These working people felt the urgency of the times and the importance of fulfilling the teachings of Jesus in their daily lives.

Scientific theories of the fifteenth and sixteenth centuries had changed the view of a mediaeval world picture. This picture of God, Christ, Angels and archangels up in the heavens, and of mankind led by a chosen few in the middle, and of Hell below a flat Earth, for many, and particularly for free thinkers, was seen as a structure of creation that was physically not so. Some began to realise that the Earth revolved round the sun and so Heaven and Hell were in need of restructuring to make sense. The idea that our political action held cosmic repercussions was becoming at least questionable and for some unacceptable. Quite a few people began to look at human institutions such as Monarchy, Church and Parliament objectively and began to question whether in fact they were under God's guidance and able to bring about God's Kingdom on Earth. Certainly such institutions seemed unaware of the Ten Commandments as was only too clear to any with knowledge of the moral behaviour of the times. There are plenty of examples of the lack of moral standards in the working of human institutions during the sixteenth, seventeenth and eighteenth centuries in, for example, Shakespeare, Pepys and Goldsmith to illustrate the rather dreadful situation of those times. Too many establishment figures did not appear to follow New Testament teachings about honesty, simplicity and respect for one another.

So it came about that independent thinkers felt that each person should be a tool of the Spirit and be individually and directly in communion with God. They should each be responsible for their own soul and conscience, and work to uphold each other in these principles. They felt that they were Disciples of Christ, *fighting the lamb's war* as George Fox, the Quaker founder, liked to put it, and thus they were impelled to be questioners, criticisers and active participators in creating a *Righteous Kingdom*.

Certainly George Fox had works written by the continental mystic Jacob Boeheme in his collection of books and this tradition was reconsidered at the time:

Every man's life is inwardly bottomless and opens from within into all theimmeasurable depth of God. Eternity springs through time and reveals itself in every person, for the foundation property of the soul of every man is essentially eternal, spiritual and abysmal - it is a little drop out of the fountain of the life of God, it is a little sparkle of the Divine splendour. There is only one place to look for God, and that is your own soul. We should take heed and begat that which is good out of ourselves. If we make an angel of ourselves we are that:if we make a devil of ourselves we are that....God's presence itself is heaven, and if God did but put away the veiling shadows, which now curtain thy sight, thou wouldest see, even where thou now art, the Face of God, the heavenly gate. [2]

Another development throughout these times and very much in the seventeenth century period was that, in effect, the industrial and technical revolution had begun. You did not just follow what had happened for generations blindly. The population was growing and towns and cities were getting more prosperous and things were beginning imperceptibly to speed up. This was especially obvious to the artisans and craftsmen of the time, the very people who traded and had opportunity to share the new knowledge to improve the lot of mankind. These were the practical application of technical problems, and discussion about social needs and changes of a political nature to bring this about. People were not prepared to accept the old order of King, church and land owner getting a disproportionate share of the wealth. The Levellers were perhaps a spent force by the time George Fox was gathering his Seekers together, but their ideas were not to die. Some Quakers had been Levellers and many felt that too few were owning and wasting too much.

The poorest he that is in England hath a life to live as the greatest he, and therefore… every man that is to live under government ought first by his own consent to put himself under that government. [3]

Of course this feeling, of holding themselves to be of some material and spiritual worth, that these Seekers after Truth had, involved theological discussion of new ideas about how to worship God and what Christ really meant in his teachings and example. What did the New Testament really mean for the day? It led some to re- think their ideas about the place of the Bible in worship and about the best way of being open to the Spirit of God. This was Dissension with a capital `D' from the `Established Church' view. It led to various groups seeking a new, reasonable direct relationship with God. Out of some of these groups the *Children of Light* and/or the *Quakers* came into being in about 1652.

Anabaptists were around in the Vale too with some Lollardian ideas. The custom of adult Baptism was their special teaching. It is quite possible that they were of the non-Calvinist sort and taught the doctrine of General Redemption, that all could achieve salvation. They tended to be involved in trades and crafts. There are entries in the Faringdon church records of both Anabaptists and Quakers being buried in the seventeenth century. The vicar possibly had entries in his records of Baptism either as Protestant Anglicans or Anabaptists and therefore felt these particular individuals could have a decent burial in `his' consecrated ground. Theremust have been many who started life as Anglicans or Anabaptists or Lollards, or even as Roman Catholics, perhaps, who in later life changed to become Baptists or Quakers. Families were mixed too, some remaining faithful to the faith of their parents and family, and some becoming independent and striking out as seekers into an exciting and creative new covenant with God. Early Quakers certainly thought they were experiencing and replicating the early Christian movement of the first century, the simplicity of the gatherings that Jesus and his Disciples led on hillsides and in ordinary homes.

In the Parish registers the following who possibly later became Quakers were baptised. 1 say possibly, because with families constantly calling the next generation by the same Christian name it is difficult to know in Quaker minutes which member of a family is present. Is it the father or the son, both of the same name or the mother or the daughter? Is an Aunt a member and not a sister? This problem continues to be a complication right into the Victorian period and leaves one guessing far too many times.

Entries in the Faringdon Parish Register:
Baptisms
1589 Mary Reynolds, daughter of Thomas Reynolds
1616 Thomas Reynolds
1618 Marye Reynolds
1620 Jone Vokens
1621 AnnieReynolds
1621 Anne Collier

Burials
1678 Thomas Whitwick
1679 John Whitwick
1679 Daniall Bunce's child
1683 Widow Langley
1696 Richard Vokens

In 1641 there were, according to Christopher Hill, eight Baptist churches in England; yet by 1660 there were two hundred and ninety seven. At least three of these were in the Vale: Abingdon 1652, Faringdon 1657 and Wantage 1648. In his book *History of the Baptist Church in Abingdon,* May 1895, Thomas Pumphrey states that Faringdon Baptist Community started in 1572. However the official date according to the present Baptist research for the Faringdon Baptist church is 1657, certainly before a Quaker Meeting House was built. There were no Quakers, as such, in 1640 and no Quaker Meeting Houses, but by 1660 there were hundreds of meeting places up and down the land, some in the Vale. Often the place used was someone's home or barn. By 1660, though, the movement was widespread with Quakers in all counties and especially strong in the North, Yorkshire and Westmoreland, in London and the counties north of London, in Bristol, Somerset and Wiltshire and in Warwickshire, Gloucestershire and Worcestershire. By 1668 when written minutes were kept there are references to Meeting Houses in all areas, and in the Vale too.

If you think about it, many of the routes in and through The Vale of White Horse connect with the strong Quaker areas mentioned above and with the woollen trade with which many of the first Quaker yeoman were involved. It was natural that a network of ideas, dissenting ideas, circulated amidst these peoples. Quakerism was swept into an already spiritually fertileand thirsting people. Soon they knew who they were and became *The Seekers after Truth*.

> *Nor would the Quaker movement have spread as rapidly as it did had there not been a multitude who discovered that they had been travelling on similar spiritual journeys and whose fellowship was warmer and more lasting as they found that they were not alone on those journeys.* [5]

William Laud, Archbishop of Canterbury under Charles I and before that, an influence in James I time, may well have held church and state together and founded a new order for the established church.

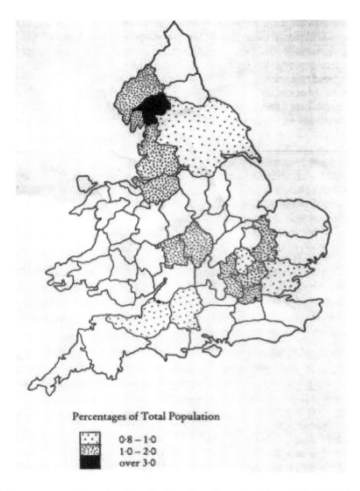

Percentages of Total Population

0·8 – 1·0	
1·0 – 2·0	
over 3·0	

Major areas of Quakerism in England and Wales 1654-64' from
Barry Reay's book *TheQuakers and the English Revolution.*[4]

The King James edition of the Bible is still well loved and Laud's Prayer Book a basis of the liturgy used in the established Anglican Church today. He swung liturgy away from fundamental Protestantism and reintroduced a more catholic rhythm to the church calendar and worship. Nonconformists and Protestants, especially the Scottish Presbyterians, were suspicious of Archbishop Laud and disliked the things that were happening. They thought he might be shifting the established church back into the Roman Catholic fold, certainly the Vatican wished England and Scotland to be united again with the *One True Church*. Also some felt that these reforms were opening the door once again for abuses of 'pure' Christianity or leading it away from the `purity' of Primitive Christianity and that the discredited aspects of the Church were creeping back. Those of a Puritan turn of mind were suspicious. The *Seekers after Truth* people were suspicious too.

Archbishop Laud needed revenue to revitalise his `church' and this had traditionally been through the tithe system. This system particularly irritated Yeoman farmers, and Craftsmen; sometimes the very ones who were Seekers. In fact Nonconformists objected to the system. None were to suffer more than the Quakers for this principle that *the church* should not have revenue and goods from those who did not worship there.

The question of tithes was potentially the most revolutionary issue of the English Civil War, because it could unite the economic grievances of the mass of small farmers with the religious programme of the separatists.[6]

An established church stood and fell by the tithes and later a loosening of the system went hand in hand with religious toleration. But time and time again during the seventeenth and eighteenth centuries the church stood firm and felt it spiritually right to penalise those who refused to pay. Certainly as we shall see the Vale Quakers seemed to get more than their fair share of punishment from the church, and from those who enforced the law of the land. They felt that as they did not worship in the *steeplehouse* and did not hold with a priesthood then they had no obligation in the Kingdom of God to pay tithes to the establishment.

To force our consciences that Christ set free, and rule us with classichierarchy, so that men whose life, learning, faith and pure intent would have been held in high esteem with Paul, must now he named and printed Hereticks by shallow, Edwards and Scotch and

28

what d'ye call...[7]

The hungry sheep look up and are not fed ..[8]

John Milton left London during the plague time and settled in Jordans, Buckinghamshire, where a Quaker meeting was in full flowering under the Penington family. He made friends with the newly convinced Thomas Ellwood. Thomas Ellwood published his own journal and *the journal of George Fox*. Milton wrote Paradise Lost at this time and Ellwood is reputed to have suggested Milton should now write *Paradise Regained*.

In fact Heretic is quite a reasonable thing to be. It comes from a Greek word meaning *one who chooses* hence heresy means choice. A heretic is one who chooses their own creed under God's guidance instead of agreeing to accept one imposed by human authority. With Quakers it was and is today a choice they gladly make. They chose not to have any creed because they felt that putting such important matters into words was stepping on holy ground, and as Seekers any verbalised rules seemed too limiting and even misleading, bound as words are by the human language. As Isaac Penington wrote:

The end of words is to bring men to the knowledge of things beyond what words can utter. So learn of the Lord to make a right use of the Scriptures: which is by esteeming them in their right place and prizing that above them which is above them.[9]

There was a feeling in some non-conformist circles of the time that the Nicene Creed, decided in AD 374 and said in Latin, was not really understood by many who recited it. It was as if the mere saying of it was the commitment to God and a protection from the Devil. Some other ceremonies, such as Baptism and Holy Communion, were criticised and even thought to be unnecessary, thought to be a misunderstanding of Christ's teaching. Seekers really believed that they should seek the Truth for themselves. They felt that the `steeplehouses' were giving second hand and false notions of religion to their flocks whereas they themselves were seeking the purity of God in Spirit and waiting for Christ to come into their midst. They felt thatChrist did come into their midst if they waited patiently in silent prayer and that then the spiritual guidance given was suitable for them and out of Christ's direct love for them. It was fresh for them, alive and contemporary.

By the middle part of the seventeenth century the Friends or Quakers as they had, by then become, assembled for worship and waited upon God. They felt words, music and symbols were man-made interventions that impeded a right relationship with God, and that they should gather and await God's guidance and teaching calmly, silently, in stillness. This Meeting for Worship was to be a time of turning away from their personal thoughts and for suspending the imagination in order to feel the presence of the Lord, which they often referred to as the `light'.

The first that enters into the place of your meeting, be not careless, nor wander up and down either in body or mind, but innocently sit down in some place and turn in thy mind to the light, and wait upon God singly, as if none were present but the Lord, and here thou art strong. Then the next that comes in, let them in simplicity of heart sit down and turn in to the same light, and wait in the spirit, and so all the rest coming in the fear of the Lord sit down in pure stillness and silence in all flesh, and wait in the light. A few that are thus gathered by the arm of the Lord into unity of the spirit this is a sweet precious meeting, where all meet with the Lord...Those who are brought to a pure, still waiting upon God in the spirit are come nearer to the Lord than words are.. .though not a word be spoken to the hearer of the outward ear.[10]

George Fox wrote the following in his Journal:

So I opened to the people that the ground and house was no holier than another place, and that the house was not the church, but the people which Christ is Head of...[11]

In the end both Archbishop Laud, in 1644, and Charles I, in 1649, were beheaded. The bloody battles fought in and near the Vale of White Horse and elsewhere during the Civil War were also over.

Many of the yeoman farmers, the Separatists and others must have fought in those armies mainly on the Roundhead side. The Long Parliament era under Cromwell, to begin with, at any rate, enabled them to worship in their own way. This was the time of Quaker consolidation meeting in each other's homes, in barns and listening to preachers from the north. By the time even the Parliamentarians were concerned to stop these Quakers it was too late. The spiritual fervour had taken hold and George Fox and others were travelling about from county to county, gathering the Seekers together. This had become a `church of people'.

Quaker meetings for worship were being held all over the Vale. In Faringdon, Uffington, West Challow, Appleton, Blewbury, Bishopstone, in homes and barns and in the open air. Even the Cromwellian government and certainly the Restoration government sought to counter `these wayward peoples 'by introducing Act after Act to stop the movement in its tracks, so those punished ones, facing hardship for their principles, consolidated both spiritually and socially. These new Acts and regulations were not especially all directed at the Quakers but at all the different sects that sprouted up at this time and also at Roman Catholics. Many officials confused or chose to confuse one sect with another and even accused some Quaker preachers of being secret Jesuits. The Government aim was to prove that a `peoples' government' could bring about law and order as well as a *King's government.*

We are utterly out of hopes of this party or the other party, for we know whatsoever men profess, they cannot rule for God in our nation till that themselves be reformed and ruled by him... And we are not for names, nor men, nor titles of Government, but we are for justice and mercy and truth and peace and true freedom, that these things may be exalted in our nation [12]

Edward Burrough, a Quaker, expressed these words in the troubled times between the death of Cromwell and the Restoration of the monarchy. This was the Quaker view of toleration. It needs to be held to today, but sadly is being over-shadowed by political agendas which most certainly do not have a spiritual basis.

NOTES

Part 1: The Beginnings

[1.]FOX (George), *The Journal of George Fox*, text prepared by Thomas Ellwood 1694,edited by John Nickalls and revised in 1952, p19. When George Fox was inNottinghamshire.Cambridge University Press 1952.

[2.] BOEME(Jacob), quoted by Dr Alexander Whvte *Jacob Behem.. .An Appreciation* p/3 1894.

[3.] HILL (Christopher),*The Century of Revolution 1603-17/4*, p110 as being said byColonel Rainborough in the Putney debates.

[4.] REAY (Barry*), The Quakers and the English Revolution*, P28, St Martin's Press 1985.

[5.] MILLIGAN (Edward H.), *George Fox: the seventeenth century background, p14,George Fox, 1624-1691, our living contemporary'*, Farrand Press 1992.

[6.] MANNING B., *The English people and the English Revolution*, Penguin

[7.] MILTON (John) *Lycidus v125*.

[8.] MILTON (John) *On the new forces of conscience under the Long Parliament*.

[9.] PENINGTON (Isaac), *letters of Isaac Penington* edited by John Barclay,1 828 p39-40 3rd edition 1844, letter undated, Quaker Faith and Practice,1995, 27.27.

[10.] PARKER (Alexander), *Quaker Faith and Practice*, 1995, 2.41, a letter l4xi of1660.

[11.] FOX (George), as (I) above, outside Sedburgh church, 1652.

[12.] BURROUGH (Edward), *Quaker Faith and Practice*, 23.11, To the distracted andbroken nation 1659, The memorable works of a son of thunder l672, part II p604.

CHAPTER TWO

Part II:
THE SUFFERINGS

Love is the hardest lesson in Christianity; but, for that reason, it should be most our care to learn it. [13]

I think it is useful for the reader to have a brief summary of the legislation that affected Quakers and that also, in the long run, channelled the movement in certain directions, especially the Separatism that marked the Quakers in this country and in America during the eighteenth century. They had not particularly wanted such a thing to happen. Whilst being somewhat over-evangelical and enthusiastic about their faith yet they sought freedom for all to worship in the way they wished. They were prepared to suffer in the name of the Lord and they did. Their non- compliance with the laws of the land were punishable offences, sometimes by either removal of animals or goods, *distraint,* or by fines, ducking or flogging. In New England, then still an English colony, Quakers and others were very severely punished. Some were punished with death, such as hanging or certain death when left in the stocks during winter. In both the old and new world many Quakers were imprisoned and often in terrible conditions. Very often the punishment for ignoring the law was a combinationof several of these things. Children were also involved and some Quakers sold as slaves.

Quakers had hoped for a better time when Charles II became King in 1660 as he had promised `*a liberty to tender consciences'* under the declaration of Breda. However the new King did not manage to control the actions of his militia or judiciary and Quakers continued to be harangued and punished. The authorities were still frightened that these dissident groups were a threat to stability in the land. One such group to cause trouble was The Fifth Monarchist people, who felt that the prophecy of Daniel was to be fulfilled in their time. They terrorised London and took it over for a few days. In the wake of the abortive Fifth Monarchist upheavals, which had nothing to do with Quakers, the authorities had an excuse to blame them and others. They were taken out of meetings, out of their houses, from their places ofWork and from the streets and by March some 4,230 Friends were in prison, according to some estimates.

If the King would authorise me to do it, I would not leave a Quaker alive in England.. .an Oxford Deputy-Lieutenant told Thomas Ellwood [14]

The Cart and Whip Act of 1661 and *The Quaker Act* of 1662, both led to incredible sufferings for Friends. Men and women were sentenced to be stripped to the waist andwhipped at the cart's tail through one town after another until they reached the limits of the jurisdiction. This was in winter as well as summer. A really barbarous law that to this day makes me suffer mentally and makes me feel bitter towards the sort of regime that can judge, condemn and punish in such ways. It was cruel and not of a Christian nature. Yet the Church fully backed all of these legislations and was actively involved in reporting Quakers to Justices.

As we shall see, Vale Quakers were to suffer very greatly under this legislation, some of it a re-hash of earlier Elizabethan and Anti-Catholic Laws, and some of it hurriedly passed to deal with a perceived emergency. The Quakers themselves felt that they were truly following Christ's teachings and upholding the testimonies of the Holy Scriptures. They believed that they were fulfilling their Christian duty in disobeying these laws. They couldn't help themselves and inevitably they were punished for breaking the laws of the land.

The following were some of the laws of the land that Quakers and other dissenters, such as Baptists, felt God expected them to break. They held the Law of God to be sacred and were later respected for their integrity and steadfastness. The Quakers especially were very open about their disobedience and were therefore an easy target for the Constables and Justices. They did not meet in secret for worship, or travel about in disguise.

Non-attendance of the local state Church on Sundays and holy days and therefore in *nottaking Holy Communion* were all punishable offences. Quakers felt they were doing God-like and spiritual worship in their own meetings where they waited in stillness to be moved by God and did not wish to have planned worship controlled by a priest. They wished to conduct their own weddings and burials under the spirit of waiting in silence and simplicity. So Church authorities lost revenue from collections and payments for services if Quaker people were not involved. Altogether the Church disliked these heretics who set a bad example and who they felt should pay their dues as had always been the custom.

Non-payment of church (steeplehouse), rates or tithes was punishable. Quakers felt that they should not have to give financial support to the church which they did not attend. They had the upkeep of their own buildings and congregations to see to. Also morally they felt that God did not wish them to support works that `He' did not approve of. They also felt that the many clergymen lived too well and selfishly off the fat of the land.

Quite an amount of legislation was brought in to counter the non-conformist habit of *travelling about and of holding meetings and evangelising* in market squares and in the fields and commons. Praying or preaching in public became an offence that Quakers were bound to break. They called their preaching *Publishing the Truth* and to begin with there was nowhere else to be moved to minister the `Word' except in fields and open squares. And the wild enthusiasm of the early days included a compulsion to share the good news that *God's light shone for all and could be experienced inwardly.*

Attendance at a dissenting religious gathering itself became an offence even if conducted inside a building and with order and quietness. As Meeting for Worship was the arena for Quaker worship and Quakers felt impelled to meet and worship in their chosen way openly and devoutly and regularly, they were in for trouble.

Quakers also were against the custom of *taking off their hats* as a homage to mankind, they only took them off for God. So they were punished by Judges and Justices for this lack of obeisance. There was an element of the Leveller in all this stance.

Language also was a problem as Quakers insisted in addressing all by familiar terms *thee* and *thou* and refused to use legal and formal language when addressing judges and gentry. All were equal before God. This could be held against them in court as showing lack of respect and was punishable.

Robert Barclay became a convinced Quaker in 1666 and his writings became very influential in Quaker circles. His *Apology* written in Latin was published in 1676. He could by then base his thoughts on knowledge of the sufferings that Quakers had undergone. He was able to put very clearly the thoughts of the Quakers and explain why they stood firmly to their principles of faith. The following passage is translated into modern English:

First we have no intention of destroying the mutual relationship that exists between prince and people, masters and servants, or between parents andchildren. On the contrary, we will show how these natural relationships become better established by our beliefs, rather than harmed. Next let no one conclude that men must have all things in common because of these beliefs, or that any levelling will necessarily follow. Our principles allow every man to enjoy peaceably whatever his own industry or that of his parents have purchased for him. His only instruction is that he use it properly for his own good, for that of his brethren, and to the glory of God. 15

In 1662 *The Quaker Act* was passed amongst other legislation, in which Quakers became liable to punishment if they assembled for worship in numbers of more than five. Further penalties were also introduced for both the refusal to take oaths and for those who maintained in public that the taking of oaths was unlawful. At this time the *Act of Uniformity* was passed and this restored the Prayer Book and regularised public worship. Soon Quakers all over the country were suffering for their Quaker beliefs and practices.

All the above legislation was strengthened in 1664 when Parliament met to consider non-conformity in the land. All Puritan sects were brought under suspicion by a Northern plot. Barry Reay in his book `The Quakers and the English Revolution p109 -110'is clear that in fact some Quakers were involved in plotting an uprising against Charles II in 1663. Quakers were not at that time especially all pacifists and some were not happy about the return of the monarchy. They could see all the old royalist powers returning and they were not happy with the prospect of monarchy overturning the freedoms so hardly won during the Civil War. The promises of Breda were not being carried out. Most Quakers by the 1660's were more concerned with their spiritual life than with political intrigue and the above mentioned legislation was well beyond what was needed to deal, with law and order in the land. It wasbrought in by the power of the establishment, which included the Church'. There was a wish to quash Quakerism and its independent spirit. There was ignorance about the movement.

The liberty we claim is that of the primitive church justifiably sought under pagan emperors. It is the liberty of men of sobriety, honesty, and peaceable conduct to enjoy the freedom and exercise their conscience toward God and among themselves. It is the right to be unmolested by the civil authorities forreceiving among them those who become convinced of the same truth by their persuasion and influence.[16]

So in July of 1664 *The Conventicle Act* came into force. It made it an offence for more than five persons, over the age of sixteen and other than a household, to meet at a conventicler or religious meeting in any other manner than that allowed by the liturgy of the church. Later *the five-mile Act* was introduced, which prevented ministers from teaching or even living within five miles of any corporate or parliamentary borough unless they swore never to attempt any alteration in Government, Church or State. Breaking these laws could lead to being transported to work on plantations in the American colonies, except Virginia and New England. In Fact sympathetic jurors were reluctant to convict Quakers and other Puritans to transportation and the shipmasters were reluctant to take on board `freeborn' Englishmen for transportation. The following incident illustrates this:

When 55 Quakers were brought down to Bugby's hole, Greenwich to be so transhipped from Newgate prison in 1665, but they maintained their innocence by passive resistance and the tough old seadogs of the Black Eagle refused to manhandle them on board. Five were got on board and a fortnight later soldiersfrom the Tower were sent to Newgate to force the Quakers on board. In fact as the Plague was raging in London many of those who were boarded carried it with them from Newgate and died. [17]

I doubt if any Vale Quakers suffered in the above case but they would hear all about it via Quarterly Meeting at Reading.*Refusal to swear or take the Oath of Allegiance* arose from the Quakers' general attitude to truthfulness, based on the expressed prohibition of Christ.

Matthew 5:33-37...Ye have heard that it has been said by those of old time, thou shalt not forswear thyself, but shalt perform unto the Lord thine oaths: But I say unto you swear not at all; neither by heaven for it is God's throne, Nor by earth for it is the footstool...but let your communication be yea, yea; nay, nay; for whatsoever is more than these cometh of evil.., also James 5:12

These quotations are taken from Yearly Meeting Minutes 1693 and taken from the King James's Bible. It all ties up with sentiments of trust that your word is your bond. Honesty was very important to a Quaker following Christ's example. On several occasions this principle was pointed out to Stuart Kings and to Oliver Cromwell, to judges and justices of the peace, both in interview and in writing but to no avail. This particular Act caused Quakers more trouble and tears than any. It could be, and was, used to catch them out time and time again. Apart from the misery this Act caused to Quakers it also prevented them from entering many walks of life right up to the end of the nineteenth century and even, I believe, the shadow lingers today in certain areas of public life.

Quakers were excluded from Universities, Professions, Church schools and some trades. They were not the `Establishment'. All of these circumstances led to Quakers setting up their own schools and institutions and to their turning to the sciences and trade for their bread and butter. It set them apart which was not good for the country as a whole or for the Quaker movement itself.

Quakers opened shops on Christmas Day if it did not fall on the Sabbath or First day as they did not celebrate Christmas or Easter as the established church did. They held to the testimony that all days were God's days. The first day was the day for worship (Sunday). They shunned using the day names or month names which they felt were heathen and not Christian. Similarly they felt that the celebrated days on the church calendar were nothing to do with Christ's teaching and often had pagan origins. They talked about Sunday as the First day and March was the First Month. This practice set them apart too. [First Month was March until 1752 when the Julian Calendar was replaced by the Gregorian Calendar.]

The Quakers were again in trouble with the Church for not baptising their children with holy water, but they felt that they were spiritually baptised and that the words that Jesus used in the Bible meant that he had come to do away with man-made ceremony especially that linked to pre-Christian and heathen practices.

Just as there is `one Lord and one faith' so is there `one baptism' (Ephesians 4:5) which is not the removal of dirt from the body but... an appeal to God for a clear conscience, through the resurrection of Jesus Christ. (1 Peter 3:21) This baptism is a pure and spiritual thing (Galatians 3:27), namely the baptism of the spirit and of fire, by which we are buried with him (Romans 6:4 and Colossians 2:12) so that being `washed' of our sins we may walk in newness of life. (Romans 6:4) The baptism of John was figurative, and was commanded for a time, but was not to continue forever (John 3:30 I Corinthians 1:17).

Quakers whilst accepting that for some Christians the outward rite of baptism is important, for them it is the spiritual transformation that changes the way we live as God's children that matters. It is a commitment that must continually be renewed. *To Lima with love says much that is helpful. Responses 27-32* .This pamphlet explains why Quakers do not accept that water baptism of infants is the only way of becoming a member of the Christian Church nor do they find this rite referred to as *an inescapable inference from the New Testament's account of Jesus's life and practice.*

This stance has always been the understanding of British Quakers and Quaker groups worldwide. In response to the World Council of Churches the following passage was written quite recently.

Even today Quaker understanding of Baptism is that it is not a single act of initiation but a continuing growth in the Holy Spirit and a commitment which must continually be renewed. It is this process which draws us into a fellowshipwith those who acknowledge the same power at work in our lives, those whom Christ is calling to be his body on earth. [19]

It is God who establishes us with you in Christ, and has commissioned us; he has put his seal upon us and given us his spirit in our hearts as a guarantee.
Paul in 2 Corinthians 1 21-22

After Oliver Cromwell died in September 1658, Friends in London and the Home Counties sent a list of one hundred and fifteen Friends who were in prison at the time. They also gave the names of nine who had died in gaol. After this some forty were released and a letter was sent to justices giving advice on dealing with such cases. It was pointed out that Friends were, in the opinion of the court, misguided rather than malicious or rebellious, and might be dealt with more leniently. However as one can see above, such guidance was mostly ignored and hard times were still to come.

Although the records of those Seekers who came from the North describe them as coming to Banbury and Oxford on their way to London and Bristol, there seems to be no direct mention of them coming to the Vale towns. Yet they came near to the Vale and 1 think possibly passed through. They may have worshipped with Vale groups of Seekers. Certainly those seekers from the Vale who went to gatherings addressed by these preachers from the North, in perhaps Oxford, Banbury, Reading or even in Bristol or London would come back and tell their own local groups about the message.

42

They became convinced of the Truth and in turn encouraged others to stand up for Truth. The good news spread very fast from market town to market town. The little gatherings suffering so much from the authorities must have been greatlystrengthened in purpose by such contacts from those with missionary zeal.

Many Quaker evangelists came to Oxford. Amongst them were people like John Camm and John Audland. Soon there was a Quaker group in Oxford. As early as 1654 Thomas Loe (Looe) and others were being imprisoned for *speaking the Truth*. Thomas Loe himself, as well as Richard Greenaway, was one of those who convinced seekers in Witney *of the Truth*. Kester Hart and his wife allowed their house to be used for worship as they were *blessed with the Truth*. Witney Quakers seem to have escaped much persecution and a special part of the Anglican Church graveyard was set aside for Quakers to begin with. The first recorded Monthly Meeting was held in 1675 at North Ly. North Leigh parish contained Wood Green where the Witney Quaker Meeting House most likely was by then. It is quite likely that Vale Seekers might be engaged in trade in Witney and hear all about these meetings and return totheir own place with the news and encouragement.

The beginnings of Quakerism in Faringdon or Charney, in Blewbury or Bishopstone must have stemmed from such Spiritual leaders as John Camm and Francis Howgill who passed through Banbury and Oxford on their way to and fro across the land. Their wives were in Banbury (1655). Thus Quaker women knew that they were involved in the `lamb's war `just as equally as their menfolk.

These Northern evangelists were part of the group of some sixty-six men and women who devoted their lives to the Truth. They were persecuted in all ways. They left their homes in the service of the Lord and they were heard about amongst the Seekers all over the land, including those in the Vale of the White Horse. They were examples to follow and a beacon of light in the difficult times to come. These Publishers of the truth were afterwards called `*The Valiant Sixty'*. Edward Burrough was one of these and had this to say:

While waiting upon the Lord in silence, as often as we did for many hours together, with our hearts and minds towards him, being stayed in the light of Christ within us from all thoughts, fleshly motions and desires, we received often the pouring down of the spirit upon us, and our hearts were made glad and our tongues loosened, and our mouths opened, and we spake with new tongues, as the Lord gave us utterance and his spirit led us, which was poured upon sons and daughters. [20]

Edward Burrough was a husbandman from Underbarrow in Westmorland, who was already a seeker when he met and heard George Fox preach when he was about nineteen years old. His parents disinherited him and he was turned out of his home to be a wanderer all the rest of his years. In certain respects he was another one of the Founding Fathers. George Fox seems now to be so important in developing and settling the Quaker movement, but from the beginning he was not alone and at first not especially important to Seekers everywhere. Vale Quakers probably came into being through any one of several Quaker evangelists, especially those who first came to Oxfordshire and Berkshire, Gloucestershire and London.

These first Quaker missionaries left comfortable homes and lived, often in very uncomfortable lodging houses, never quite knowing where they might lay their weary heads. Travelling in those days was uncomfortable and difficult too. The Authorities punished them in all kinds of ways including imprisonment in dreadful places. They were often misunderstood and abused by the general public, stoned, spat upon, shouted down and laughed at. They felt they were only re-living the trials of Christ himself and of the early Christian martyrs.

Sarah Cheevers and Katherine Evans, were imprisoned in horrible conditions in Malta from 1659 to 1662. They managed to write letters to their families:

To my right and precious husband, with my tender hearted children, who are more dear and precious to me than the apple of mine eye.. my prayers are for you day and night without ceasing... Pray for us believingly, all things are possible with our God. [2]1

We don't know if George Fox ever actually visited Faringdon, though there was a hint that a letter to the Reynolds family of Faringdon was found in the attics of The Farmhouse in the 1960s. It thanked them for their hospitality and told of riding to London, changing horses but once. It mysteriously disappeared! In his journal he writes about visiting Berkshire:

In 1663...Soe I past through ye countrys of visiting Friends in Wiltsheere andBarksheere till I came to London. In 1668 he speaks of. .setting ye mens meeting in Barksheere when most of ye emminant Friends were in prison...and thence to Barksheere where I had many large and precious meetings. [22]

Fox certainly visited N... Crisp in Marlborough and also Oare in Wiltshire where there was a burial ground a few years later. In 1676 George Fox writes -

to my ancient friends Thomas and Anne Curtis (of Reading) and George Lamboll (of Newbury) and all the rest in Berkshire. My desire is that you may keep in the first love and holy life, light and power and spirit of Christ. [22]

In 1676 George Fox had another meeting at Oare and then a large meeting at Warborough, so to Lambourne Woodlands and Marlborough. One can imagine someone like Oliver Sanson and Joan Vokins (Vokens} having been present at some of these meetings. Oliver had become convinced in 1657 and was struggling with the authorities at this time.

Margaret Fell, later to be the wife of George Fox, travelled all over England with her daughters until they came to Bristol and the South West. This was in 1663. So she may also have travelled through the Vale area and met some of those who were suffering for the Truth. One can be certain that these happenings were talked about in `Seeker' circles and strengthened the enthusiasm for their way of life. Women played their part in the strengthening and growth of the movement. They had to bear the brunt of the hardships. Margaret Fell and others were an inspiration and very early on women were organising themselves to cope with husbands, fathers, brothers and sisters away from home, preaching or in prison, and also, for them, when they returned home exhausted and often ill from ill-treatment in prison or from diseasescaught whilst travelling about.

For those who became Quakers it was a way of life all the time in every aspect of human activity and endeavour, it is so today. Our Advices and Queries says, *Quakerisin is a way not a notion.[Book of Discipline 1995]*

Not by strength of arguments or by particular disquisition of each doctrine, and convincement of my understanding thereby came [I] to receive and bear witness to the Truth, but by being secretly reached by [the] Life. For, when I came into the silent assemblies of God's people, I felt a secret power amongst them, which touched my heart; and as I gave way unto it I found the evil weakening in meand the good raised up; and so I became thus knit and united with them.. .[23]

Fortunately we have a very good record of Quaker sufferings for their `Truth' in *Besse's Sufferings of Quakers 1655 - 1688* compiled in 1753 from records kept in earlier times. In his book *Portrait in Grey*, page 68, John Punshon mentions that Friends claimed that over 3,000 had suffered for conscience sake down to 1660. (I have the figure as 3,170 Friends suffering for conscience sake prior to the restoration of King Charles II to the throne from a source I cannot find!)

The first recorded suffering of a Quaker was a Leonard Cole of Abersfield for non-payment of tithes (1655). The first in our area seem to have been Joseph Cole, of Newbury, I think, and five others in 1656, *for offering to speak by way of Christian exhortation to the priest and people when assembled in a place of public worship at Reading.* They were sent to Reading jail. I do wonder if these Coles were related in some way. They could have been in Oxford when Johm Audland and Johm Camm preached. That might have convinced them of the Truth.

In 1655-56 Joseph Cole, Dorothy Waugh, George Adamson, Hannah Mills, Thomas and Anne Curtis and John Evans were imprisoned for delivering the Truth in steeple houses. Leonard Cole was again in trouble in 1658 and imprisoned and a horse worth four pounds seized. He was later in a London prison and corn from his barns was seized and turned over his threshers. This was worth £100 when the tithe he had refused to pay was £6.

In 1660 rough treatment of Quakers at Newbury, Reading and Abingdon for refusing to take the Oath of Allegiance and for recusants (non-attendance of church). In the Berks and Oxon Quarterly Meeting Minutes of 1660 it records these men as being husbandmen, labourers, a tailor, a millwright, a comb-maker, a chandler, a mason, a shoemaker.

On the 27th May 1660, Quakers were meeting for worship in the home of Mary Slade at Kingston Lisle when in came the local militia. They wounded Richard Ballard, John Clark and Hugh Penston with the points of their swords. They broke the heads of Robert Cook and Edward Ware and cruelly beat Bartholemew Maylin, an aged man. They dragged Richard Greenaway, a London Tailor, who often travelled in the vale to share in worship, out by his hair and threw him into a pond. Others were also thrown into the pond.

Later in the same year, about the 8th month Richard Sanson (1 wonder if this was a brother or cousin of Oliver Sanson because his father Richard never became a Quaker, I think) meeting at Steventon was attacked by the constable and many others who rushed in with pitchforks, staves and suchlike weapons and Thomas Curtis was thrown into the pond and had his coat torn to pieces. Other Friends were thrown into the muddy water and some women and men were trodden on and later these innocent people were driven along the road.

These wicked actions were said to have been done by the instigation of a drunken Priest in the neighbourhood - who sometime before being told that hisweapons of warfare ought to be spiritual, said that he would fight Quakers with such weapons as he had. [24]

Thomas Curtis was rather an eminent Quaker in the Vale story; he seems to have had a cloth warehouse and cloth shop in Reading, so you can see that he was in touch with the wool trade, with farmers, merchants and tailors. He had also helped on the Parliamentary side in the Civil War and had risen to high ranks in the Berkshire Force.

Another meeting at Kingston Lisle again at the home of Mary Slade was broken up and the Quakers taken to a nearby Justice of the Peace. Having refused to swear the Oath of Allegiance they were committed to jail until the Quarter Sessions. So John Giles, Leonard Cole, Humphrey Knowles and Andrew Pearson were soon also joined by Richard Greenaway. Around this time Richard Greenaway was preaching at Faringdon after the priest had finished, and he then refused to take the Oath of Allegiance and perhaps to take his hat off to the justice and so to prison he went.

Braithwaite in his *Second Period of Quakerism* says that in 1661 at least 4,200 Friends were simultaneously in prison, this being a conservative guess, and that many counties were completely empty of adult male Friends. (Some authorities suggest nearer 5,000 were in prison at one time.) He writes:

At Reading jail some 28 conscientious sufferers were incarcerated and this included some 22 who were kept in a deep filthy dungeon - no air and no covering, they were treated more severely than the worst murderers and felons. Ink and working tools were taken from them and often they were refused the food and other necessities brought by their friends and families. The jailer a notorious man in Quaker circles mocked and insulted them.

In 1662 17 Quakers were held in Reading jail, including a John Reynolds, for meeting for worship and refusing to swear the oath of allegiance to the crown on the Bible. J.Sowle mentions in his notes that a paper was handed in to the judge by the Men's Meeting setting out the reasons why the Quakers could not swear:

Eternal God, from whom no secret can be hid, sees your days and the eye of the Lord beholds the way that now you walk in.Our Lord and master Jesus Christ who hath said `swear not at all.. .their yea is their yea and their nay is their nay...'

Later still in about 1662 seventeen Vale Quakers were in Reading prison, for one reason and another, but always also for refusal to swear the Oath. John Reynolds from Faringdon was one of these. as well as John Whitehead who was a renowned Friend and must have been travelling in the Vale area at that time.

Sir William Armorer, a Reading Justice of Peace, was a particularly nasty piece of work, he was out `open- mouthed' to get the Quakers by fair means or foul. He came to Thomas Curtis's house and dragged some forty away from Meeting for Worship to prison. The next First day he went again and found just two or three men and women had gathered for worship, as the rest were in prison:

`What the devil are you met again? I will send you all to prison... What the devil? Are you dumb!' said Armorer. `We have chosen the Spirit of Jesus Christ,' said John Boult, `The Spirit of love, meekness, patience and humility.'

In 1664 Armorer came again to the gathered flock at the home of Thomas Curtis and this time only women were gathered. Menfolk were kept in prison and often without trial going on and on missing the Quarter Sessions. These women gathered on that day were Anne Curtis, Sarah Lanbolls, Judith Smith, Katharine Woodward, Martha Cheesman, Elizabeth Hampon and he sent them all to prison too.

In 1664 many Quakers were in trouble because they would not swear the Oath of Allegiance to King and Country at Abingdon and they set forth a paper to the magistrate explaining why they could not swear, but that their word could be trusted and that they did uphold the basis of the oath:

(As explained already) Sir William Armorer really tried to get rid of the Quakers in a big way. In March 1664 34 or even 40 Friends were arrested at Meeting under the Quaker Act and taken to the dreadful prison. Each Sunday more Quakers were hauled out of meeting until there were only very old and children left no women or men. However the children continued to meet though even they were bullied as they sat in silence. Once they had cold water thrown at their faces with violence and force. [26]

Violet Hodgkin has written a wonderfully moving story ofThe Children of Reading Meeting,meeting at Thomas Curtis's house. It ends with the following letter:

Thankfulness and joy last freshly through the centuries, as an old letter, written at this time by one of the fathers to George Fox proves to us today: `Our little children kept the meetings up, when we were all in prison, notwithstanding that wicked justice when he came found them there, with a staff that had a spear on it would pull them out of the meeting, and punch them in the back till some of them were black in the face. His fellow is not, I believe, to be found in all England a justice of the peace.'...'For they might as well think to hinder the sun from shining, or the tide from flowing ,as to hinder the Lord's people from meeting to wait upon Him. [27]

By now Sir William Armorer held some 60 Quakers in Reading Jail. They refused to swear the Oath or to remove hats. They said that as he had imprisoned them for holding a Meeting they should be tried on that and not the oath! He was furious. Eventually they were brought to the court and Thomas Curtis said:

`He didn't refuse to take the oath so as not to bear his allegiance to the King but because Christ had commanded him not to swear at all. He was persuaded that he was as good a subject to the King as most in the country since he came in. Could the court show him how he could take the oath yet not break the command of Christ [28]

In 1667 Oliver Sanson was up for non-payment of tithes in Boxford and he was excommunicated, had goods distrained valued at £6.8.0 and the miller was told not to grind Oliver's corn.' In 1669 he again refused to pay tithes for conscience sake and was sent to Reading jail where he met more like-minded Quakers and had much to gain spiritually.

In 1670 John Stevens of Uffington punished and distrained of goods for holding a meeting in his home. Richard Thatcher, Richard Ballard, May Johnson and Thomas Leadbetter were also distrained for attending that meeting.

1674 Thomas Curtis of Reading was ministering to his people and a priest informed on him and he was distrained of calves and cows being all he had - not considering his family of small children. They also took 2 brass pots, 2 pewter platters etc.

Sufferings of Joan Vickers of Bourton in the parish of Shroovham - poor ancient widow with only half an acre of ground- because she (for consciencesake) refused to pay `tythes' - Kinshon ye priest of Shroovham caused to be taken by force from her as much hemp as was judged worth 6s.8d., which was all she had grow...and in fact was £ 1.6.8 ... .So they robbed this poor widow of a fourth part of what she had grow in one year for one year's tythe. [29]

Michael Reynolds of The Farm, Faringdon for non-payment of tithes and refusal to take the oath suffered under Robert Pye 1677. He was distrained of hay and wheat they took what they pleased, but he was also arrested and taken to Reading prison with others:

John Knowles of West Challow 1677
John Lambolls of Stanford 1677
Daniel! Bunce of Charney 1677

In 1678 Michael Reynolds was arrested by Robert Pye for non-payment of tithes again and was distrained of 9 cows, 2 colts and a barn of corn, beans and peas. He was kept a prisoner in an Inn in Faringdon (was it the Bell or the Crown?). Then they took a mare and more corn for one year's payment of tithe, yet the rent of his land was £55. This was far more than a tenth of his income. It was in fact ten times more than Michael should have paid. The following tract was found in the attic at Michael's farmhouse in 1966. It must have lain there for centuries.

Here followeth A BRIEF RELATION of the late sufferings of MICHAEL REYNOLDS of Farringdon, in the same County; because he could not forconscience sake pay tyths, to Robert Pye, impropriator. And therefore it is evidently manifest, how cruelly and unjustly Robert Pye hath dealt with his neighbour Michael Reynolds (althou in other cases we have not had much cause to find fault with him) who for the denial of scarce 10 1.0.0 demanded, hath caused to be taken away cattle and corn the value of £971. 16s.9d which is near ten times much more. Oh horrible injustice, that ever such actions should be found.

[30] *[Appendix II Copy of Sufferings of Michael Reynolds]*

Of course to lose young animals was devastating for a farmer. Also he needed some seed for next year's crops as well as some for themselves on the side.

Also with this tract about Michael Reynolds of Faringdon was one about a man called William Dobson of Brightwell in Berkshire entitled: The Ancient testimony of the Primitive Christians and martyrs of/Jesus Christ. This man refused to pay tithes in 1664. His tithe monger was one Ralph Whistler. William Dobson was kept in Reading jail for 15 weeks. The following year he was sent to Westminster and was made a prisoner at the Fleet. His sufferings continued with Ralph Whistler and his lot taking corn, beans, barley, cows and carts, horses and tools from the farm. Each time William tried to get some cows from Wallingford market for his wife, to have milk for his family, Whistler (encouraged by the local Priest) would find some pretext ofdistraining William Dobson of his rightful goods. He was continually in prison because he refused to take his hat off to the judge and so on, and was often put with felons that had distemper and smallpox. In the end though William owed the Church nothing, yet he was kept in prison where he died for conscience sake on last day of the third month, called May 1677. At one point William was in Reading goal (1675) and was very weak and ill with distemper. Many Quakers and others were dying all about in the foul place. He rose and is reported to have given all courage and faith to face the future:

And at that season the living Power of God, as a spring of love and life, filled his heart, and burst out as a stream, in uttering forth many heavenly expressions, and wholsome exhortations to his friends and Brethren; to prize the love of God, and to be faithful to him, signifying how good the Lord had been unto him. [31]

Thomas Withers was beaten by Thomas Reynolds, a Constable in Faringdon, and Thomas Reynolds later died which to Quakers was a judgement. (It is confusing as I have mentioned before when all these cousins, fathers and sons have the same names. This Thomas was not a Quaker whereas Thomas Reynolds of Buscot was a Quaker - more of him in another chapter.)

1683 Richard Vokens at West Challow was distrained of corn worth £16.17.0. For non-payment of tithes.

Also in 1683 Thomas Reynolds *of Burscot* [Buscot] was fined £32 10.0 for not paying his church rates. At the same time John Knowles and Daniel Bunce of Charney and Joseph Stevens *of Baulkin* suffered too. And so again and again in 1684, 1685 and 1686 these same Quakers suffered. I shall mention a frightful story concerning Oliver Sanson in chapter four when 1 am setting down his life story in more detail.

The fact is that in spite of all these troubles Quakerism had not been squashed out of existence, neither had it gone underground. It had become more firmly established by the late seventeenth century than ever. This was due to strongly felt unity of faith, almost cemented by the *Sufferings* which gave followers a reality of Christ's sufferings. They had their Way and their Truth to support them throughout. Also Quakerism flourished because a structure had been devised. It is their church governmentthat has kept the Society of Friends together in this country over the centuries. Their way of worship may well have been open to individual interpretation but their structure had a firm foundation to underpin their faith.

When George Fox was released from Scarborough Castle in 1666, weakened by his long imprisonment, he rode slowly to London to find the greater part destroyed by fire. The Society he had founded was at breaking point. Persecution and internal strife about the way forward were leading to disaster. So for the next two years he set about organising the system of Church Government that broadly speaking exists today. Local *Particular Meetings*, now called, *Preparative Meetings*were gathered into *Monthly Meetings*. So the particular meetings of the Vale were gathered into the Vale Monthly

Meeting and the minutes of these Monthly Meetings, from 1666 onwards, are in the Oxford Archives now. Men's Monthly Meetings and Women's Monthly Meetings were formed. The Vale Monthly Meeting became part of the *Berkshire Quarterly Meeting*. Representatives and any Quaker could and did attendthese meetings and so the Society of Friends came into being and was well knit with worship and business meetings.

The Vale Monthly Meeting covered more than the geographical Vale and stretched over the White Horse Downs to the south including meetings in the valleys of the Oare and the Lambourne. In those days the shepherds and farmers themselves moved between these wider market areas. The area north of the Thames was not part of Berkshire and was then run by Oxford and Witney Quakers.

Thus it was that by the mid-sixties of the seventeenth century the Religious Society of Friends was a fact. They held meetings for worship and for business. They conducted marriages and burials. They had Meeting Houses and Burial Grounds. They worshipped in silence with ministry based on the principle of 'the priesthood of all believers'. Men sat on one side of the meeting house and women on the other, as they do in Kenya today. Women or men might equally be moved to give ministry. The numbers of Quakers in England might have numbered over 50,000 or as much as five per cent of the population in some counties. They were by this time peaceable people and refused to take up arms. They were on the whole honest. If they met to worship they did so openly and they kept to their principles of equality and simplicity in their worship and daily life.

In the Faringdon Parish register of the period there is a list of people not coming to the Parish Church on a Sunday for Divine Service or on holy days and for not taking the sacrament at Easter time. These were all punishable offences. There are thirty three names in 1675. Oliver Sanson and his wife Jane and Widow Townsend are amongst those mentioned. Their stories will be told in the coming pages. Those that were dissenting were shopkeepers, a sheepsher, a ropemaker, a maltster, a mercer, a shoemaker, a *taylor* tailor, a corn chandler, a baker and several farmers. All independent tradesman and craftsmen. In 1681 the entry states that 'we present that all

Dissenters and sectionaries of our Parish were excumunicated two years ago.'

At last under King James 11, in 1686, a General Pardon and Royal Warrant was issued followed in 1687 by a Declaration of Indulgence and Friends were about to begin a less troubled era of Quakerism. In fact James wished to show tolerance to the Roman Catholics and many dissenters and others were not altogether certain about the outcome of this tolerance toward all worshippers. The Quakers were relieved and grateful for they had suffered so much.

On May 24th 1689, The Toleration Act became law and the long battle for religious liberty was more or less won. The principle was won and this country never went back to the intolerance of the previous years. I like to think that the Quakers played their part in this. The suffering did have a good outcome and I certainly am glad to live in a country that allows religious freedom. It was hard won by faithful followers of Christ and this should never be forgotten. This freedom still needs to be cared for and those of both Christian and non - Christian persuasion, that live in our midst, should not take their privilege to worship in their own way lightly. Others suffered greatly and very greatly for them. We all still need to understand and cherish toleration.

The Humble, meek, merciful, just, pious, and devout souls are everywhere of one religion; and when death has taken off the mask they will know one another, though the divers liveries they wear here makes them stranger. [32]

NOTES

Part II: The Sufferings

[13.] PENN (William), *Quaker Faith and Practice* 1995, 22.01, *Somefruits ofsolitude*,1693, collection of works 1726, Vol 1, p843, Select works 1782 Vol5, p166.

55

[14.] ELLWOOD (Thomas*),* *The history of the life of Thomas Ellwood*, 1714, plo1,Friends House Library MS i20.

[15.] BARCLAY (Robert), *Barclay's Apology*, p 392, Edited by Dean Freiday,1967,New Jersey. .Original version in Latin 1667 and in English 1678.

[16.]BARCLAY (Robert), p365, as note (15).

[17.]VIPONT (Elfrida), *The story of Quakerism,1652-1952*, p95, Bannisdale Press,1952.

[18.] BARCLAY (Robert), *Proposition 12, Baptism, from his Apology*, 1676, see note(15).

[19.]*To Lima with Love Baptism eucharist and ministry* QHS 1987. (This book waswritten as an answer to the World body of Christian churches. Whilst making clearhow far short Quakers may seem to fall from the point of view of mainstreamChristian churches yet it demonstrates how consistently interested Quakers have beenand still are in Christian understanding and respecting each other. Quakers do feelthey hold insights and ways of worship in trust for the whole church of God.)

[20.] BURROUGH Edward, (1632133-1663), *The Epistle to the reader in George FoxThe great mystery of the great whore unfolded,* 1659 prelim leaves bl-b2 QFP19.20

[21.] EVANS (Katherine), Letter written between 1659 to 1662 from prison in Maltaand quoted in *The Valiant Sixty*, Earnest E.Taylor p68, Bannisdale Press 1951

[22.] CADBURY Henry: These entries are mentioned in *the Annual Catalogue ofGeorge Fox's papers* collected by Henry Cadbury of Massachusetts in 1939, and alsoin *The Journal of George Fox* and *The short Journal and itinerary journals of GeoFox in commemoration of the tercentenary of his birth* (1624-1924) both Ed. ByNorman Penny 1911 and 1925 respectively.

[23.] BARCLAY Robert CFP 19.21, *Apology for the true Christian divinity, prop 11,*sect 7 1678 London Edn.

[24.] SOWLE J, *An abstract of the sufferings of the people called Quakers* Assigns of J.Sowle 1733 Vol 111660-66 1738 Berkshire

[25.] SOWLE J., *extracts taken from an abstract of the Sufferings of the people calledQuakers ,1650-1660,*Vol.li Assigns J. Sowle 1733 at the Bible in George Yard.

BESSE J., *A collection of the sufferings of the people called Quakers.* TwoVols,1753

[25.]SOWLE J., Vol II *An abstract of the Sufferings of the people called Quakers* 1733.

[27.] HODGKIN Violet, (Mrs. John Holdsworth), *Book of Quaker Saints* Macmillan1924

28. SOWLE J., see note (25) and also from *Victorian History Berkshire* Vol 111927and *Besse's Sufferings* 1753.

[29.]*Victorian History Berkshire* Vol 11,1927, also from J. Sowle and J. Besse as note(25).

[30.] A tract printed in the year MDCLXXX (1683). A copy of this tract is in theIronbridge Gorge Museum Trust in Shropshire.

[31.] Sufferings: *Extract from the Tract to William Dobson,* Ironbridge Library

[32.] PENN (William), *Quaker Faith and Practice,* 1995 27.01, *Some Fruits of solitude,1693, maxim 519* from his *collection of works 1726* vol I, p842.

The Sufferings of George Fox (1624- 1691)

He was in prison eight times, as far as I can tell, and how he survived some of theseevil places was a miracle in itself. He was also many times brought before magistratesand also badly treated by any who felt they could get some fun out of throwing thingsat him or shouting abuse or otherwise ill-treating him.

First: 1649, Nottingham. Prison for blasphemy...preached that God was not necessarilyin churches but most definitely was in people... This implied that the priesthood andchurch authority was irrelevant. Truth is the interpretation of the scriptures throughexperience, not the scriptures themselves.

Second: Derby, 1650. Prison again Blasphemy... They asked me whether I wassanctified. 1 said, 'sanctified yes, for I was in the paradise of God'. They said, `had I nosin?' Sin, I said. `Christ my Saviour hath taken away my sin, and in him is no sin.'They asked how do we knew that Christ did abide in us? I said, `By his spirit that hehas given us. They temptingly asked if any of us were Christ. I answered, `Nay,weare nothing Christ is all.' So they committed me to prison as a blasphemer as a manthat had no sin.

Third: Carlisle prison, 1653 as a blasphemer, a heretic, and a seducer.

Fourth: Launceston Prison, 1656. (Doomsdale cell) for travelling in ministry,refusal to take hat off, refusal to address defference to authority, refusal to swear onthe Bible to tell the truth etc.

Fifth: Lancaster,1660. Refusal to swear the Oath of Allegiance to King and countryand the other usual things as above mentioned. So the authorities accused him ofrising against the King and disturbing the peace.

Sixth: Leicester,1662. Refused to take the Oath of Allegiance by swearing on theBible.

Seventh: Lancaster again,1664. Refusal to take the oath...holding Quaker meetingsetc. Let your yea be yea and your nay be nay (the testimony of honesty).`I told them my loyalty to the King lay in a yea and a nay, which was more than anoath, for I was a man of tender conscience.'

Cont.. Scarborough, 1665. Moved from Lancaster to Scarborough prison. A placeset on the cliffs where the east winds blew across the North Sea into his cell. His cellfaced the open sea. He was only allowed bread and water, and soon got very illsleeping and living in these terrible conditions. The more Fox stood by his convictionsthe more was he tormented by the soldiers in charge of the prison within the castlewalls.

Eighth: Worcester, 1673. Because he attended meeting for worship at Armscote in abarn instead of worshipping in the established church.

Taken from *the Journal of George Fox* Edited by John Nickalls 1952.

CHAPTER THREE

THE MEETING HOUSES

`We came to know a place to stand in and what to wait in; and the Lord appeareddaily to us, to our astonishment, amazement and great admiration, insomuch thatwe often said one to another with great joy in our heart: `What, is this theKingdom of God come to be with men?....
[1]

So for one reason and another great numbers of folk flocked to the Quaker meetings. Homes and small uncomfortable barns were not sufficient and it was soon realised all over England, Scotland, Wales and New England that proper Meeting Houses were needed for worship and business. Quakers from the beginning stood for outward honesty, and, whatever the punishments might be, they would not be secretive about their worship. This was one reason why they were so obvious and easy to accuse and punish. They met for worship freely and openly, they travelled to minister all over the place, they did not go to church, they would not swear the Oath of Allegiance, they would not doff hats for judges or aristocrats or speak withdeference to them. They very early on became peaceable people and so they did not fight their case with weapons and skirmish.

Abingdon Meeting

Abingdon *`Friends in Truth'* most likely began meeting in each others'homes to begin with and were eventually part of the Vale Monthly Meeting for a time. Land was acquired in 1679 and this was situated on the river Ock banks adjoining Holy Bush and soon used as a Burial place for Quakers. By 1697 there was also a Meeting House. The meeting transferred to Warborough MM in

1791. In 1865 the building was sold for £725 since there had been no Friends using it since 1839. This money was used to alter Reading Meeting House. In 1896 there were again enough Quakers to rent the Primitive Methodist Chapel in the Vineyard. Later this was purchased for £400. Later again in the 1960's it was sold.

At the present time Abingdon Friends do not have a Meeting House and meet in rented accommodation.

Blewbury Meeting

There was quite a long standing Non-conformist following in Blewbury well before the seventeenth century. Certainly by 1668 Blewbury Meeting was represented at Berkshire Quarterly Meeting. In the following year the meeting was sufficiently strong to be visited by Steven Crisp, a prominent East Anglian Quaker, while on a journey to the West of England. In his journal he tells us of joining the meeting `at Edward Hide's at Blewbury, Dec. 1669'. The Meeting House must have been built after 1669. It was North West of the Manor in the long meadow running alongside the stream and just off the Hagbourne footpath near an old tanyard. The place is now called Quakers Croft. We do not know what it looked like but it is represented in the Enclosure Award Map of 1805 as being a simple square form. Perhaps it was a bit like the one in Uffington. Three weddings were solemnised there between 1675 and1710. Blewbury Meeting was last represented at Quarterly Meeting in 1757. After that it ceased to function. The Meeting House was demolished by Richard Badcock, who was farming the Manor, soon after 1805.

There is some possibility of Quakers having been buried near the meeting house or in their own gardens. Some burial stones were found in a passage of the old malt house but seem to have been lost in recent times. It is quite possible that such a malster might have been a Quaker, many were. As they had not been `christened' with water baptism they could not be buried in consecrated land. So unlike, for example, gypsies [who would seek infant water baptism and would consider it the right thing to do, though they might never again enter the church alive, but were thus eligible for burial in consecrated graveyards], Quakers stuck to their principles and if they had to make their own arrangements for their dead, so be it. They considered that they were still children of God and felt satisfied that they were spiritually clean.

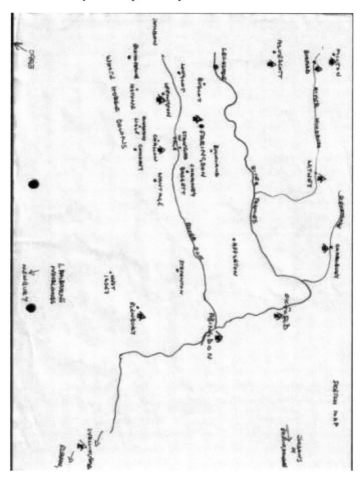

A map of the Meeting houses in the Vale and beyond around 1680.

After the meeting closed those in the Blewbury area wishing to worship in a Quaker way, could, and still can, go over the downs to **East Garston** which was part of the Vale from 1687 to the mid-18th century when it closed. They could also get to **Wallingford** Meeting which has a lovely old Meeting house built in 1725 and used more or less ever since, coming under **Warborough** and then **Reading** Monthly Meetings. [2]

Lambourne Woodlands

Possibly a Meeting House here or use of a barn. I need to do more research into this. There was a Burial Ground by 1670. Conveyance signed on 7th June 1669 between Joseph Minden Halt of Reading, a Mealman, and James Reynolds and Charles Reynolds of Faringdon, Yeoman, and John Snelly, a Cheese Factor... etc.

West Challow Meeting

The Meeting house at West Challow is a bit of a mystery today and I have been unable to find any trace of it. To begin with `Children of Light' or `Friends in Truth' met at the home of Adam Laurence. A Monthly Meeting also took place here in 1669. At some time perhaps a barn was built by Richard Vokens in about 1680. This could have been a meeting place for Anabaptists or `Children of light', but does not appear to have been a Quaker place initially. Later a strong Quaker group formed in this part of the Vale with regular Sunday and Monthly Meetings. There was a burial ground in use in the seventeenth century and up to about 1731. [3]

A proper Meeting house was built or a barn converted at **West Challow** by the 1680's for there are minutes about the upkeep of it. It may well have had a thatched roof. This was later replaced in 1706 and there is a letter dated 1802 from Benjamin De Horne (Faringdon*) `I return the receipt for the receipt for the deeds, built 1706, of Challow Meeting House'* After that its use as a meeting was terminated in 1731. *The building was called Box Cottage situated beside the village pond near Manor Farm.* According to Violet House, the Baptist Chapel might partly be built on the original Quaker Burial ground and the Meeting House, but it has gone now. Reference is made in the Vale Women's Monthly Meeting of money being paid to `Chawlow' Meeting House for wood and cleaning. Violet Howse gives the date as 1731, but in Title Deeds held at

Oxford now, the hand over from the Vale Monthly Meeting to Witney Monthly Meeting was in 1795.This was the time when Berks and Oxfordshire were consolidated into one Quarterly Meeting.

The former Trustees being mostly deceased ... Meeting House and burial ground in West Challow Trustees handing over to John Townsend and Henry Snelling to have and to hold for 2000 years.

So I am not quite sure what happened.

The Vokins family, especially the Joan (Bunce) and Richard Vokins marriage and their large family must have been the strong point of the meeting. Perhaps they were themselves married there in a barn used as a meeting house. Joseph Woodrofe of Uffington married Mary Hayes of Watchfield there in about 1684. Thomas Franklin of Great Coxwell, Thomas Bunce of Goosey and Jonothan Thatcher of Uffington desired to have certificates signed to go to Pennsylvania in 1685 and this was done at a meeting at Challow.

Hopeful Vokins in her legacy 25th February 1729 left 20 shillings per annum for Monthly Meeting people called Quakers in West Charlow for use and benefit of poor belonging to the meeting there. To be paid out of rents and profits on an estate lying in the parish of Tetbury called Hillsome farm.

Berks and Oxon Quarterly Meeting schedule of Friends' properties Reading XVI c1850.

This legacy was finally managed by Witney Monthly Meeting well into the twentieth century. By the mid eighteenth century the Quakers in West Challow had died out or left the area or even possibly joined other Christian denominations.

Nearby there were also Quakers in **Childrey.** Here Thomas Clarke held meetings in his home well before 1660's and up until his death in 1669. In Sufferings it says: *"He was in prison for refusing to swear (on the Bible,) in 1669 and has been there ever since", says Jane Clarke*[4]

Goosey never had a meeting house but it certainly had Quakers. This was a little island in the floods of late Winter and early Spring and so much of the land around was commonly used for grazing in the lush meadows of Summer and for catching of wild geese and ducks at most times of year.

Abbey Farm as it is today was originally a cell established by the monks from the Abbey of Faringdon and noted for excellent cheese. Both Charney and Goosey were given to Abingdon Abbey in 785 by Offa the King of Mercia and Wessex. In the seventeenth century it probably was still very much an open field area as the enclosures only began in about 1657. A John Bunce had to pay tax for three hearths in the seventeenth century which is quite a large house and the Bunce family became Quakers. A John Vokins had one hearth and again that was to become a Quaker name in the area.

Charney Bassett Meeting

Charney Bassett is a Quaker village of the early movement and the Bunce family farmed there for centuries. It had been part of Abingdon Abbey and a rather large Manor house was built where the monks could supervise their lands. An Abbot was appointed to do this and live there. After the dissolution the manor passed through several hands and seems to have been a Catholic stronghold until it was sold to Sir William Dunch, auditor of the mint to Henry VII and, his son or grandson, squire extra-ordinary to Elizabeth I. Soon this family owned Pusey as well, and could have been involved in persecuting Daniel Bunce, a Quaker, for refusing to pay tithes. Daniel's household nurtured the seeds of Vale Quakerism and his daughters and son-in-law were to particularly uphold the movement when they grew up during the seventeenth century.

**Picture of Charney Manor today. Drawn by Bob Elkington when Resident
Friend at Charney Manor [later Warden of Oxford Meeting House].**

It was most fortunate that during the 1940's, some three hundred years later, Henry and Lucy Gillett visited and got to know the then owner of the Manor House and that when the owner died they had the means and the inspiration to buy it and to give it to the Society of Friends to be used as a place of peace and recreation and for educational purposes. So today that village where the Bunce family lived is a Conference and a retreat centre. Here too, in the 1950's to 1970's, a Preparative Meeting found its home, serving the Vale once again with Quaker light.

The farmhouse where the early Quaker Bunce family lived is still lived in and is situated on the South side of the village green. More will be mentioned about this family in another chapter. (See reference 4)

Faringdon Meeting

Faringdon Friends may have met in a barn to begin with, some

Faringdonians seem to have a myth that they did. This barn behind the present site has since been pulled down. Certainly they appear to have purchased some land from an Edward Brooks of Childry in the 1660s and were meeting regularly from 1668 and burying their dead in their own burial ground. The building of the Meeting house was most likely begun after the purchase of the land in the 1670's, probably around 1672, and we simply do not know whether or not it was thatched. But the inside may well have been similar to the Wallingford Meeting House which is still in use today and includes its original furniture, benches and a small preaching gallery at one end. Vale Monthly Meetings were held at Faringdon.

These are to certifie all friends of ffarringdon Meetings or any other friendswhom it may concern that we Warmen Townsend, Adam Lawrence, JohnLangley, John Willis younger, Richard Vokins the younger, John Stevens and Thomas Reynolds who are all of us equally interested according to law in a plott of ground in Ffarringdon bought or purchased of Edward Brooks of Childry as by an indenture of lease...the last day of the tenth month'1672'And since that time our Meeting house has been erected upon the sayed plott of ground and part of it is appoynted and made use of as a burying place. We do hereby acknowledge and declare in the fear and presence of the Lord God that all right of tithe and interest in the sayed premises is for no other and nor intentbut that it may always remain and continue as it is now for the sole use and service of friends. And if at any time friends shall soo cause to require any or all of us to surrender or resign our right tithe and interest we do own andacknowledge that it is our duty to submit to the judgment of friends concluded and given forth from the Monthly Mens Meetings and upon notice given we shall freely and willingly with all readiness resign and yeild upon interest according. And that this writing and declaration be read once or twice every year at the Mens Meeting and notification made thereby who or how many of the said partys are disclosed - and hereunto we set our hands this 26th day of the second month 1679.

In y presence of y friends
at the Monthly Mens Meeting at Ffarringdon
thereto aforementioned

signed
Warren Townsend
Adam Lawrence
John Langley
John Willis
Richard Vokins
John Hanny
thumb mark of Thomas Reynolds

This is a copy

Deed of Assignment feb.3rd 1668

Upon trust that the said premises may be continued as a public Meeting house and burying place for the Friends in and about Great Farringdon when and as often as they shall seek occupation or so long as they shall be suffered without molestation from the civil magistrates and etc and to convey to others within six months after the decease of any four. [6]

So a Meeting house was built by about 1672 and it was in use continuously as a Quaker worshipping place until the 1880s. The last Quaker Certificate of burial appears to be that of John Gardner in 1902. But that interment may have been in the Non-Conformist Burial ground in Canada Lane. Today there are only three obvious tomb stones in the Meeting House garden.

The place lay unused for a bit and fortunately was never sold. Its subsequent history will be told later in the book. Today it is very much in use as a Quaker worshipping place once again, the only Meeting in the Western Vale of White Horse.

The present building is a Grade II listed building "late C17[th] or early C18[th]" built of limestone rubble [ragstone] with brick dressings. Pevsner dates it early C18[th], original gabled roof, steep pitched lipped stone slate. Original windows near road had to be blocked to prevent damage. At some point a high wall was built to protect the Meeting House.

Faringdon Meeting House entrance

Uffington Meeting

Further into the West of the Vale another Meeting House was built and still exists though now converted into a bungalow. This one is situated right under the White Horse hill in Uffington. A village named after King Uffa of Offersdyke – Uffa's town. This building is situated a quarter of a mile South East of the church and opposite Garrards Farm where John Betjeman had his home for a while (1933-41). The Quakers met for worship in the village from about 1668 onwards as a recognised First Meeting within the Vale Monthly Meeting structure. Friends met until I680's in each others' homes or barns until a Meeting House was built. A meeting is recorded at the home of John Stevens in 1673 and later at the home of William Ballard, and of Richard Thatcher. These people paid Hearth Tax so they were comparatively well off farmers or craftsmen. William Lockey, another Quaker, was the Miller. [7]

The Uffington Quakers appear to have come from the same sort of background as elsewhere in the Vale. They were persecuted for non-payment of tithes, for not swearing the oath of allegiance and for non-attendance of Divine Service. They were small independent producers, such as farmers and shepherds, traders such as bakers,wool dealers, and shoemakers and craftsmen such as blacksmiths.In 1673 there is a Monthly Meeting minute:

Uffington Meeting House

`It was convenient that a meeting for every first day might be established at Uffington'....*

`William Ballards house 1680 to the barns which Friends judged to be very coldin winter.....*

Remember in those early heady days of waiting upon the Lord a Meeting for Worshipcould last for four or more hours. To be cold must have been very unpleasant.

In 1762 a Quaker Committee meeting noted *that the meetings on*

71

First days are not always attended and the keeping up thereof was recommended, but shortly after meetings were discontinued. Some of the names that crop up in Quaker minutes in Uffington are as follows:

William and Martha Ballard, Elizabeth Chamberlin, Ann Downs, John Geering of Wool stone, Ann and Oliver Lockey of Moor Mill, Ann and Thomas Pottinger, John and Rebecca Stevens of Baulking, Giles, Richard, Sarah, Joan, Danial Stamp, Richard and Jane Thatcher. In some minutes of 1677 it was agreed that a Friday meeting should be held **at Charlow, Faringdon and Uffington and Bishopstone.**

A Meeting house must have been built soon after the 1680's and a cottage was attached in 1710. This Meeting house was rebuilt in 1730 at an estimated cost of £34:8:6.

Deed of Trust for Uffington for 2000 years 1731

Richard Stamp of Challow Yeo . John Townsend of Loncot Yeo. EdwardSlatter and Robert Reynolds of Westbrook Faringdon Yeo. John Vickers Bourton cord winder

The Quakers were busy keeping their affairs in order and presumably these people were the trusted ones to see to things such as proper up keep of buildings and documents. These people are local and mostly farmers or connected with the woollen trade.

Assignment for Uffington June 1795
signed:
Jos Morris of Reading gent. Josiah Allen of Abingdon cutler. John Hankins blanket weaver, Thomas Smith Hatter, John Fardon Grocer all of Witney,William Barritt cord wainer, Thomas Minchin distiller, Joseph Cowdrey grocer, Joseph Huntley school master all of Burford.

Again these people must have been the Trustees, but by now some lived beyond the Vale area. They are the General Meeting Trustees and are all in business. This was the late eighteenth century and many Quakers were now well-to-do.

Quakerism died out in Uffington village for one reason and another. Certainly a Baptist Chapel was built in 1831 and flourished and may have drawn Quakers through its doors. The Meeting House was finally sold in 1821. It has been used as a private dwelling since about 1960.

Bishopstone Meeting

Further up in the head of the Vale there were Quakers and they met in a barn in **Bishopstone,** but never in large enough numbers to actually build a meeting house. Geographically that area is near to Wiltshire and Quakers got pulled that way towards **Lambourne Woodlands**, now gone or to **Oare** with a burial ground. In the late nineteenth century those wishing to worship in a Quaker way did so in Swindon.

George Fox certainly visited the Lambourne Valley and that may well be where some seekers from Blewbury, Uffington or Faringdon first became convinced of the Truth. In 1681 George Fox records that he attended large meetings at Oare and on page 373 (Penny edition of his journal) he gives reference to Samuel Burgess of Oare singing (or speaking singingly) in prayer or in preaching or with a vocal voice as an abomination and he reflected *on SB. of Oare who sung a new way of merry jiggs.*

I have been unable to discover to what extent reasonable landowners and parsons enabled meetings to exist and flourish, even if not with their unmitigated blessing. It would not have been wise or expedient to be seen accommodating Dissension if you wanted promotion and acceptability in Establishment circles. Certainly there seemed to be an anti-Quaker situation in the Shrivenham area. Some unreasonable punishments were levied. Lord Fettiplace of Kingston Lisle was also rather against Quakers. How it came about that Challow got its meeting must have had something to do with the strength of the yeoman farmer Richard Vokins. Wantage never had a meeting and neither did Shrivenham. Yet Faringdon did and so did Blewbury. Oxford Meeting as we have seen had a chequered history, which undoubtedly was connected with the antagonism of the establishment there.

On the northern side of the Thames in Oxfordshire Quakerism also flourished. The following Meetings were linked with Vale Meetings at some stages.

Milton under Wychwood and Burford Meetings

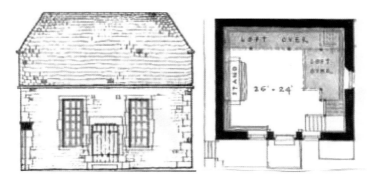

Burford Meeting House
Taken from Hubert Lidbetter's Book - The Friends'Meeting Houses
- left 1710 exterior, right plan.

The first group of Quakers seem to have gathered at Milton under Wychwood. A meeting house was built there very early on. Quakers met there until 1813 when the building was sold as a private dwelling which it is today. Not long after this group built their meeting house, another was built in **Burford,** which is still used for worship. Vale Quakers will have worshipped in these Meeting Houses from time to time. So I feel that the plan we have of Burford can be included here. It gives an idea of the early structures.

Also the meetings of **Alvescot** and **Charlbury** were eventually part of the Monthly Meeting to which some Vale meetings belonged (see dates in the table at the end of this chapter). The footings of the Alvescot Meeting House can still be seen (1996) and Charlbury Meeting is up and running.

Charlbury Meeting House today with 1991 extension.

Witney

It is almost certain that Witney Quakers had their first Meeting House in what is now Marlborough Lane. There was no graveyard and they were allowed to bury their dead in the church yard. In 1674 the Meeting transferred to the Woodgreen which included a burial ground. This area was then in the parish of Hailey. At this time meetings were held in the home of Kester Hart. In 1677 John Hart the son of Kester transferred property to Thomas Minchen of Burford. and John Harris and Silas Norton gave T. M. £383. (Perhaps this went towards Burford Meeting Funds.) John Hart eventually sailed away with William Penn to Pennsylvania. The Early(Witney Blankets) family were also involved in the meeting in these early times and into the eighteenth century. [9]

Oxford Meeting

Although Oxford is not in the Vale as such, it is very much a city at the mouth of the Vale and trade from the Vale was drawn to Oxford. So it seems right in my journey round the Meetings to include Oxford. Eventually Oxfordshire and Berkshire became one General Meeting as they are to this day.

Oxford, the university town, was not a happy place to be for Quakers. The first evangelists from the North often travelled to Oxford on their way to London or Bristol and stopped to preach. They spoke with Northern accents and were treated mercilessly by the students. These Seekers would criticise the young men for their theological ideas and forms. The young students and their Tutors were accused by these travelling Quakers of not understanding the reality of Spiritual Truth. This sort of criticism of the established church did not go down well. It led to riotous disorder and so sometimes the constable would imprison the preachers or leave it to the students to do with them as they pleased. Elizabeth Fletcher and Elizabeth Levens were dragged through a dirty pond. Elizabeth then felt called to walk naked throughthe streets of Oxford as a sign of the way God would strip them of their profession as clerics. The young students were enraged and excited as women were at that time not allowed to preach and engage in religious argument. These two girls were dragged into St John's College, tied back to back and had water pumped onto them until they choked. The University Authority had enough and when the girls, having been cared for during the night by friends, held a meeting for worship the next day, they were arrested and brought before the Vice Chancellor, Dr Owen, and the justices. They stated that they had come to Oxford to declare `against the sin and ungodleyness' which they saw the students lived in, `as pride and covetousness, lust and all uncleaness, self righteousness and all false worship'. They were whipped out of town as vagrants. Of course they were too fanatical and evangelical and did their own movement a disservice in retrospect. At the time the girls felt they were under theLord's advice. This view of religion scandalised the University Authority and seemed sinful and subversive. Always is the question, "How do you know it is God and not the Devil advising you?" Girls rushing through the streets nakedly and men riding on donkeys as James Naylor did in Bristol were indeed extravagant ways of demonstrating a peaceful loving way of worship.

The Mayor of Oxford was more friendly towards these Seekers from the North, many of whom were more sober and quieter, or were men which helped! The mayor's son became convinced of the Truth. A regular meeting of Quakers was established in the home of Richard

Betteris by 1654. Of course some of these events and happenings must have percolated through the grapevine of traders, farmers and travellers to the Vale Seekers. So though the Oxford story is a world away from rural Berkshire of the day yet it was in some respects not so far apart. The Quakers in Oxford had a very difficult time during the Restoration Period, so they met in each others' homes and were especially concerned with succouring all those Quakers who languished in gaol there. The Journal of Thomas Ellwood includes some evocative descriptions of those Quakers held in Oxford Prison.

So Oxford did not get their first Meeting House until after 1686 when James I issued a general pardon and a royal warrant for the release of Friends from prison, followed by his Declaration of Indulgence in 1687. Land was bought at the back of Silus Norton's house, at 63 St Giles. Quarterly Meeting ordered general collections throughout the county between 1687 and 1693. Vale Friends were therefore not especially involved in this but they must have been aware of it all as I have already hinted. Some may even have visited meetings in the homes of Oxford Friends from time to time. The building was probably not ready until 1688 or 89, when theToleration Act was passed. This Meeting struggled on in Oxford with continuous struggles with the authorities and the students. Original families such as the Nichols family died out and their young moved away. By 1746 the Quarterly Meeting was compelled to record that `there are not sufficient Friends left in Oxford to keep the meeting there'. This state of affairs continued on and off, until the Meeting house was sold in 1867.

The rest of the story is told in Stephen Allott's booklet - *Friends in Oxford.* [10]

Since 1939 Oxford Friends have met at 43 St Giles and today it is by far the largest group of Friends gatherings in Oxfordshire and in Witney Monthly Meeting to which the old Vale area belongs.

Reading Meeting

I am not covering the history of Quakers in Reading for that is well told elsewhere. It has always been an important Meeting for Vale Quakers. It has always been the strong and large Meeting in their General Meeting area. Here was the prison that most were sent to. George Fox visited Reading often as did other Publishers of Truth and Vale Quakers will often have been at these gatherings. The meeting has been there since the beginning of Quakerism and is still active. Reading Meeting certainly had difficult times in the early days due to a particularly unsympathetic Justice of Peace as we have seen in the last chapter, but the meeting has always kept going.

Bristol Meeting 1747
[from Hubert Lidbetter's Book of Meeting Houses]

I think that several Vale Quakers will have worshipped in **Bristol Meeting** and in the **London meetings** and elsewhere as their families married into wider Quaker circles. Certainly this was so with the Faringdon Reynolds family.

NOTES

[1.] HOWGILL (Francis), *Quaker Faith and Practice* 19.08 Francis Howgill's testimony concerning... *Edward Burrough, 1663,* in Edward Burroughs *The memorable works of a son of thunder, prelim leaf e3.*

[2.] Northeast (Peter), *The Venerable village - some notes on Blewhurv 1981*

[3.] HOWSE (Violet), *Parish Records of West Challow, Goosey and Charney*

[4.] Drummond Jane, *Quakers in Childrey* 1984

[5.] SALISBURY (Harriet), *Charney Manor*Quaker Home Service 1990

[6.] Oxfordshire Archives for the original deeds and assignments of the Vale meetings, see appendix at the end of the book.

[7.] *LITTLE (*John E.), *Ecclesiastical History of Uffington part I*

[8.] SCOTT (Sharon), *Uffington Parish Trail* 1994. The Uffington Museum alsoholds some records about the village.

[9.] GOTT Charles and Joan, *The book of Witney* MCMLLXXX Barracuda Books Ltd

[10.] ALLOTT (Stephen), *Friends in Oxford The History of a Quaker Meeting 1952*

List of First day Meetings in the area
(Preparative)

	Dates	Monthly Meetings
Abingdon	1668 - 1790	Vale
	1791 - 1810	Warborough
	1810- 1837	Reading
	1894- 1948,	
	1978	Witney
Alvescot	1709 - c18th	Witney
Appleton	1668 - 97	Vale
Bishopstone	1668 - 1730	Vale
Blewbury	1668 - c18th	Newbury
Burford *	1668 - 1855	Oxford !Witney
	1891 - 1921	Witney
	1956...	Witney
Challow	1668 - cl8th	Vale / Witney
Charlbury	1 1668 - 1918	Oxford! Witney
	1919- 1957	Witney
	1985...	Witney
Charney	1949 - 82	Witney
Faringdon *	1668 -1790	Vale
	1791 - 1880	Witney
	1982..	Witney
East Garston	1675? -1687	Lambourn
	1687-cl8th	Vale
	1939- 1975	Witney

Milton	1668 - 1813	Witney
Lambourn Woodlands		
	1673 - 1687	Lambourn
	1687 -c18th	Vale
Marlborough	1965...	Witney
Oare	1668 -c18th	Newbury
Oxford	1668 - c18th	Oxford/Witney
	1889 ... Witney	
Swindon 1892 - 1909	Nailsworth	
		and Gloucester
	1909 ...	Witney
Uffington	1668 - 1790	Vale
	1791 - c19th	Witney
Witney	1668 - 1890	Oxford/Witney
	1893- 1919	Witney
	1922 -48,59-66	Witney
	1997.	Allowedunder Witney

* Burford and Faringdon were one Preparative Meeting 1798 - 1817 under Witney MM.

The following Preparative Meetings are currently (1998) part of Witney Monthly Meeting, which includes much of the original Vale of White Horse area:

Abingdon (no meeting house), Burford (meeting house), Charlbury (meeting house), Faringdon (meeting house), Headington (no meeting house), Marlborough (meeting house), Oxford (meeting house), Swindon (meeting house), Witney (Nominated - no meeting house).

CHAPTER FOUR

THE LIVES OF EARLY QUAKERS IN THE VALE

`Sing and rejoice, ye children of the Day and of the Light; for the Lord is at work in this thick night of darkness that may be felt: and Truth doth flourish as the rose, and lillies do grow among the thorns, and plants atop of the hills, and upon them the lambs doth skip and play. And never heed the tempests nor the storms, floods nor rains, for the Seed of Christ is over all and doth reign. And so, be of good faith and valiant for the Truth.' George Fox 1663.* [1]

The Vale Monthly Meeting was quite a prosperous one containing at least fourteen yeoman families. They owned their land and seem to have been literate and in touch with the outside world. **Thomas Bunce** of Charney Bassett appeared to have had a very well organised household. The farmhouse is still lived in and is thought to be the building situated on the South side of the village green. His wife must herself have been well educated and seen to it that her children were tutored. Her daughters Jane and Joan were to become very important in holding the Monthly Meeting together. As their lives unfolded, Jane was like the Biblical Martha and Joan like the Mary. Oliver Sanson of Boxford in the Lambourne Valley was sent to this household to be educated as a boy and later became Jane's husband. At that time none of them were Quaker and yet they were open to the influences of radical Protestantism.

Oliver Sanson

Oliver Sanson, born at Beedon in Berkshire on the 8th day of 7th month 1636 was baptised 14. 7th 1636 at the Parish Church. His father was John Sanson and his mother was Elizabeth. He appears to have had one brother and two sisters who also later seem to have become Quakers. His father was honest and of small substance, but with care was able to educate his children.

When I was six I was put to school to a woman to learn to read and write and I could read the Bible within four months. After I was seven I was sent to board with a sister at Charney to learn Latin and writing.[2]

At ten years old he returned to his father's farm helping with the business.

Whilst these family links were helpful at the start of Quakerism and gave stability to the families facing those difficult times, yet later on too close marriages within the Quaker movement was not so healthy either physically or culturally. In the nineteenth century such closeness and inwardness nearly led to the demise of the Society of Friends as we shall see. It became a small and inward looking sect and cousins did marry cousins far too often in some families.

Oliver Sanson says that he was always interested in the Holy Scriptures and other Godly books, that he listened to many preachers and was waiting and seeking. He says in his journal that at times `I felt alone' and `lost'.But He that tendered me was withdrawn and I knew not where to find Him ...I cried in distress.'.* [2]

At the age of twenty-one he was still in turmoil (1657) of uncertainty when:

`I was invited to a meeting of people called Quakers and there I heard one of them declare the Truth - the inward principle - the light within, shining in the heart and discouraging darkness there, which when I heard, I came to be fully convinced and satisfied in myself that that was the TRUTH and the WAY OF GOD which was a matter of great joy and comfort to me.[2]

Of course he had problems because his parents disapproved, so for a time he still went unhappily to church with them. They encouraged him to follow the pleasures of the world and find a nice girl and forget all the silly Quaker stuff He tried to do this, to go dancing and singing and living `*loosely*' as he puts it. But in 1661 he became ill and lame (was this polio?) but the Lord brought him through. He married Jane Bunce, who also at that time went to church and presumably enjoyed country dancing. But he was changed and thankful to God he now wished to be `*an inward worshiper'.*

There must have been quite a crisis for the newly wedded couple and their respective families. Oliver seems to have moved to Charney and read books and become a bit of a recluse. He read a book by Isaac Penington also recently convinced and the step father of the girl who was to become William Penn's wife eventually and who was running a Quaker Meeting in Jordans, Bucks (still a Quaker place today). The title of the book was `*The way of life and Death made Manifest and set before me*.' It was at this time that Oliver became a convinced Quaker. Sometime later Jane also became a Quaker and they brought up their children as Quakers. [3]

Not very far away, in Buckinghamshire this other couple were also becoming Quakers at about this time, Isaac and Mary Penington. She wrote the following which gives us an idea about the problems for those joining Quakers:

My relations made this cross very heavy, but as at length I happily gave up, divested of reasonings, not consulting how to provide for the flesh, I received strength to attend the meetings of those despised people which I never intended to meddle with, but found truly of the Lord, and my heart owned them. I longed to be one of them, and minded not the cost and pain, but judged it would be well worth my utmost cost and pain to witness such a change as I saw in them - such power over their corruptions... Thus by taking up the cross, I received strength against many things which I had thought impossible to deny; but many tears did I shed, and bitterness of soul did I experience, before 1 came thither...But oh! the joy that filled my soul in the first meeting ever held in our house at Chalfont. [4]

So it came about that Oliver Sanson was far more than interested in Quakerism than ever he was in farming. He became a Publisher of Truth and wished to uphold their testimonies and preach their truth. But he also had a young wife and family to support and so in 1663 he and Jane moved to a farmhouse (the old farmhouse) next to the church in Boxford where his father gave him a small farm to manage. In fact he employed men to do the work and probably therefore had time to do his Quaker work too, attending meetings on First days including business meetings. Here he kept up a constant feud with the priest over non- payment of tithes. This came to a head when part of the church tower fell into his garden in 1667. Tradition has it that he refused to allow the material to be taken away saying that `as God had sent it to him, no man should take it away.' The rector got his own back and laid information against Oliver Sanson for non-attendance at church and non-payment of tithes. He was sent to Reading jail and a distraint was laid on his property.

In prison Oliver caught smallpox and Jane came to nurse him in the prison. She also caught the illness and so returned to Charney to recover.The family must have been in crisis, the younger generation forging a way for itself in supporting the new movement and the older generation supporting them as best they could.

In his autobiography Oliver Sanson relates of the rector's painful death, which he regarded as a judgement! The trouble between Oliver and the church became too much. On one occasion whilst in prison the crops in his fields were harvested and sold and he got no chance to do anything about it. Far more revenue was gained by the church authorities than was legally allowed, far more than a tenth. Eventually he and his young wife Jane and the family moved to Faringdon, where they set up a draper's shop, selling woollen materials and some finished garments. As he wrote in his journal:

The thoughts of moving to Faringdon came afresh and more strongly to me. And because the exercise it brought with it was very weighty upon me, I laid the matter before Friends at a men's monthly meeting. And as I related my condition and the exercise that was upon me therein, the Friends were much tendered and had great unity therewith and found clearness to encourage me to go in my purpose for they were sensible that I might be of more service to the Truth in Faringdon than where I was ... 1673.5.[2]

By 1676 Oliver was away from home much of the time leaving capable Jane backed, no doubt by her family to manage the shop whilst she also managed the Vale Meeting. He visited Liverpool and crossed over the Irish Sea to Dublin, Droghuden, Lurgin, Ballymury and Wexford. In a letter to Jane from Dublin he wrote:

Dear Jane, In that love which sea and land cannot separate doth my soul salute thee and truly reach unto thee and the secret breathings of my life are often poured forth unto the Lord that thou mayest daily partake with me of the same heavenly comfort and sweet refreshment which the Lord in his love hath opened as a spring to me... I sent a letter to thee by first post after we came ashore and about ten days after I sent a letter to Joan Vokins (his sister-in-law) to whom I desire thee to mind my very dear love and to her husband and family, to M W and D.A. whom I desire may not be negligent in their endeavour for setting up a Womens' Meeting... and mind my dear love to all Friends belonging to Faringdon, Uffington and Charlow meetings. [2]

In 1678 Oliver wrote:

Thomas Blagrave, steward of Sir Robert Pye, Lord of the Manor of Great Farringdon, kept a court Leet there. I was ordered to appear, I was sensible a share was intended, yet I was going but got too ill to go. So I wrote a note explaining why (I could not go). In 1680 1 was nominated as Constable, but could not swear the Oath (of Allegiance). [2]

So once again Oliver wrote to the Court...

But if I may be excused, then this I request of thee, to admit me to take the said office and perform it without having an oath imposed... and I shall endeavour, through the Lords assistance, to perform my duty faithfully... [2]

In the end he must have been called to the court where he refused to remove his hat or swear the oath and so he was fined £5 and did not become a Faringdon Constable. Later he was distrained of goods worth 18 shillings and some more worth £6: 6 shillings. It was no doubt his wife Jane that had to find the money from the shop. This was easier than having to pay with breeding animals and farm seed as had been the case when they were farmers.

Oliver asked himself

Why did this man (Robert Pye) appear so implacable against me in the matter seeing he was well known in the county, of late years especially, to be in general against persecution for religious dissent'... [2]

He went on to wonder if it was due to his writing letters in defence of other dissenters regarding their non-payment of tithe! I suspect that Sir Robert Pye realised that Oliver would be open and outspoken about any accommodation they might have come to. If he made allowance for one principled Quaker, then where did his law and order responsibilities go regarding all the other dissenters and factions around? These were times of intrigue and a wrong step reported to the King and his minions could spell disaster. There were plenty of those looking to make something out of another's mistakes. It is one thing to think tolerantly and another to act.

The following is a complicated little story which occurred in 1683 and is written about in the Sanson journal: In Shrivenham there lived a man called Eustace Hardwick. He was not a Quaker, and was disliked by the justices because they had constantly to deal with his `malpractices.' So he wanted to get his own back on Sir Robert Pye and Thomas Fettiplace and make them look bad in the eyes of the law. He thought they were too lenient with dissenters and that he would curry favour with the Government informers if he could catch his local justices out and also be seen to be helping the informers against law breakers. So it was that`on the 4th day of the first month 1683 Eustice Hardwick rode over to Faringdon just at the time he knew the Quakers would be worshipping. He flung open the Meeting House door, just as Oliver Sanson was on his knees making supplication to the Lord. Hardwick commanded his *men to stand guard over the worshipping Quakers lest they slipped away...*

"if he had known our principles he need not have done!"

Meantime whilst Hardwick rushed to inform Sir Robert Pye of this illegal meeting, those left on guard were `moved to feel that these people were good'.`Soon the officers came and charged us with meeting illegally (in our own Meeting House). Names were taken and two went before Pye and were fined £20. Sir Robert asked who the informers were, [2]

Apparently on being told that it was Hardwick and his men, who had ridden quickly away, Sir Robert Pye was furious that they had got away and sent his own men to catch the informers and bring them back to Faringdon. This was done and Hardwick was disarmed, there and then, of his sword and two pistols and he was held for *misdemeaners he had made afore'*. Thomas Fettiplace was sent for and the two justices made a mittimus for Hardwick and sent him to Reading Jail. So this time anyhow his scheme to curry favour didn't work. The following day Oliver apparently met Sir Robert out riding and asked him,`Why am I wrong to worship?`" Not very tactful in the circumstances for Oliver knew the law of the land and in fact Sir Robert had scotched the plot of one informer and fined Quakers fairly leniently. Oliver did not record an answer.

Of course Faringdon had been in the midst of some of the Civil War due to its position with East/West routes along the hill top and the Radcot Bridge. It had many inns for the soldiers and was a useful market centre for feeding the war weary. Sir Robert Pye senior is known to have given money to the King's side, and at one time the Cavaliers were in the town and occupied the old Elizabethan Faringdon house.

Sir Robert Pye kept himself in London and out of the way during the skirmishes in and near the town. He kept his distance and somewhat played the game on both sides or none. His son and heir also Robert, though, was a staunch Roundhead and he raised a troop of cavalry and spent most of the time campaigning against the Cavaliers. It is with this younger Robert Pye that our Friend Oliver Sanson was dealing and so as some of the Reading Quakers such as Thomas Curtis had been officers in Cromwell's army one can understand why the Oliver Sanson might, afterwards, expect sympathy and understanding from the younger Pye. In 1645 Cromwell had come to root out the cavaliers from Faringdon town but only partly succeeded. He did not get them out of Faringdon House and had to ride away on more pressing matters to Newbury. Finally after the surrender of Oxford to Cromwell the young Pye was sent to capture his house from the Cavaliers. As he had no intention of damaging the property that would one day be his, he settled down to a siege and finally allowed the cavaliers to ride out of town unmolested. He did indeed take over the house when his father died in 1662. He helped the townsfolk to rebuild their damaged town.

At one point soon after the Eustace Hardwick incident, in 1684, Oliver was distrained of goods worth £21.13.6 because of his Quaker principles. He wrote *that James II declaration, some four years later, all the shop goods were given hack untouched...Some serge cloth was a hit moth damaged and the books were lost.*

So probably the heart for punishing Quakers had gone, and those in charge of law and order had better things to do with their time in Faringdon and they realised the unfairness of the law as it stood. Quakers were seen as honest traders and generally as law-abiding citizens minding their own business.

Towards the end of his life in 1690 Oliver Sanson and his wife Jane moved to Abingdon. Oliver wrote in his Autobiography that the only three men friends in Abingdon were lately removed by death and that the meeting needed help. He was soon in trouble in Abingdon for refusing to pay church tax and distrained of materials worth £19.5 and there he died in 1710. He had testimonies to his life signed by William Penn, William Lamboll of Uffingion, Thomas Nickolls (publisher of the first Fox journal), Thomas Eliwood, Jane Sanson and Danial Bunce of Charlow.

Thomas Ellwood published the journal of Oliver Sanson and included the followingTestimonies:-

He was not only a preacher of good works but practiced them. `He hath dispersed, he hath given to the poor, his righteousness endureth forever psalm cxii...and his testimony was against all pollutions of the world, against all pride, and vain fashions and customs there of- and he laboured that Truth might be in dominion amongst us.. .He was a good husband, master and neighbour and a serviceable instrument in the hand of the Lord for turning many from Darkness to light.,.he was mindful to entertain strangers, to visit the prisoners that suffered for Christ's sake, sympathized with the afflicted and was careful overthe widows and fatherless... He admonished the disorderly walkers and laboured with them and backsliders to bring them to repentance and amendment of life...'

Thomas and Robert Withers, Daniel Bunce, Jim and Adam Lawrence, William Orpwood, Jeremiah Harman

This was read at Reading 10th 6th month 1710 either at a Quarterly meeting or a Meeting to give thanks for the life of Oliver but it was also then signed by more friends from a wider area who... `had unity with the above':*

John Buy, William Lwnholl, John Thorn, John Reason, William Penn, William Lawrence, Richard Hoskin etc.

Other testimonies were read ... `His memory remains sweet to us `... Oxford Friends.

Thomas Ellwood wrote:

`The like may be truly said of the deceased friend and brother Oliver Sanson that he was a just and upright man, one that feared God and eschewed evil.. [5]

Jane Sanson his widow wrote most touchingly:

This testimony I give forth concerning my dear husband whom the Lord in his great mercy has pleased to give me which I can truly say was a great blessing from the Lord to me for he was convinced of the blessed Truth before me and very helpful to me in my convincement, and always very careful for my prosperity in it. So that the loss of him is very great and a trying exercise for me...[5]

The Vale Quakers in general

Many Quakers left their farms in the latter half of the seventeenth century. It was easier to manage with goods being distrained for non-payment of tithes and other, so-called, misdemeanours, than to replace breeding animals and farm seeds. Winters were difficult in those times and if your newly born calves, piglets and lambs were sequestered what could you do? If your breeding bull was sequestered what could you do? There was little justice or kindliness shown to the `dissenters'. On the contrary the aim was to force them with privation and poverty to mend their ways, or at least to put others off following their example. In fact with Quakers, so full of their spiritual zeal, it merely drove them on to earn their living in the 'fields' of business and manufacture, where they could also worship in their chosen way with less direct harassment. So the second generation of Quakers were much more likely to be business people. These businesses were still connected with farm products such as wool and food.

George Fox had decided to set up a more formal structure whilst he was held prisoner in Scarborough Castle and he set about doing this in 1667, some ten to twelve years after Quakerism first came to the Vale.In the Vale Quarterly Meeting minutes 1673-78 you find the following people involved in the running of the Quaker affairs: **Thomas Bunce** of Charney and **Richard Thatcher** of Uffington, and **Oliver Sanson** and his wife **Jane (Bunce) Sanson**. There was **Warmen Townsend** of Longcot and **Thomas Reynolds** of Buscot and **Michael Reynolds** of Faringdon, **John Langley** of Idstone. There were women as well. **Joan (Bunce) Vokins** of West Challow who was Jane Sanson's sister. She was now married to **Richard Vokins.**

The Quakers met for business meetings nearly every month in different villages around the Vale area. Childrey, Appleton,

Lambourne `church of Christ'`, Uffington and Faringdon are all listed. The Tull family from West Ilsey on the Downs were at Monthly Meetings. In 1674 **Philip Tull** was at Faringdon MM, and **Jane Tull** witnessed at the meeting in Reading held after the death of Joan Vokins 1691. They may have been related to Jethrow Tull the inventer of the Seed Drill. [6]

It is amazing that the men and women and children travelled so frequently to each others' homes for worship. They went on foot and horse to these gatherings and of course representatives had to go to the Quarterly Meeting at Reading as well. They were often joined at their monthly meetings by Friends from other parts of the country. From time to time some Vale Quakers attended Yearly Meetings in London and they travelled about far and near on business too. So though in one sense they were living in the small Vale countryside yet they were in touch with the outside world and the main Quaker movement.

First Day must have been a busy one. The farm work to be seen to, hasty family prayers and Bible readings, followed by breakfast and then off to the gathering. They took lunch with them and expected to be away all day. The Meeting for Worship held in the morning was held under God's will and could last for hours. The children were there too and one has to assume that women went in and out to answer the calls of nature and to feed babes. Men also must have gone in and out too. During the lunch break there was time for the swapping of news of sufferings of Friends, and about what was happening in other countries, especially in New England. Who was to be married to whom and who had died or given birth. In the afternoon it was a business meeting after the manner of Friends. This was held in a silent frame and clerked and minuted. By the end of the seventeenth century, when Quakerism had been formalised, the epistle from Yearly Meeting might be read or a minute from Quarterly Meeting discussed. A lot of the business concerned the needs of those in prison and their families in the early days. Vale Quakers were themselves sufferers and often nearly all the men-folk were in prison. The business meetings were divided into men's Meeting and women's Meeting, but the women could send a representative to the Men's Meeting.

The early minutes are full of sympathetic love towards those who stray. Standards are expected of Quakers and those values and guidances taken from Yearly Meeting Epistles are to be upheld by members. Gradually as the century wore on a Puritanical leaning came to the fore and a strong moral tone reared its sometimes rather judgemental head. This was to become even more strongly stressed in the eighteenth century.

In a meeting at Faringdon in 1674:

' mention made concerning the poverty of William Parsons by reason of his late sickness and it was thought fit to give him ten shillings to supply his present outward necessity'...[7]

`It is ordered that John Goring and Oliver Sanson do go to George Green and admonish him concerning some misgivings which he had lately been found in'

One longs to know what these misgivings were about. Perhaps he had paid his tithes, or got drunk and disorderly or got mixed up with dubious money fiddling.

At a Faringdon meeting in October 1675 Joseph Nobbs came from Oxford and confessed that he had:

`sinned and done wickedly with his servant mayd and then to cover his shame he went to a priest to be married. For both these actions he sayed he was sorry and troubled and condemned himself and desired Friends to breathe joy and love for him that he might be redeemed from y unclean spirit which had overcome him so he might have unity with the Lord and with his people.'

Friends felt that time was not yet. And committed him to wait *for ye righteous judgement of God to redeem his soul from the unclean spirit'~*

Another entry is full of innuendo. This minute was recorded at Appleton in December 1675.

`The accusation charged upon John Butcher was by Friends examined according to order and he hath not changed himself in any way to their satisfaction although he flatly denies it: Yet a strong suspicion of guilt seems evident in the sight of those Friends who have been concerned with it. And Friends of this meeting can do no less but deny and abhor such wicked and unjust doings... and until John Butcher do clear himself of this charge he shall henceforth have nothing to do with the keys of this meeting house nor digg any more graves.'

Was this a barn in Appleton or was this misdeed elsewhere, one wonders?

Piecing together various entries about Warmen Townsend is interesting. It is the start of the Quaker stance against things they saw as too pagan and earthy. It was a strand of Calvinistic Puritanism: music and dancing, drinking and gaming were not allowed. In November 1677, at a Faringdon meeting, mention is made of some miscarriage of Warmen Townsend, that he was among dancers at Lambourne and danced with them. He was exhorted to repentance and asked to give a paper saying he condemned his evil doings. He must have been present because he said he was sorry for it but the Friends wanted time to consider the matter of forgiveness.

The next meeting (January 1678 at Childrey). Warmen was not present, nor had he written his apology. So John Goring, Oliver Sanson and Joan Vokins were asked to visit him and seek his repentance. At a later meeting he again is reported to have repented but refuses to do so publicly again. In fact during a visit made to his home:-

`Warmen Townsend did in words acknowledge that he was sorry for his miscarriage in dancing and etc. and did hope that he should never do the like again. But he refused to give out a paper under his hand to clear ye truth and own his own miscarriage according to Friends desire...   (17.2.1678)

For a while Warmen is not listed as an attender of meetings for business. Then there he is back in the fold again. He possibly worshipped on Sundays but sneaked away from business meetings. At a meeting in Uffington in February 1679 the matter continued again and Warmen refused to have his repentance recorded because;-

Oliver Sanson did not speak to him privately about the matter before he brought it to Monthly Meeting. So Oliver in `true tenderness to him and desiring his recovery confessed he was sorry'. Warmen then accepted the apology and `confessed and acknowledged his transgression and did condemn it'. Perhaps he was not a very good writer and producing a paper was indeed beyond his capabilities!

Meantime in 1678 at a Quarterly Meeting of Berks and Oxon, William Townsend of `Longcut' *has been reported of several miscarriages and a group asked to seek his repentance and also to visit Warmen at the same time.* We do not know if Warmen is the son of William but I think he must have been and that these matters were running concurrently over the years.

At a meeting at Standford *26.2.1678 John Goring and Oliver Sanson gave account that they visited Longcot `on the 7th day of ye 2nd month at 6 hour in the morning'. They found him guilty of deceit and hypocrisy in his payment of tithes and covenant breaking in selling a parcel of land at Clanfield. And to other things also. However William himself was not there and it was left to his wife and children to explain things.* At Childrey (26.5.78) mention is again made of William Townsend and his family.

`Friends were grieved to see their love to them so slighted and their tender careand labour in visiting them so little esteemed. Yet nevertheless it is still ye earnest desire of all faithful Friends that W.T. and those of his family concerned might yet turn to the light and truth which did at first convince them to condemn their overall doings and come thereby into unity with God and his people'.*

Once again a group was asked to visit them at their home *that where there is tenderness it might be preserved and if possible they might be recovered and saved…*

Unfortunately minutes in this Men's Vale Quarterly Meeting Minute book are not signed but they could have been written by Oliver Sanson and already one can discern an over-zealous tone, an intolerance of the failings of weaker souls that several preaching Quakers or ministers cultivated. The minutes could equally have been written up by Reading Friends, but one does not know.

It has to be remembered that many of these people were in their twenties or early thirties. John Langley of Idestone may have been a yeoman farmer or a husbandman. From time to time he gave quite large sums of money to the meeting. He attended many meetings and became a trusted Quaker eventually, but to begin with he was a bachelor and had to sort out his love life.

In about 1678 Mary Harris of Bourton, near Shrivenham, made known to some Friends that she was troubled and dissatisfied at John Langley's carrying and dealing with her that `after he had drawn out her affection and promised to marry her some years yet he delays to perform it'. So a group were appointed to speak with John Langley.

At another meeting it was reported that *John Langley was visited and also his servant maid (Ann Barnard). Things not well, and contrary to the Truth, in many particulars in their deportment. John appeared very penitent and sorry for what he had done. So the meeting desired that John Langley and Ann Barnard should give forth a paper in the fear of the Lord condemning all these things.* Further the Meeting suggested they should live asunder and then get married.

Even today the hamlet is very isolated and it certainly was then. One is left wondering if John Langley's parents had died whilst he was in his early twenties and so that was why the maid had come to the farm. it was sometimes customary, particularly in country areas, for the poorish parents of a daughter to get her into service, off their hands and to hope or assume that in fact marriage might eventually occur if the two got on. A wealthy young bachelor was quite a catch. So what John and Ann apparently did was a fairly common way of pre-marital dallying. But it was a system open to abuse, and not the standard of chastity expected within puritan ideals. Again one has no idea if Ann was pregnant by then or whether or not they had children. They may in fact have not done very much of a carnal nature at all.

On the eleventh month 1681 John and Ann were present and their paper was read condemning his former miscarriages and Ann said she was sorry for what had been amiss in time past. Later the proposal for their coming together in marriage was brought to the meeting. They were asked to wait a bit until things were clearer.

At a later meeting John and Ann were married and all seems to have ended happily for them. We do not know what happened to poor Mary Harris of Bourton. Perhaps she left the Quakers and married into some other denomination.

Quakers were from the beginning very particular about marriage that it should be a spiritual union but fully witnessed and that the arrangements should be according to the custom laid down in fairly lengthy advices drawn up by elders at the Quaker gathering at Balby in Yorkshire in 1556.The Marriage Act of 1556 allowed such marriages too.

For right joining in marriage is the work of the Lord only,and not priests or magistrates'; for it is God's ordinance and not man's; and therefore Friendscannot consent that they should join them together: for we marry none; it is the Lord's work, and we are but witnesses. [7]

Indeed marriage was taken very seriously, recorded and witnessed in a Meeting for Worship. It was not to be undertaken lightly and those wishing to marry were expected to consult with their families and take time to ensure that this was what God intended.

It is quite impossible to sort out family trees because the births and deaths were not recorded very meticulously at the time. Also parents had a habit of calling their sons by the same name as father or grandfather, and, as often the three generations were born in the

Oldfield [may have been re-built; certainly re-roofed]

space of forty or fifty years, it is a nightmare trying to0 decide who is father, who is son or cousin.

It is interesting to look at the minutes of the local meetings for business and these give some indication of the lives being lived. For example to note that Thomas Reynolds of Oldfield in the parish of `Burscot', Buscot, a husbandman, married Mary Davis at Childrey in 1679.

`*Thomas Reynolds declared 2nd time his intention of taking Mary Davis to be his wife and she Mary Davis declared the 2nd time her intention of taking TR to be her husband. A certificate was produced from ye Marys mother signifying her consent.*

A paper was read for a collection to redeem such friends as were taken captive by the Turkes. Agreed 3th of our stock to supply eservices.'

Later at a meeting in Challow (29.9.1688) *Thomas and Mary are reported as having triplets and then in 1688 great want of nurses for Thomas Reynolds children his wife lately had three at one birth.*

My final story, taken from the minute books of both the Vale Women's and the Men's Meetings, and pieced together with some guessing is about **Elizabeth Wightwick**. I think she was possibly the sister of Oliver Sanson and so perhaps she too was educated with her brother at the Bunce home in Charney Bassett. She was therefore related to Joan Vokins and Jane Sanson and a very much loved member of the family. On the other hand Thomas Bunce of Goosey had a daughter Elizabeth in which case perhaps Elizabeth Wightwick was in that way part of the Bunce family and cousin to Jane and Joan `Bunce'. One does not know.Elizabeth married John Wightwick and they had a family. At a Monthly Meeting at Appleton (26.7.79) the decease of John Wightwick is recorded and a group asked to go and advise the widow.

At a men's meeting at Childrey (31.8.79), Joan Vokins reported *that Widow (Elizabeth) Wightwick is causing concern to the Women's Meeting by her deeds and practices, living with Edmund Parker, so soon after her husband had deceased. She had said she wanted to be with Friends but is not listening to their advice.*

At a Men's Vale Meeting at Charney on (26.10.79) the following is recorded:

`Not withstanding friends have time after time given their judgement that she will ruin herself if she shuns it, wherefore in concern it was spoken to her that seeing she had refused friends council and followeth her own way, and if it should come to pass that by this means she do make a rod for herself and suffer under it, then how could she expect that friends (whose council she had rejected) should anyway stand by her. Then she answered that if it did so fall out that she comes to suffer she would expect no help from Friends. This and much more was spoken to them both on the 30th day of the 9th month last past.And it was agreed that notice shall be given to the WidowWightwick'sLandlord that he may not have any dependence for his rent upon Friends that so Truth may not be blamed if she do in any way fail.'*

So we do not know if she had children out of wedlock with Edmund Parker. At a meeting in March 1682 Widow Wightwick asks Friends if they could give her and her children a transfer Certificate to Pennsylvania, but friends felt they could not.

A Vale women's meeting granted Widow Wightwick money in May 1682 to pay for her children's schooling so she can go `abroad' to work. I think `abroad' simply meaning to a neighbouring farm or something. She is present at the memorial meeting held for Joan Vokins at Reading in 1691.

The Vale Monthly Meeting Women's Business Meeting

Women's business meetings were encouraged from the time the Quaker structure was put into place from 1667. However it took time as women in those days were not thought fit to run their affairs. Most churches did not have much of a role for women in their church government and most women were not able to read and write. So it is interesting that women in Quaker families were taught to read and write and to keep accounts. They were considered equally as children of God and could take a full part in 'preaching' and Ministry in Meeting for worship. The Women's Meetings for Business Affairs were formed for mutual support. In those early days many men were away from home preaching or in prison and those left behind needed to be cared for. The poor, the sick as well as those in prison. So the women were concerned with the welfare of the group and acted in the role of the Quaker Overseer of today. Later they were often the meeting that looked after the heating and cleaning of the meeting houses too. The Vale Monthly Meeting Women's Meeting officially may have started in 1667 at the instigation of George Fox and Oliver Sanson. It was very much held together by Jane Sanson and spiritually by her sister Joan Vokins. The first minute book that we still have runs from 1676 to 1730 and we have a wonderful transcription completed by Nina and Beatrice Saxon-Snell.

I have to digress at this point to the wider developments in Quaker Business structure and the disagreements that it led to. This will later colour the problems that our Vale Women had to face when holding their meetings. The first Quaker Yearly Meeting was held in 1660 at Skipton in Yorkshire and, in 1661, another such Meeting was held at which it was decided that each County should send two friends and London 6, Bristol 3, and Colchester 2. This was a men's meeting in those days. It was decided to hold such a gathering annually. Ireland had its first Women's Yearly meeting in 1679 and England had its first in 1784!

Two Early Publishers of Truth, John Wilkinson and John Story who came from the North and had mainly preached in Berkshire Wiltshire and the South West, were also at the first yearly meeting. At first they apparently agreed with Fox when, at this same gathering, he said

Keep your women's meetings in the power of God... in the restoration byChrist into the image of God and his righteousness and holiness again in that they are helpmeet man and woman as they were before the fall Epistle 291

As the days went by John Story in particular felt that the business side of things was getting too formal and also that some were meeting secretly to avoid friction with the law. The purity of the Quaker simplicity of the individual meeting openly before God was being polluted. He and others began to feel that all this Church Government controlling things was a backsliding into an imitation of traditional church practices. Some so-called Quakers were performing christenings and marriages in secret. I wonder if some of these things were being done in women's meetings or due to women wanting their babies christened and their children married in the way that they had been before ever Quakerism was. Anyhow all of this culminated in a schism led by John Story and John Wilkinson and their Reading friends Thomas and Ann Curtis, who we already know were very influential Quakers in the Berks/Oxon General Meeting. They felt Women's Meetings were not a good idea except in the large cities where there might well be poor and prisoners to see to. They felt that recording condemnation papers was taking over from the role of God and taking up time that should be used in spiritual matters. They disliked Friends groaning and singing in Meetings especially whilst another was ministering. They objected to the way George Fox was structuring the Society. So they returned to their own area and as the years went by their views presented a problem for The Vale Women's Meeting. Fortunately the Wilkinson - Story faction was no match for the spiritual fervour and resilience of the sisters Jane and Joan (Bunce) who were, it has to be recorded, also supported by their husbands.

Although the Vale Women's meeting was rather frail, as there seem to have been quite a few widows in it as time went by, yet it held itself together against outside interference. Nina and Beatrice Saxon Snell suggest that as the area was damp and low-lying the men were particularly subject to tuberculosis and rheumatic fever. Many also had been in terrible prison conditions in their fight for religious toleration and against payment of tithes for a church they did not worship in. So this minute book is full of oversight of these widows.

`It was done with sympathy and tact and where possible' [8]

The mothers were paid for small tasks such as sweeping the Meeting Houses, so that they had a feeling of independence. Money was also sent to the Men's Meeting from time to time and a legacy was paid into the Women's funds by the men too. So these Vale women had means of their own, perhaps inherited or through selling cheese, butter and cream, we don't actually know. Perhaps some of them had payments made by their husbands to them for their own use.

When the Sansons moved to Faringdon in 1674, Jane must have begun to help the needy of the meeting informally. She appears to have become the first Treasurer of the Women's Meeting. As mentioned above George Fox had encouraged the setting up of such meetings, as part of the 'church government' of the Society of Friends. Jane was often alone managing the Draper's shop and bringing up her children, as Oliver was away preaching and also spent several periods in prison. Her letters to him in prison or on his journeys are full of love. She obviously supported him in his work for the `Truth'.

`My true and entire love doth sincerely reach forth unto thee.'
`My very dear love once more to thee.'

There are all sorts of little entries that give a colourful picture of the concern for the meeting houses.

Paving was paid for at Challow Meeting House and also for *'disburse of a parcel of wood'*.

Ten shillings was given to Thomas Reynolds for the upkeep of the motherless boy. More money was given for this task by women and men's meetings and finally to pay for the boy's apprenticeship....Faringdon 1677

> *Agreed to pay for John Clark's son who was lame and needing a surgeon... at Alice Deans' house Uffington 1679*

> *Two pounds twenty was given for the relief of the poor of Lechlade as many of the families had members in Gloucester jail...West Challow 1678*

Poor relief was often given in kind ... bacon, clothing, linen, cordials, food, wood, wool for spinning ... money for doctors and for schooling

Joan Vokins

It is time to tell the story of Joan Vokins who was a very special Quaker. Some of her influence has already been mentioned. It is clear that Joan and her brother-in-law Oliver Sanson held the Vale together spiritually.

She was born in Charney and her father was Thomas Bunce, her sister Jane Sanson. She probably did not become convinced until after her marriage to Richard Vokins of West Challow. At the time she went through great exercise of conscience and endured much opposition from her near relations. Through her eventually her father, husband and children became convinced. In some records she seems to have been an attender of Newbury Monthly Meeting. This must have been the area where she first met Quakers and possibly heard George Fox and others minister to the spirit. Once a proper organisation developed and she called herself a Quaker, she was an active member of the Vale Monthly Meetings. *Charlow* meeting was on her doorstep and she obviously must have worshipped there regularly when at home. But Joan Vokins must often have clerked the Vale Women's meetings and I think she has written those minutes that we read today, she and Jane between them. She is often recorded as being present at the Women's Meetings and is the one who represents them and reports for them at the Men's meetings. She was most concerned with the spiritual life of these meetings. Today she would be an Elder and her sister Jane an Overseer. Together, against all odds, they ran a remarkably successful Women's meeting.

A Cockermouth printer printed Joan Vokins's Works in 1721. Her husband seems to have been instrumental in getting this accomplished. I take much of the following information from this text:

`God's mighty power magnified: as revealed in his faithful handmaid Joan Vokins who departed this life the 22nd of the fifth month 1690...'

Oliver Sanson wrote to the reader:

`these papers have been collected for thy benefit and were not written and given forth by the will of man or worldly wisdom but by the will and hidden wisdom of God - which is (and ever was) a mystery to the learned scribes and wise disputants of this world and as foolishness to them.'

Joan must have been a child of light or something similar all her grown up life. She was very spiritual and was as well educated as could be in the circumstances of her background. She got married, had at least four children and helped on the farm. She seems to have been sickly in later years, possibly tuberculosis. In spite of this problem, once the children could manage without her and whenever she was well enough, she felt called to travel preaching the *Word* and sharing the *Truth*. She travelled around England, sailed to America and to Ireland. Always she wrote home and to friends, she wrote to and prayed for the Vale Women's Monthly Meeting.

The following is such a letter mentioned in the foreword to the transcription of Nina and Beatrice Saxon Snell. I am not sure of the date or if it was written in Ireland or America:

Dear and well beloved sisters whom I cannot forget, but in that love that reacheth over sea and land, do my soul dearly salute you, hoping that the pure mind he stirred up in every one of you to consider the matchless mercies of our tender God which I do here put you in member of...

Oh how hath He manifested His almighty power when we have been together in our Women's Meetings, and how have we been relieved and horn up over all our oppositions both inwardly and outwardly and in the Gospel Light have seen the great Goodness of the Lord and in the Gospel Power have been strengthened when we were very weak and supported when we were very needy. Hath not our Heavenly Father's love been sufficient to engage our hearts in faithfulness?

Oh that it may be an Obligation to us to everyone of us to keep to the Gospel Light and to live the Gospel Life and to love the Gospel Order. For our God is a God of order and he affords precious opportunities to wait upon him and if we abide in good sense in his love we will not forget our times and hours to wait for the seasons of the Lord for they are so sweet to the thirsty souls that itcannot be satisfied without them and therefore many times thinks in long(ing) ere the meeting day come, that it might he replenished with the virtue of Christ Jesus the head and strengthened with the rest of the members; for as we truly gather in his name (praises there unto) he has made us partakers of His divine nature.

Oh that we may take heed that we give the enemy no advantage by slighting the mercies of our tender God or neglecting our duties but that in remembering of his tender mercies and Fatherly love we may double our diligence in our places of Service, that our God may be honoured, feared, obeyed by us all that we may receive the blessed and sure reward in the end, when time here as to us all shall he no more and be in his safety from all harms for ever and evermore be it

106

saith the soul of your dear sister in that which is strength to the weak and help to the helpless, that sea and land cannot separate.

When her beloved sisters were in serious trouble she returned from America and put off journeying until things were settled. This was the time when the Wilkinson Story schism alluded to above caused so much trouble to the Women's Meeting. It was the time of the half yearly Quarterly meeting for men and women at Reading. Wilkinson and Curtis locked the door of the place where they were to meet so the meeting was as far as one can gather cancelled. This was not approved by mainstream Quakers and the women decided to meet next and as soon as possible at Faringdon far from the homes of Story Wilkinson and Curtis. Lo, when the women gathered at the appointed time at Faringdon, Ann and Thomas had galloped over and barred the way!

They went with intent to spoyle ye meeting'

Joan must have been in America at this particular time and presumably Jane wrote to her about these terrible events of Quakers quarrelling with Quakers. Joan `had a service laid upon me to go back and labour for the settlement of theWomens Meetings in our Count of Berkshire.' So she did return and writes `thorned Amaleks' lay in wait by the way (Thomas Curtis) armed with the opposite spirit which did strongly strive. Yet our Good Shepherd did visit his hand maids and (blessed be His name) filled us with His overcoming power.'*

Yes, the Women's meetings gathered even more vigorously and eventually seem to have been left in peace. The Wilkinson - Story separatists lost their desire to continue in their differing views and George Fox and others persuaded them to return to the Yearly Meeting.

Apparently Joan arrived in New York 4th of 3rd 1680, and was accompanied by Sarah Yorklet. They travelled to Oyster Bay and Long Island. She had, no doubt, met those who had been to these new lands of North America before her, when they returned to England and she felt called to go too. She had no sooner got to

America than she was *inspired* to return to her Berks Women's Meeting `which was no small cross to take up'` she wrote. This could be interpreted as the travelling back again on awful ships and dangerous waters or in the thought of dealing with the men who were so against the Women's Meeting back home. One has to remember the travelling problems in a country just opening up and the frightfully hazardous Atlantic crossing in small sailing ships. When she was back with her beloved women friends she wrote:

> `I felt the Good Shepherd did visit his hand maids and filled us with his overcoming... The Lord Owns our Women's Meeting...`

She was sick and lame, so perhaps she suffered from arthritis as well as some form of TB, but she felt called once more to America. She knew that the women there were having a very rough time in many areas. So in 1681 she was once more in New York, Long Island, where a Ranter oppressed the Quakers. She nearly died here but rallied. At Rhode Island `with Thomas Case the Grand Ranter ..bawling away...She spoke with God~ living power and Thomas Case went his way.` She travelled to Boston and East Jersey with Elizabeth Dean and then on to Pennsylvania.

Joan was very dear to those New England Quakers and had possibly met Elizabeth Hooten and others who were called to America in England. Others she met there. But she must have known about Elizabeth Hooten and her work for the Lord, though Elizabeth had been dead some nine years by the time of Joan's American visit. Elizabeth had died in 1671 but her works lived on for the Joan Vokins's of Quakerism.

I will include a little about **Elizabeth Hooten** who came from Skegby near Mansfield. She was a well-to-do, middle aged woman, a mother and already a popular preacher, when George Fox first met her at the age of twenty-three (1647). Their friendship lasted until death and they must have influenced each other. They found the answer to their questions in `the light within `and called themselves `the children of light'`. She was recognised as the leader of the Nottinghamshire `children of light'` by 1649. It was here that George Fox first came into collision with the authorities. He was on his way to attend meeting in Nottingham one day when he felt called to go to the church of St Mary. The minister was delivering his sermon on the text *'we have also a more sure word of prophesy; whereunto ye do well that ye take heed, as unto a light that shineth in a dark place, until the day of dawn, and the day-star arise in your hearts '(2 Pr* 1.19) The minister went on to explain that the sure word of prophesy was in the *Scriptures. George Fox could not bear it. 'Oh no, it is not the Scriptures,' he cried. 'The Holy spirit is the one sure guide to Truth and did indeed inspire the Scriptures*.'

It was not an offence to speak in Church after the sermon was over in those days, but it was a punishable offence since Queen Mary's day to interrupt the sermon, and so this young George Fox had his first imprisonment in the 'nasty stinking' Nottingham prison. Elizabeth was soon in prison herself for similar reasons. She later felt called to go to New England and once again was often in prison or barbarously treated for her faith. Quakers were whipped from town to town, women stripped and whipped, branded, had ears chopped off, imprisoned and hung. Elizabeth as a sixty-year old suffered much. She was put in the stocks for days, imprisoned without food and water for two nights once. She was whipped and then carried to a remote place and left to face the perils of wild beasts and starvation. She really was a Quaker martyr. She did finally return to England. But you can see how inspiring such a person was to our Joan Vokins.

In 1671 George Fox, broken in health himself after long imprisonments, took twelve Friends with him including Elizabeth Hooton, who went especially to look after him. They landed in Barbados and stayed a while with the Quaker community. They moved on to Jamaica and there Elizabeth was suddenly taken ill, perhaps malaria and so departed this world *'in peace, like a lamb.'*

A letter to the Governor of Barbados from George Fox, probably mainly thought about on the voyage over in 1671, is quoted below:
Whereas many scandalous lies and slanders have been cast upon us to the rendering us the more scandalous, (vizt) that we do deny God and Christ Jesus and the Scriptures of Truth, this is to inform you that we do clearly testify to the contrary...

109

That God who is only wise, omnipotent, and everlasting God we do believe in, who is creator of all things both in Heaven and Earth, and preserver of all that he has made, who is God over all, blessed for ever, to whom be all honour and glory and dominion and praise and thanksgiving both now and for evermore.

And that Jesus Christ is his beloved and only begotten son in whom he is well pleased, who is conceived by the Holy Ghost, and born of the virgin Mary, in whom we have redemption, through his blood even the forgiveness of sins,who is the express image of the invisible God...

Now concerning the Holy Scriptures, we do believe that they were given forth by the Holy Spirit of God through the holy men of God, who spoke, as the Scriptures of Truth saith, As they were moved by the Holy Ghost (2 Peter 1.21) and that they are to be read, and believed, and fulfilled and that he who fulfils them is Christ (working in us).

Another slander is that we should teach the Negroes to rebel....for that we have spoken and declared to them is to exhort and admonish them to be sober and to fear God... George Fox

The Quakers encouraged their Negro servants (slaves) to become Quakers, to hold their own meetings and to order their affairs which included marriage and burial. All were children of God whether black or brown or white, said the Quakers of the time. All this must have been known by Joan Vokins who also visited Barbados and the Leeward Islands, Nevis and Antigua. There she wrote letters to her husband Richard and to her sister Jane and brother-in-law Oliver:

had meetings amongst black and white people [separately I think] *and the power of the Lord Jesus was mightily manifested, so that my soul was often melted therewith, even in the meetings of negroes and blacks...*

She is pleased that the children in the West Indies have meetings and learn George Fox's catechism (he wrote this in 1657) that they may come to learn of Christ and the Light, the Truth and the Way that leads to the Father, the God of all Truth.

Some recent studies in America suggest that the Feminist Movement was begun in the hands of those early Quaker Women. Indeed their new found independence, upheld by their direct relationship with God, was threatening to men and that possibly led to their being whipped and ducked, imprisoned and burnt, sometimes on the flimsiest of proof. However these martyrs for Spiritual Toleration, including a belief in the equality of all before God, male and female, black and white, poor and rich, was not to be dampened by punishment. They continued to do, with God's help, that which they believed they were called to do. They did these things for the spirit, for God not for themselves or for a political change. They were good mothers and wives. Once their children were old enough, those married to Quakers were encouraged `to stand up and be counted'. To preach and minister and run their own affairs, to take risks and spread the Quaker ways.

Of course, as I have written elsewhere, there were some women who were so emotionally involved and so led by the spiritual excitement of the times that they did break conventional ways and may well have upset fathers and husbands and children who did not themselves `get caught in a net' and could not understand this behaviour. I think though that this awakening of the role of women in the Quaker movement was more to do with the feeling that they were equally children of God and equally open to the Spirit and could take a full part in the seeking for and the experience of God rather than a feminine stance as we have had this century. So I might suggest that their behaviour and accomplishment was a beacon and an example to women who were downtrodden or unrecognised but that was not their aim. Their aim was to fight *the Lamb's War*.

Finally Joan Vokins died on her way home to West Challow at the home of John Buy in Reading, in 1690. She must have been buried there or at West Challow, though I have not been able to find out. In the New Year a special Meeting was held in her memory. Over forty Friends were witnesses and signed their names. Elizabeth Wightwick was there so not in America and many of those we have already met in those early days of Quakerism in the Vale. Testimonies were read and recorded

Theophila Townsend of Cirencester 10.2.1691 wrote:

She was a virtuous woman truly fearing God and one that was full of zeal and courage...and that did the work of the Lord with boldness and holy confidence and much cheerfulness. I have known her about twenty years and had correspondence with her by letters, have been to her house and she to me - she was of tender spirit ready to hold forth a hand to the weak, to help them on the way to peace, to watch over them for good and encourage them in well-being- and delighted in seeing those that know the Truth grow up into the life and nature of it. Great was her care for her husband and children - her care was great for her children that they might come to a sense of Truth that (she said)when she saw them cumbered with their minds hurried with their worldly business that she would call them together to sit down and wait upon the Lord and sit with them that he might compose their minds into inward retiredness and said the Lord was with her in it and often refreshed her spirit among them.

An Epistle probably from Joan Vokins written to the Vale women (1669) reads:

Therefore dear hearts, think not your time long, neither let the world hinder, but keep your meetings frequently, there to wait with sincere hearts, for those that so wait, never lose their reward: therefore be encouraged to wait upon the Lord, that in pure refreshing life your souls may come to have an habitation. Therefore dear Friends it concerns you all to dwell in the patience and in the wisdom that comes from above, which is first pure, then peaceable, gentle, easy to be entered, full of mercy, and good friends without particularity, and without hypocrisy. And so the God of peace establish your hearts to his encircling truth and righteousness for ever.

If Quakers had Saints I think Joan Vokins would be our Vale Saint. She really stands out in her service to the Lord. She demonstrated remarkable fortitude in spite of her illnesses and the pain she suffered for she travelled thousands of miles in very difficult situations. She travelled mentally too from accepting a given role for her in the established Church of just being a lay mother, and a given mindset, to being a pioneer of theology and spiritual pathways as she grew into her Quakerism. She also showed that as a woman one could be true to that role as mother and wife and yet give service as a preacher and spiritual healer in its own right. She never gave up and was an inspiration for her own generation. Her example and Quaker principles are an inspiration for today and forever.

By the end of the seventeenth century the children of the original Quakers were marrying more widely within Quaker circles as the Society became more organised and Quaker business and educational networks strengthened. The Sansons moved to Abingdon, some Reynolds's moved to Bristol and Banbury. Many had gone to Ireland and many more to New England to Pennsylvania.

NOTES

[1.] FOX George, *A collection of. Epistles, 1698, Epistle227* (1663), p99 in *QuakerFaith and Practice 1995*

[2.] SANSON, OLIVER *An Account of the remarkable passages in the life of OliverSanson 1710 Autobiography*

[3.] ELLWOOD Thomas, *Journal of Oliver Sanson , published by Thomas Ellwood.*

[4.] PENINGTON Mary, *Experiences in the life of Mary Penington , No 29 ChristianFaith and Practice 1960*. Mary came from a well to do background and was part ofthe establishment as was Isaac Penington. Her first husband was killed in the Civil War and her daughter by that marriage(Gulielma Springett) became the wife of William Penn. Mary with her husband became the nucleus of the Jordans Meeting in Buckinghamshire.

5[.] see3

[6.] OXFORDSHIRE Archives, for Men's and Women's Vale Monthly Meetings. BothOXFORDSHIRE and BERKSHIRE Archives for Quarterly Meeting minutes. (Theseare well catalogued and can be found relative to the dates concerned. See the list at the end of this manuscript.)

[7.] FOX. George 1669 and entry 16.01 *Quaker Faith and Practice* 1994.

[8.] SAXON SNELL Nina and Beatrice, *Transcription and notes Vale of White HorseWomen's Meeting 1676-1730* BOQM XV2

[9.] VOKINS Joan, *Gods Mighty power magnified as manifested and revealed in hisfaithful handmaid Joan Vokins 1691* Edited by Oliver Sanson

CHAPTER FIVE

THE VALE CONNECTIONWITH PENNSYLVANIA

0! you young men and women, let it not suffice you, that you are the children of the people of the Lord; you must also be born again, if you will inherit the Kingdom of God.

[William Penn][1]

Pennsylvania was given to William Penn in 1681. On his deathbed his father Admiral Penn in 1670 had asked King Charles II and James, Duke of York (King James) to befriend his wayward son, his only son and heir. This they tried to do, but the King was a Catholic and young Penn was the Quaker! They both came from religions that had not been tolerated by the establishment. It was the debt that the establishment owed the Admiral that got translated into the lands in the new world. They named it Pennsylvania in memory of Admiral Penn. Thus it was that William Penn, who was then 37 years old, inherited the lands. Here was the opportunity to found a Quaker State along Quaker lines in the New World.

The first settlers sent back good reports to their friends in England, Wales and Germany. They told of fertile lands to be purchased cheaply, of kind natives, of easy government and of the possibility of worshipping in their own way without hindrance and punishment.

In 1682 Penn sailed to the place of which he was the entire owner, inheriting it from his father who had been honoured with it by the King. He sailed in the Welcome, a ship of 300 tons and he took a hundred colonists. Thirty died of smallpox on the voyage but I do not know if any were our Vale colonists.

Our people are mostly settled upon the upper rivers, which are pleasant and sweet and generally bounded with good land. The planted part of the territorie is cast into six counties, Philadelphia, Buckingham, Chester, Newcastle, Kentand Sussex, containing about four thousand souls. Two general assemblies have been held, and with such concord and dispatch that they sate but three weeks, and at least seventy laws were past without dissent... [2]

This extract was taken from a letter sent by William Penn to the Free Society of Traders of Pennsylvania in London 1683.

On the whole there seemed to be a delightful peace and harmony in the early days:

At the two `aforementioned' Yearly Meetings (Burlington and Philadelphia) we had such a blessed harmony together that we may say we know not that there was a jarring string amongst us. A great multitude came of hundreds, and the gospel bell made a blessed sound. There was a men's and a women's meeting in both places in the precious services to inspect into Truth's matters in what related to them~ and God gave them wisdom to do it, and all was unanimous.. . The majesty of the Truth is great here, and does prevail and grow...yea it will increase more and more to the ends of America... The day of its great visitation is come, and his great power and holy authority is rolling hither like the inundation and breaking and overflowing of waters... [3]

It is estimated that by 1700 about half the population of Pennsylvania was Quaker. The proportion probably never reached this amount again. Perhaps there were twenty thousand Friends in the wider area. Samuel Bowness speaks of meetings in Chester County having 1500 members. In Philadelphia the Meetings were `exceedingly large... more like Yearly Meetings than First Day Meetings.'

From this point on one reads of Vale Quakers asking for a Certificate of recommendation to go and live in Pennsylvania. Some are listed in Vale minutes, some in Quarterly minutes. Once or twice collections are made to help Friends to settle in America.

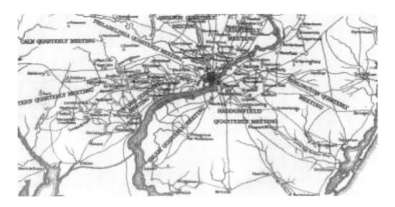

Map of Meetings around Phladelphiaia

Mary Webber has lately been afflicted with the distemper wishes to go to Pennsylvannia. This was agreed to at a meeting in Faringdon 27. 1 .1682 - *hoping it will do her good evervway* was included in the minute.

Certificates of Removal to Philadelphia (Pennsylvania):

> Joseph Austic from Oare.
> John and Richard Bunce of Faringdon -1682.
> John Mason of Faringdon 1682. He went with his wife Mary and three sons.
> John,Robert and Richard. He had purchased 1000 acres in England before leaving for
> Philadelphia, Pennsylvania. His surviving son Richard appears to have settled inChester County, Pennsylvania.
> Elizabeth Newman of Faringdon 1682.
> John and Richard Wormwell of Oare 1682.
> Thomas Franklin of Great Coxwall 1685.
> Thomas Bunce of Goosey 1685.
> Jonathan Thatcher of Uffington 1685.
> Richard Thatcher of Uffington 1685 or 1687 when it was

recorded at Concord PA.

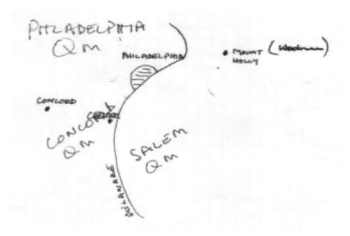

Concord Quarterly Meeting, Chester County Area

So some of these Friends possibly sailed with William Penn in 1682. Some may have died of smallpox on the voyage. But Richard Thatcher seems to have sailed to Philadelphia on The Bristol Merchant on the ninth month 1685 with Jonothan (18) and Jane or Jeane (15). His wife Jeane (Jane) Stevens (M. April 1667) had died in Uffington. The Thatchers first settled in Thornbury Township, Delaware County, PA where they were leased some 124 acres. Jonothan seems to have purchased or leased land in Concord Township in Chester County, Pennsylvania an area of rolling farmland. Here he and his descendants farmed and continued to be Quakers. The local town was and is Willistown. In those days it was expanding rapidly.

Jane married William Brinton and they had a large family too. The Brintons are around today as well and some are still Quakers.Jane or Jeane Stevens, the mother of Jane and Jonothan, had also been a Quaker and is most likely the daughter of John Stevens of Uffington who held meetings in his house. The Officers of the law set guard upon the house to keep the Quakers out one Whitsunday in May

1670, so apparently, they held their meeting for worship in the street. Thus were they accused of breaking the law and were punished by being distrained of goods. The local people would not buy their goods. Those suffering with John Stevens were Richard Thatcher, Mary Johnson, Clement King, Anthony Pearson, Thomas Leadbeater. They were all fined five shillings and distrained of goods.

The above information has been taken from Sufferings of Friends VOL. 1 page 28 and quoted in a document about family history sent to me by Edward Thatcher, a descendant. 29.1 97.

A May Thatcher in one minute in the Vale women's meeting did bring her problem of having a difficult husband to them (1679).

So reading between the lines perhaps the Uffington Thatcher men were hard on their women. Richard does not sound an easy man or a very loving father, or Quakerly in parenting. He was possibly about forty years old when he arrived in America and about fifty five when his son by then himself thirty years of age wanted to marry. This was very much against his father's wishes and Richard in fact sounds a cantankerous old man by this time. His daughter Jane had married in 1690 and so perhaps he just did not want his only son to have other interests.

At a Monthly Meeting at Concord Pennsylvania, in Robert Pyle's house, in 1699, Jonothan Thatcher (Richard Thatcher's son born in Uffington, England 2. 1 5.69) and Hannah Dix or Dicks laid before the meeting their intention to marry,

`this being the second time ye persons were appointed to make inquiries in that respect as also concerning the life and conversation, make report to the meeting that they do not find but that it is clear for all other women in relation to marriage, his life and conversations being orderly: But his father told them that he would not give them his consent, therefore this meeting appoints Nathaniel Parke and Nicholas Pyle to go to him again and order him to appear at the next monthly meeting to show his reason wherefore he do not give his consent.

119

Hannah Dix or Dicks.'

`At a Monthly Meeting held at the house of Nathaniel Parke, Nicholas Pyle... reports that he accidentally met with Richard Thatcher at a friend's house and after some friendly discourse he was given the news.. and having heard the demand of the meeting.. Richard replied that he would not come to meeting and after further debate he said it mattered not the order of the meeting no more than dirt under his feet and that if it were but two steps to the meeting, he would not come, further adding so to tell them.'*

In the end the meeting gave Jonothan and Hannah permission to marry and they had nine children.

Concord Meeting House circa 1850

The Thatcher family are spread now all over America. Some have even become Mormons. The descendant that I have communicated with is a Quaker, Edward Thatcher living in Western States in Oregon. His Great Grandfather Thatcher married his Great Grandmother Mary Hibbard of Williston in 1826 (1876) and they had 17 children.

This branch of the Thatcher family became Hicksite Quakers. This split in Quakerism finally was formally recognised in America in

1827. By that time the Evangelical Movement affected all denominations and the Quakers too. The feeling of Evangelical Quakers was that the Quietist tradition was thin on Christianity and did not teach directly from the Bible as it should. They split away from traditional Quakerism and set up separate Yearly Meetings, employed Pastors and had programmed Meetings with set Bible readings and hymns and sermons. But more about this in chapter seven. Elias Hicks and his followers emphasised the Spirit in the midst of silent worship and especially the awareness of the God within. Theycontinued to hold traditional Quaker meetings where all were responsible for the quality of worship and they did not have employed ministers or hymns. Edward Thatcher, a direct descendant of the Uffington family, with his wife Monette, attend a Hicksite meeting in Eugene, Oregon up to this time. So in many ways Richard Thatcher who left the Vale in 1685 would simply walk into meeting on First Day and find things very much the same, even though three hundred and fifty years have gone by. I have not traced any other Vale Quakers with descendants still Quakers and still going strong, but I am sure there must be some out there too, perhaps some Bunces, Masons or Reynolds.

NOTES

[1.] PENN William, *Preface to George Fox journal*, 1694, prelim leaves L3-L4; bicentedn,1891 VolI, pplvi -lviii, Quaker Faith and Practice 19.59 1995 edn.

[2.] PENN William, *The Peace of Europe, the fruites of Solitude and other writings ofWilliam Penn*, Dent Everyman series.

[3.].JONES Rufus, *The Quakers in the American Colonies*. Macmillan 1911.

[4.] Haverford College Library Haverford PA has helped a lot with references from its Special Collections and checked out my leads from the following records: *Dictionary of Quaker Biography*. Cope's

History of Chester County, PA, McCracken's, Welcome Claiments, *Hinshaw's Encyclopedia of American Quaker Genealogy and other materials.*

[5.] CONCORD Meeting, the clerk of Concord Meeting itself probably has more details about certain Quaker settlers. Their records are kept at Friends Historical Library, Swarthmore College Swarthmore PA. 19801.

The Holy Experiment ... William Penn :

* A true democracy without any class distinction.

* No army or navy.

* A home of religious liberty (a belief in Christianity being the only qualification for office and this qualification may have been imposed from the King of England).

* No established church but toleration for all who believed in God. (Penn felt the Indians knew about the one God) his letter from Philadelphia 16.6.1683 a description of Pennsylvania.. .*these poor people are under a dark night in things relating to religion, to be sure, the tradition of it; yet they believe in one God and immortality without the help of metaphysics...*

* No distinctions of race, and all foreigners to be at once naturalised.

* A humane penal code with reformative punishment.

* Just and generous treatment of aborigines and neighbours.

* No oaths.

* Some regulation of slavery.

* Strict regulations against puritan sins such as swearing, lying, duels, card playing etc. *`According to good example of Primitive Christianity and for ease of creation' no common Daily labour on Sundays.*

* Provision for Education.

CHAPTER SIX

THE EIGHTEENTH CENTURY AND THE QUIETIST PERIOD

Disorderly walking, and evil practices.[1]

Those Quakers still living in the Vale of White Horse had by now settled down to a peaceful life after the passing of the Toleration Act. They recuperated and re-grouped, many had emigrated to the New World or had left the Vale altogether for various reasons. Marriage was one reason; if you had a son perhaps the prospects were better working with or for a Father- in-Law in another town, if a daughter, perhaps her father thought prospects for her were better married to an up and coming Quaker merchant elsewhere. Apprenticeship was another reason for leaving the Vale. The Quakers in businesses and trades were becoming strong in Birmingham, London, Bristol and such towns and that was where opportunities occurred. It was not so easy to be a Quaker in a village where you were ridiculed for wearing `plain' dress and for avoiding military service. In the village a Quaker still upset the church authorities byrefusing to pay tithes and taxes. Whereas in earlier times rural situations seemed to enable `Seeking' to flourish, now with increased communication and speeding up of life this was not the case. As most Quakers were now self-employed and getting involved in the pre-industrial Revolution, they got on with their lives and did the best they could outside the professions and mainstream business life. They formed Quaker trading and business connections as they moved into larger towns and cities and overcame the challenges they faced imaginatively and prudently.

In 1689 the customs duty on the export of corn was removed. Exports rose rapidly with the exception of some bad harvest years. So it became profitable to drain more land to put it under plough and to enclose land. At first all farmers did well, so our Quakers must have made some money during the end of the seventeenth century, hence the ability to build the Meeting houses and to enable some members of the family to travel in ministry. But the eventual result was that large landowners did well and small yeoman farmers did badly. This led to bigger and fewer farms and especially hit the Quaker Vale farming community. The Agrarian Revolution was coming along and soon not so many would find employment on the farms. The growing cities offered more security and reward.

Only a few Quakers continued to farm in the Vale, such as the **Reynolds** family in Faringdon who still had their farm for the one son and the rest of the family went into trade in Faringdon or elsewhere. The **Vokins** were farming in Challow and the Uffington Quakers were still farmers as were the **Bunce** family in Charney and Goosey. Also it is fair to say that no longer were so many Vale Quakers so closely involved in the production and distribution of wool, though in other parts of the country Quakers still were. They were independent and expanding business people honest and fair for the most part.

During this second century many Quakers became a more middle class, urbanised people. At the same time because they wore plain dress and used plain speaking they cut themselves off and became a peculiar people'. They had survived as a group by adhering to strict codes of behaviour and Quaker `church' government. **Margaret Fell** Fox, the wife of George and often called `the mother of Quakerism`, warned Friends against undue regard for outward forms:

`It's a dangerous thing to lead young Friends much into observation of outward things, for that will easily be done.. But this will not make them true Christians; it's the Spirit that gives life.'[2]

She noticed that rules and formalities were increasing. The testimony for simplicity in dress and against slavish following of fashion was fast degenerating into an obsession. Margaret thought it a silly poor gospel. But it seems that those second generation Quakers were not listening. Margaret died in the arms of her youngest daughter, Margaret Abraham, in 1702, and her last words were `I am at peace.'

According to John Punshon (p.103 Quakers in Grey) by 1715 Quakers possibly had at least 696 worshipping congregations which was the largest number of any dissenting community in England and Wales. Of course the average size of the group may not have been large. Perhaps there were about 39,000 Quakers as against 179,000 Presbyterians and 59,000 Independents or Congregationalists. I simply do not know how this breaks down in the Vale but it probably replicated the national picture, though the Quaker element must have been less than even the national average as so many had moved away from the Vale by 1715.

As non-conformists were excluded from the universities, the professions and from public service, Quakers had to set up their own schools and arrange for their own apprenticeship schemes. They had to become very self-sufficient. This had its good points as we shall see. For example Quakers could embrace the new scientific and technological ideas and were well placed to make the most of the industrial advances soon to come. Steam power and mechanisation into railways and industry and so on all became Quaker strongholds of innovation and ownership.

The first Affirmation Act was passed in 1696 after much lobbying by such men as William Penn, William Meade and Thomas Lowe. This lasted for seven years. It was supposed to enable those who objected to taking an oath the opportunity to affirm instead:

I A…… B…. do declare in the presence of Almighty God, the witness of the truth of what I say.

In 1722 the final Act of Affirmation was passed, still in use today, and used by me quite recently in an estate transaction upon my mother's decease:

I J... I....R....do solemnly, sincerely and truly declare and affirm......etc. etc.

So the Toleration Act whilst permitting differences of worship was not the end of the struggle. The persecuting laws were not removed from the statute book, but there were to be none of the penalties for breaking them that there had been. The prisons were no longer filled with Quakers. There was still no relief from payment of tithes. The corporation Acts were still in place and as Quakers would not swear and were still excluded from public service and Higher Educational institutions. So they were still kept apart from mainstream society, and kept out of civil posts, Parliament and the professions as such. So the rift in society was hardened and the non-conformists had to look after themselves. This rift was not really to be bridged until the twentieth century. I have to mention that even today there is sometimes an air ofmistrust around the matter of affirmation and other Quaker stances of principle based on their religious testimonies to honesty, simplicity and peace.

In and around the Vale, in the early eighteenth century, families became more closely knit within the Quaker culture and somewhat cut off from great world affairs. They had their own philosophy of life but it was becoming rather inward looking. Some Elders and Ministers held a rather high moral expectation of members of the Meeting. At the same time the Vale Quaker families had ties with Quakers in other places through family links. By 1771 it is recorded in the *First Directory of Faringdon* that:

The Stroudwater to London coach passes through Thursday, Sunday andTuesday and it came back through Faringdon again. The Tetbury coach also came through the town and back [3]

So Friends and other townspeople could get out if they wished and their friends and relatives might visit them.

In **West Challow** the Quakers probably met in a converted barn, but by 1706 there was a burial ground. *The Deed of Assignment says on third day of the second month of 1706 land was purchased.* In 1731 land was purchased for a Meeting House to be erected. It appears that this was built, possibly of wattle and daub and with a thatched roof. By 1762 numbers had diminished and the meeting was discontinued. The meeting house seems to have become a home called Box Cottage, near the village pond. This also seems now to have been demolished because I have been unable to trace it. (see chapter 3)

In 1737 the meeting house at **Blewbury** was rebuilt. Repairs were also undertaken from time to time on **Uffington** and **Faringdon** Meeting houses. As the century wore on the Vale Quakers diminished in such numbers that the only meeting houses still used for worship were at Uffington and Faringdon.

There is a document in the Reading archives of the Reynolds papers that reads as follows:

1740 Joan Wilde and Richard Southby Buckland. upon Trust that they shall [?] premises for the teacher or preacher of the congregation of Protestant dissenters at the Meeting House in **Buckland.** *~*

This was found in the same Quaker farmhouse that the Reynolds's have owned throughout the periods that Quakerism has existed. This paper does point to the Faringdon Quakers being involved with Buckland, and so one imagines that at that stage the congregation in Buckland was very much in tune with 'the children of light' or `Friends of Truth'. However Baptists and Anabaptists did also use these terms about themselves in those days so it may have been a sort of Anabaptist group.

Another document of 1783 is between William Wheeler of Buckland and Robert Reynolds of Faringdon and again it is money to help with preaching. I feel that by now the group had perhaps become Baptist.

Some families reverted to Anglicanism and their names begin to appear in the births, marriages and deaths of the Parish records. The Bunce family in Charney seem to have become Anglicans and a Bunce served as Church Warden in 1748. Daniel Bunce is recorded in the Longworth (Charney) register as being on the PCC and caring for the church. Others moved away. Anthony Home 1758-1816 born in Southwark and a coal merchant married Elizabeth Reynolds (1760-1787) of Faringdon. They had three children. She died either in childbirth or shortly after and he married again. But soon after Hornes and **De Hornes** began to live in Faringdon and feature in the minutes. Whether these were Elizabeth's children come to Faringdon to their maternal grandparents, I do not know.[I have come across Quaker De Hornes in Brigg Lincolnshire who travelled in ministry a lot in the 18th century.]

Whereas in the seventeenth century those in the Vale who became Quakers were often at the centre of events, quite well educated and informed and in touch with theological ideas coming over from Europe, now they were content to live and let live. The evangelical zeal had gone and they seemed satisfied that they had found what they had sought. They worshipped at their meetings on Sundays and attended their business meetings. I think that the Faringdon Quakers in the latter half of the eighteenth century were perhaps `plain Friends' that is that those left in the meeting were serious minded people, God fearing and upright. They observed the regulations of Yearly Meeting and wore plain clothes and Quaker bonnets and hats. They would have set Sundays aside for worship and reading of the scriptures. They would haverefused to take part in blood sports and to play cards. They would have been carefulnot to drink spirits and to avoid dancing of any kind.

The Meeting would have been held to both welcome the spirit of Christ into the midst of the worshipping group and to nourish and support the concentration toward the inner and outer voice of God. So if there was no visiting minister and if the appointed ministers for Faringdon were not called to minister the Friends would sit for two hours or more in silence. I have been unable to find out if any Faringdon Friends were appointed Ministers and so one is left to imagine many silent meetings. Some Friends may even have gone to sleep during meeting. So there was no plan, no prayer book, no music, no hymns and the room plain and unadorned with any outward Christian symbols. The earlier time when any might contribute thoughts and prayers from God to the gathered community was past or almost frowned upon as beingexcessive and undisciplined. It all sounds dry and cold and you can see how, as Methodism came to the Vale some who had been Quakers may well have become Methodists. After all had not John Wesley's mother read from George Fox's Journal as well as the Bible and other works when he was a boy. Some even called Methodists `The Singing Quakers'. However I think for those who loved the Quaker way, George Greenleaf Whittier says it all in his poem or hymn:

> *Drop thy still dews of quietness,*
> *Till all our strivings cease;*
> *Take from our lives the strain and stress,*
> *And let our ordered lives confess*
> *The beauty of thy peace*
>
> *Breathe through the heats of our desire*
> *Thy coolness and thy balm,*
> *Let sense be dumb, let flesh retire~*
> *Speak through the earthquake wind and fire,*
> *0 still, small voice of calm!* [5]

On the other hand in other parts of the country things were not so quiet. Recalling his visit to Norwich Meeting in 1798, the American Travelling Minister William Savery remarks:

> `*I thought it the gayest meeting of Friends I ever sat in, and was grieved to see it...the marks of wealth and grandeur are too obvious in several families of Friends in this place and it made me sorrowful...'*

Yet Savery's preaching had an effect he had not realised. In front of him, resplendent in purple boots laced with scarlet, defiant but troubled, sat the daughter of one of the eminent families, Betsy Gurney of Earlam Hall, known later as Elizabeth Fry who was destined to be converted and turned into a Plain Friend by this same melancholy evangelist. [6]

The Vale Quakers, the remnant still in the Vale, were not `Gay Friends'. They were still humble and lived a less complicated life than those rich families in Norwich and Bristol, Colchester and

Birmingham. They may have been directly involved in the Agrarian Revolution, but not directly in the industrial Revolution with its rich pickings for the successful entrepreneurs.

The Men's Vale Business meetings seem to have dealt with money matters. Richard Pocock, Robert Reynolds, John Townsend, Thomas Withers often attended the meetings at Charlbury, Abingdon, Faringdon and Challow. In the fifties they did not meet so regularly and usually only at Faringdon. But they picked up some enthusiasm again in vitality towards the end of the century. In 1758 they were concerned about Hannah Heydon and her bastard child. She wrote that she is sorry but they referred the matter to Yearly Meeting. That body subsequently sent for her but she did not go. Finally `*therefore being sorrowfully affected in her disservation and for the honour of Truth'*, a paper of denial was drawn up. Thus it came about that yet another member was disowned. In 1779 they desired to get hold *of George Fox's Journal, Robert Barclay's Apology* and also works by *Richard Claridge* and *Edward Turner*.

In 1762 at a Meeting in Faringdon a letter was written to Warmen Townsend:

Some Friends having acquainted thee of the report and they having been somewhat addicted to swearing and which it seems thou dost not deny, but not having opportunity to say as much as might be requisit on that subject, we have thought it convenient to supply that omission by this epistle. Also we remind you that you still have not paid us the monies your Father owed the meeting
(Vale minutes)

Swearing was frequently noted (*attended to*). Other vices of a public nature such as *drinking to excess*, and *rioting* required a *penitent confession and then forgiveness*.

`*for if we confess our sins the Lord is merciful and just to forgive us our sins and cleanse us from all iniquity...'* or *'fruit of the spirit is love, joy, peace, long suffering, gentleness, goodness, faith, meekness, temperance and as the tree isknown by its fruit.*

Finally Warmen got disowned in 1763.

John Bacon caused problems by paying tithes and Margaret Bacon because she got married by a priest. She finally did send a paper of repentance to a meeting in Lambourne and all was well there. So, much of the business is similar to the early times. Perhaps it shows that Friends in the Vale had not got their act together as well as they might and that members were not too clear about the discipline of Yearly Meeting. Margaret Bacon's father or mother, if still alive, should have known what a Quaker marriage was. The women's Vale meetings of this period do seem to record marriages of those who married in the Quaker way.

In the decades before the Vale Monthly Meeting was laid down the original Quaker names were still appearing in the records. Representatives from the Vale attending General Meeting were Richard and John Townsend and Robert Clark and Richard Stamp from Uffington. Thomas Sargood from Blewbury, and Richard Pocock and Robert Reynolds (1705-1765 - son of James and Susannah Reynolds) and James Reynolds of Faringdon. These were the daughters and sons of the early Quakers. The Men's meetings of the Quarterly Meeting were sometimes held at Faringdon and the last such meeting held and minuted was on the 7th day of the 7th month 1766. The Vale representatives were Charles Reynolds and John Snelling and the minutes were signed by Richard Vokins of Newbury. He may have been a son of Joan Vokins now running a business in Newbury.

So Quakers should have listened to the Quaker news of the day, to Yearly Meeting Epistles and should have known about the views and actions that they as Quakers should hold and take. One could say that some meetings and individuals got isolated it was partly their own fault. It was only partly because the `Active Friends' of the day could and should have done a lot more than they did to keep up the strength of the Society and that should have included much better oversight of the Quaker families in the old Vale Monthly Meeting area.

It is interesting that up to this later period the Vale people still continued as a body with their Vale Monthly Meeting as minuted in their Minute book 1673-1722. It is clear that discipline was constantly a matter for action. There are twenty cases of dealing with `disorderly walking and evil practices' probably to do with promiscuity and courting. Young men and maids could not always manage to attain the Quaker /Biblical standard of waiting until they were married before indulging in sexual relations, the wider society certainly did not. Widows and widowers also faced similar difficulties. So I suspect the evil referred to was to do with such individuals trying to get to know each other. Eight cases of drunkenness were dealt with. I think this is not very high if one compares the Quakers with the population at large. Even these cases may not have been very serious. A farmer celebrating after a good sale and getting himself more than merry might have led to his being disciplined by the meeting. Everyone drank malt ale in those days and several Vale Quakers were maltsters. Tea and Coffee were still expensive. The Warmen Townsend Family through the two or three generations of our records do seem to have been admonished for drinking too much. Seven were disciplined for not attending meetings. It is possible that this Vale Meeting Minute Book had in reality become a Faringdon Preparative Meeting Minute Book, by this time. There are no Faringdon Meeting Minute Books in the archives.

It is interesting that the Quakers were being punished by the state for non-attendance at Church not long before this and now they were disciplining themselves as severely. Freedom had a different meaning for them it would seem. Freedom to worship in their own way provided it was the Quaker way. They did not like pagan ceremonies any more than the Church did. It is interesting to see the watchfulness by the meeting of the business practices of their flock. Of course many epistles and minutes coming from London Yearly Meeting reminded some of them about these matters. Soon they would have a reputation, by and large, for honesty and fair dealing that enabled them or their children to build up major national business empires.

List of Admonitions:

For breaking promises 2
Disorderly walking and evil practices 20
Fornication 2
Marriage by priest 3
Not attending Meeting 7
Not repaying a loan I
Running into debt and mismanaging a business 3
Spreading false rumours 1
Striking a woman 1
(Vale minutes)

There are other entries placing young into apprenticeship schemes and also for paying fees and for providing clothes. Some indentures were agreed and organised.

Books were purchased for the Quaker Meeting Houses and payments made to clean burial grounds in Woodlands, Challow and Faringdon. I am sure that *The Journal of George Fox* was read widely as was *Barclay's Apology*. The most widely read and used book was of course the Bible still at the heart of Christian-Quaker worship. Money was collected to help Quakers in the Vale and for prisoners and overseas evangelism. I think these latter collections were made for those who were struggling in America. Some of those we heard about in the last chapters left legacies for the Quaker work to continue. John and Mary Langley gave a legacy to Faringdon in 1712, but it doesn't say how much. Oliver Sanson left a legacy for Challow Meeting in 1717.

In 1717 Thomas Story visited Gloucester for morning meeting and in the afternoon he had a meeting at Faringdon, he writes in his journal:

`On 29th in the afternoon we had a meeting at Farrington, This was small and heavy in the forepart but ended pretty well.

to Bishopstone 30th in a barn where some of the townspeople came in but to me the meeting was very dull and dead a long time: and after some Friends had spoken what was in their minds the meeting was silent for a while and then I stood up and told them that *there had been more mischief done among the children of men by anyone thing in most ages of the world than by men's running the name of God, as his messengers, when he did not send them.*

In Jeremiah 23 Silence might be better than false speaking. I would not have any think I have smote at any of my brethren here who have been `concerned' in the meeting. Many were overcome in prayer after this.' 7

Possibly verse 21 in Jeremiah chapter 23 is the one Thomas Story had in mind. *`I have not sent these prophets, yet they run: I have not spoken to them, yet they prophesied.'*

Thomas Story was born at Justice Town near Carlisle in about 1670. He was well educated and he kept a detailed journal of his spiritual journey. He had the means to devote his life to the Society of Friends and travelled in ministry all over England, Europe and America. He set up a business in London as a conveyancer. He was very much a friend to William Penn and was also friendly with Peter the Great of Russia who was paying a long visit to England incognito. Thomas Story was one of those who handed Peter the Great a copy of the Quaker book, *Barclay's Apology*, the Latin edition. The Tsar visited Meeting for Worship several times.

The meeting described above must have been one of the last in Bishopstone as I have found no further information about gatherings there. It sounds like an ill-disciplined meeting. Thomas dealt with the spiritual challenge but not the practical problem. There was no meeting house. They appeared to have no obvious business structure. One person from Bishopstone got mentioned in MM minutes and that was a Robert Whithers or Withers.

Thomas Story finally lived in his father's estate near Carlisle where he experimented in planting trees from the New World. He continued to propound scientific theories well ahead of his time:

That `all inert matter was generally animated consisting of innumerable animatliculae and farinae before the worlds were made of it. Nothing, in fact, was `dead'.'

When visiting Scarborough in 1738, Thomas Story made a geological study of the rocks and decided that the earth was far older than was suggested in the Bible, and that the six days of creation were long periods of time and not natural days! As Elfrida Vipont says in her The Story of Quakerism.....

A mind like this would have no difficulty in accepting the scientific and criticalapproach to the Bible that split the Established church and Nonconformity in the nineteenth century.

Changes in Quaker structures were taking place too. In 1737 Yearly Meeting stated that all friends including children, should be deemed members of their Quarterly Meeting. The Quakers still felt that true religion must be a first-hand, living experience, but henceforth they were to take it for granted that all Friends' children would enter into their inheritance. This was later to lead to all sorts of problems because some youngsters did not wish to be Quakers. The Marrying `In' was fine when the Society was growing, but when it was not, then it was impossible to find someone to marry within such a closed group. Families were large and, as it was, far too many cousins married cousins. If a youngster married a non-Quaker then they were considered to have resigned and were taken off the membership lists. They were `out'. This situation very nearly destroyed the English Quaker `church'. Either the circle became narrow in psychological and physical ways, or it diminished even further as people married `out' and were pushed out! I shall argue that this was what happened to the Reynolds family in Faringdon in the mid nineteenth century. This was possibly the main reason that led to the final decline and demise of Faringdon meeting.

During the eighteenth century, three groups emerged; Ministers who were recognised as possessing the gift of ministry, the Elders who were concerned with spiritual worship in the meeting and Overseers to deal with pastoral care. Unfortunately I have not found any contemporary minutes about who in the Vale filled the above roles as Elder or Overseer. Perhaps Richard Reynolds was an Elder and perhaps later James Reynolds was. Robert Reynolds must also have been one of the `*grounded* `Friends in his meeting. He was brought up to know about the Quaker Gospel Order and the business method. Visitors came from time to time but I do not think Vale Quakers felt `called to Visit' elsewhere. After the death of Joan Vokins and Oliver Sanson, I don't think Vale Quakers travelled far on purely spiritual matters, apart that is from attending local Monthly and Quarterly Meetings from time to time. One or two may have attended Yearly Meetings in this country. I have found no mention of Vale Friends in any material I have read. The travelling to New England is not recorded though relations were living there and perhaps there was some travel to and fro on family matters.

Other records that give an idea of what was going on in the Vale are the lists of Visiting Friends and we find that in 1744 Thomas Curtis came, no doubt, the son of the Curtis who caused such problems for the Vale women in earlier days. In 1775 Daniel Badger and others came. In 1751 Thomas Whitehead (was he the son of George Whitehead the Valiant Sixty Quaker who died in 1723 aged 87 years), and others came, very much of the London Yearly Meeting set.

These were grounded Quakers. `Grounded' for Quakers meaning someone who has breathed Quakerism and knows its ins and outs, someone who can be trusted to know the `Truth' and live out the `Truth'. In 1753 William Brown of America came, and in 1760 William Fry came (a Bristol Quaker) and soon that family would be the Fry's Chocolate people of Bristol.

In 1734 the Wiltshire representative reported that the several advices of Yearly Meeting are endeavoured to be put into practice relating to the godly education of our children and we have a very good boarding school for Friends' children. In 1736 William Townsend was the representative. Could this be a nephew or son of our Warmen Townsend family? This is a widely used family name round the Vale area and elsewhere, but this Quaker branch seems to remain faithful.

In 1737 the Blewbury Meeting house was re-built. So Quakers must have felt confident at that point. All the other meeting houses were repaired and used. Marriages were not so frequent, but those families that remained true to the Society were quite large and no doubt filled the meeting house on a Sunday.

I have found records of burials and I think the burial grounds were quite busy in the early eighteenth century. Between 1701 and 1730 about a hundred Friends died. In 1701 Jane Vickers, Elizabeth Clark and Stephen Ballard, in 1706 Elizabeth Flatten from Buscot [Burscot], in 1709 May Saunders of Uffington [Oflingion] and William Parsons of Shellingford, soon to be followed in other years by William Bunce of Stamford (Goosey) 1711, Thomas Reynolds of Faringdon 1713, Jane Bunce 1715, Warmen Towsend (the old rogue) 1719 and Joseph and Edward Lockey in 1729. So the early Quakers died. Faringdon Burial ground used to have tomb stones but many people must also have been buried without them. These may have been removed at some point in the twentieth century because only one or two are laid in the path beside the Western wall of the building today. In the years 1730 to 1765 the burials amount to forty-two and so the numbers dwindled and were not replaced by new blood in this rural area. Some of the Quakers were now abroad in the New World,where even by 1700 they could join the twenty thousand Quakers or more, that hadescaped to the new life. Others, of course, were starting new lives in the growing towns and cities of Britain, such as Abingdon, London, Bristol and Reading and elsewhere.

According to Rufus Jones, *The Quakers in the American Colonies*, meetings in Philadelphia could number 800 or more, though not all attenders were Quakers. In 1727, Samuel Bownas speaks of the size of the meetings in Chester County amounting to 1500 each. This was the area where some Vale Quakers had gone. Quakerism was still unofficially the state religion of Pennsylvania. Rufus Jones asserts that the number of Quakers in the Chester area by the mid-century was about 25,000. Franklin suggests that the population of Pennsylvania was about 160,000 in 1766 of which about a third were Quakers (53,000).

There is in the Reading Archives *a Last Will and Testament of James Reynolds in the parish of Ffarringdon -1740* (he had married Mary and he died in 1748 and his final will is dated 1748). His son Robert

(1705 died 1767) also married a Mary and he may well have been first cousin to Richard Reynolds, father of the philanthropist (1705-1769). (See Reynolds family tree.)

Here is some of the James Reynolds will:

Sibford cups to grandsons
Fields and goods allocated to different members.. .there is reference to arranging for Richard Reynolds to surrender copyhold to his son James (Reynolds papers)

I do just wonder if somehow this land had been left to the Richard who became an iron merchant in Bristol and whose son was the Coalbrookdale Richard. They would not need any fields in Faringdon. This is pure surmise! This added bit might have been a codicil written in by Robert for his son James (or grandson James,1781-1829).

The fall in numbers of Quakers can also be accounted for by the expectations of these second generation Quakers and their lack of tolerance for moral shortcomings. A Quaker must live up to the high moral and spiritual standard expected of a member of the Society. So whilst some were disowned for falling short of the strict rules expected of them, others lapsed and took themselves away to pastures new. Some became Baptists or Methodists or reverted back to being local church goers The records of some Congregational churches are not very clear and so it is hard to discover if any of our Quakers became Congregationalists, some probably did.

As already pointed out, Quaker ladies were by now wearing the plain dress with white collars and Quaker poke bonnets. The men wore the wide brimmed hats and collarless homespun coats. So, though they were quietest and withdrawn from mainstream political and religious life, yet they were obvious and conspicuous in their immediate community.

In the 1771's it is recorded in the *First Directory* covering Faringdon that **Jon Fidel** was a carpenter, **Thomas Giles** a butcher, **Robert Reynolds** (possibly the Robert 1740-1813 - married to Ann and disowned by the Society of Friends in 1813) a cheese factor, **Bryan Reynolds** a draper, **Richard Townsend** an Auctioneer, **William Townsend** a baker, and **Richard Wheeler** a butcher. These are family names that do also appear in Quaker records and sometimes branches of these families were probably members, especially in these early years. It also seems that where there was a non-conformist chapel these were the families that would support that when the Quaker Meeting folded up. In places where there was no alternative but the church they would become Anglicans.

I have been unable to find records written by the Faringdon or Uffington Quakers of this period at Preparative Meeting level, apart from the Vale ones referred to above. So one might wonder what their spiritual life in Meetings for Worship was. I have though found a wonderful description of a young woman who finally gained the power to minister after Sunday lunch at the home of Robert Reynolds in Faringdon. Thus we can tell that some of the Vale Quakers were carrying on the traditions and well aware of the living *Truth*. Often there is the difficulty of knowing if the urge to give spoken ministry, is in *'right ordering'*. Quakers discuss this matter today also and there is quite a lot of helpful advice in our *Book of Discipline* about this.

Sometimes the first time, for some, just happens, it feels right, `one is impelled to minister'*, but for others it is quite a painful process. The following description of a first time is wonderfully told.

In the Memoirs of Ann Crowley, who attended Warborough meeting are the following records. She lost her sister in 1791 and seems to have also lost her mother. Friendsvisited her: John Hull of Uxbridge and Deborah Darby of Colebrookdale and Rebecca Young from Colebrookdale. They decided that they should all go over to Faringdon.

`The thought of having more of their profitable company seemed pleasant, yet the prospect brought great awfulness over my mind, inasmuch that I was afraid to refuse, though their were feelings raised which were contrary to a quiet aquiesence because I apprehended the time was drawing near when the DivineMaster*

141

would require fresh proof of my love and obedience to him...(She finally ventured to go and in Abingdon she felt the love of God abundantly abroad in her heart insomuch that she could experimentally adopt the language of the psalmist. "Thy people shall be willing in the day of thy power" she wanted to say in meeting for worship, but so great was the fear that attended her mind lest she had not passed through needful preparation to qualify rightly to minister, that she did not.)

The next morning in Farringdon at 11 O'clock, still fearful about whether I was called to minister of the everlasting gospel of peace and reconciliation...I felt my struggle did influence the meeting of my dear Friends....We all went to the house of Robert Reynolds to dinner, but my mind was too deeply exercised to take much nourishment for the body; for trudy I desired above all other considerations that it might be my meat and my drink to do the will of my heavenly father.

After dinner many Friends came in, nearly all we had sat with at meeting: A solemn silence soon prevailed, the mighty power of Truth seemed eventually to overshadow the little gathering, and many minds were much humbled; in which precious feeling I was made sensible that (this) was the accepted time for the offering to be made.

1 ventured to stammer forth a few expressions which arose in that degree of life and power that no doubt remained, it was the operation of Divine love which influenced me to yield to the fresh manifestation of revealed duty: and oh the blessed reward of peace that flowed into my humbled heart!

Language is inadequate to describe this heavenly enjoyment.' [9]

(taken from her diary extracts in Friends House Library London)

Witney Monthly Meeting

In 1791 the Vale area of meetings got split up and Faringdon and

142

Uffington became part of **Witney Monthly Meeting** which is where Faringdon is today. Blewbury went to **Newbury Monthly Meeting**. I think this may have been a bit difficult for the Quaker families living in the Vale as their lives revolved round that area in Berkshire. Oxford, Chipping Norton and Charlbury seemed like another world. The General Meeting was much as it is today, called **Oxfordshire and Berkshire General Meeting** and eventually included Banbury, Witney and Reading Monthly Meetings.

Witney Monthly Meeting was in place earlier than this of course and included the following meetings most of the time:

Oxford Meeting (1668-17.., 1889 to present day). A Meeting House plus earliersites.

Milton under Wychwood (1668-1813). A Meeting House sold and now used as aprivate house.

Burford (1668-1855,1891-1921,1956--- to present day). A Meeting House.

Alvescot (1709-17...). A Meeting House now pulled down but foundations still there.

Charlbury (1668-1918,1919-1957, 1985----to present day). A Meeting House.

Chipping Norton (1668-1910). A Meeting House now.

Abingdon (1668- 1790) (Vale MM) Meeting House (1791 - 1810), (WarboroughMM), (1810- 37) (Reading MM), (1894 - 1948) Meeting house sold (1978)

Uffington (1668- 180?). A Meeting House. (Vale to Witney MM 1791) MeetingHouse sold and now a private house.

Faringdon (1668-1880). A Meeting House (Vale and Witney MM 1791) l980---topresent day.

Witney 1668- 1890 Meeting House (Oxford MM, later Witney MM) 1893- 1919,1922 - 48, 1959 - 66 meeting house sold. Allowed Meeting under the care of WitneyMonthly Meeting 1997.

East Garston 1675 -87 Lambourn MM ,1687 - C 1 8th. Vale MM, 1939 - 1975 WitneyMM, 1 975---Reading MM

By the mid-century C 18th., Appleton, Bishopston, Challow, East Garston, andLambourne Woodlands had closed or more or less so.

Witney Meeting itself was still held at the Wood Green site and in 1738 there were more than thirty Quaker families attending. They were shopkeepers or connected with the woollen industry. Earleys of Witney being a Quaker Family at this time. I understand from Michael Harris, an old Witney Quaker family, that quite a few Quakers emigrated to America and this gradually weakened the meeting. Also Wesley preached in the town between 1764 and 1789 and this really caught people's mood and supported a need. The Wesleyan gatherings became very strong. So this was not a good time for Vale Quakers to be amalgamated with Quakers who lived over the other side of the Thames. Also the Oxfordshire Quakers had enough to do to keep themselves going and Faringdon and Uffington seemed to be in another world.

Soon after this, though, Faringdon Quakers were not keeping up with the business side of their Monthly Meeting. In Witney Monthly Meeting minutes 1796 to 1809 there never seems to be a Faringdon Representative. This points to the fact that Uffington and Faringdon Friends did not feel part of Witney Monthly Meeting and made little effort towards it.

At a meeting held in Burford on fourth day of fourth month in 1796 it is minuted that:

This meeting being affected with a concern that the Friends of Farringdon have discontinued their Preparation Meeting and do not so well attend the Monthly Meeting as we could wish. Deputes William Barritt (Witney), Thomas Huntley (Milton & Burford), John Hankins (Witney), William Fardon (Chipping Norton ?),

Joseph Atkins (Chipping Norton) to visit them and make a report. 10

Another minute was made respecting the *reparation* of Vale Meeting Houses...

At a meeting at Chipping Norton held on ninth day of fifth month 1796 a report is made that the Vale Meeting Houses are repaired...

At a Monthly Meeting at Charlbury later in the year Friends reported on a visit to Faringdon `much to their satisfaction. (In view of the subsequent decisions about Faringdon one can only assume that the visitors got a good lunch at the Reynolds farmhouse!)

At a meeting *in Farringdon 11th day of 7th month 1796: No Friends of Farringdon appointed to attend!*

Faringdon did contribute money once or twice to help Suffering Friends.

At another meeting *in Farringdon ninth day seventh month 1797*

It is suggested that `Farringdon' meeting unite with Witney. `Farringdon' Friends are not united with this!

At a Monthly Meeting at Burford 13.8.1797 there is the following minute:
The uniting of Farringdon Friends with Witney Preparative Meeting hath beenconsidered but there still appearing unwillingness in their minds to comply with the wish of the meeting the minute is continued...

The next mention of Faringdon uniting with Witney is in Charlbury, when William Barritt, Thomas Huntley and John (Hunkins or Hawkins) are asked to confer with Friends at *Farringdon* on this subject and report back.

In the eleventh month of 1797 they report back to a Monthly Meeting in Witney:

William Barritt reports that he and other Friends have taken an opportunity of conferring with Farringdon Friends and informed them it was the desire of this meeting that they would be united with Witney or Burford (Preparative Meetings) and it appearing most pleasant to them to be united with the latter this meeting gives them that liberty.

Also at this point:

Thomas Giles of Farringdon applies to be a member of our Society and some Friends are appointed to visit him.

He was later accepted into membership and is sometimes the Faringdon representative at Monthly Meetings.

So in 1797 Faringdon and Burford became one meeting. Some monthly meetings were still held at Faringdon with Robert Reynolds reporting *`that the meeting house at Uffington is not yet repaired.* Later the bill is presented for that repair being nine shillings. James Reynolds (no record of marriage, may have moved to Wales for a time to be near his `cousin,' Richard Reynolds) and Richard Reynolds (174 1-1837 (married to Jane Winters 1782 -1859/61) and Robert Huntley seem often to be representatives from Faringdon by then. James with his brother Robert and Richard were running between them, the farm, a Malting Business, a Cheese Factor and probably other things as well, such as dealing in woollen garments and draperies. Robert Huntley had moved from Burford to Faringdon, perhaps he was apprenticed to one of the Reynolds business cheese or drapers, and later (1813) married Issett Reynolds the daughter of Robert and they settled in Faringdon for most of her child bearing life, up to 1835.

In December 1817 Burford and Faringdon separated again, so they were together for twenty years, possibly whilst the youngsters of the Huntley family in Burford and the youngsters in the Reynolds family in Faringdon were courting and then married. They might well be have been travelling back and forth on family matters. It is clear from the minutes that Faringdon First Day Meeting did not wish to be united with Witney First Day Meeting.

Meantime in Yearly Meeting minutes in 1787 Oxfordshire Quarterly Meeting reported that:

the state of their meeting is in general rather low, yet we believe there are someamongst us who through divine assistance do experience growth in the truth we know of none bearing arms...

In a letter in 1788, from Thomas Huntley to Yearly Meeting, the junction of Oxfordshire and Berkshire and Bucks is mentioned but Yearly Meeting agreed to the junction of Oxon and Berks...

Bucks have not seen their way open to affect such a junction.

Finally Berkshire and Oxfordshire united in 1790 and are so to this day.

Richard Reynolds of Coalbrookdale

I have continuously explained that attempting to work out family trees is confusing because the same names are used in each generation. However I have worked out a reasonable family tree for the **Faringdon Reynolds family**[see Appendix 1]. It will still not be absolute. I am certain that **Richard Reynolds (1735 -1816)**the Iron Master of Coalbrookdale and the Bristol philanthropist was descended from the Quaker, Faringdon stock. I think his Great Grandfather was **Michael Reynolds**, married to Alice, who lived and suffered for the Truth in the seventeenth century Vale. Also that in turn his Grandfather was the **Michael Reynolds** who married Susanna Bromley and was the one known as Michael the Honest.

In the Memoirs of *the life of Richard Reynolds* written in 1852 by his granddaughter Hannah Mary Rathbone (her mother was daughter of Richard Reynolds and Hannah Darby and Hannah was born at Ketley) there is this passage:

as the marriage Certificate of Michael,
the father of the above mentioned
Richard surnamed the `Honest' is

*dated in the year 1704, and is signed
by his father Michael as a witness,
who may therefore be supposed to have
been one of the early converts to the
preaching of George Fox in the middle
of the seventeenth century.* [11]

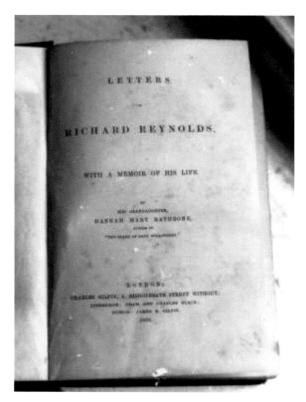

Front of Hannah Rathbone's book

The girl **Michael Reynolds II** married was called **Susanna Bromley**. The marriage took place at Stratford upon Avon meeting on *24th of 12th month called February*. So this Michael born in Faringdon and still with close ties stayed in Banbury, presumably for business reasons. The son of this union was **Richard Reynolds (1709 -1796)**, born in Banbury. He was most definitely Richard of

Coalbrookdale's father. So he would also, no doubt, keep in touch with his father Michael's Faringdon family where he had many uncles, aunts and cousins and grandparents. I think he knew the town well. As a young man he moved to Bristol where he was in the iron business and became an Iron Merchant.

He got married to Jane Donne and sent his only son also Richard Reynolds to school at the age of five years to a Mr Bennett of Pickwick in Wiltshire. I think Richard would take his young son to Faringdon to visit relatives, such as Uncle James and cousin Robert, and also to visit his parents in Banbury, whilst they were alive. I think Richard of Coalbrookdale knew the old farm house.

At fourteen, Richard junior was apprenticed to a member of the Quaker Bristol Fry family. In 1756, when he was twenty-one years old, he was sent to Coalbrookdale to do business with the **DarbyFamily**. He seems to have really done well and from this point onwards never to have put a foot wrong. Soon he became a partner in the iron business with the Darby's and indeed married **Hannah Darby.** So it is likely that the Reynolds's of Faringdon would know at least something about these events. At one level they were thus aware of the changing times. I think **Robert Reynolds** of Faringdon was very proud of his famous cousin and passed this interest and pride on to his children. They collected many of things about their famous relative such as commemorative mugs, and portraits.

In an extract from Richard Reynolds's diary on the 30th May 1763 *Supped and spent the evening with Cousin Robert Reynolds & C ye Coffee House.*

Richard was by now 28 years old and Robert was 23, they must have had much to talk about, the family, Quakerism, politics and the budding technical and scientific revolution that was part of the scene. Also they may have swapped ideas about banking money and other lucrative financial matters. Though Richard became very wealthy indeed on a national scale Robert did not do so badly in his own Vale town. They both had access to Quaker Bankers such as Gilletts of Banbury and Lloyds of Birmingham, Gurneys of Norwich and the London houses.

A wax death mask of Richard Reynolds, philanthropist
t[now in private hands]

The story of these happenings is well told elsewhere (see Raistrick in the biography section) and the Ironbridge museum itself is there to visit. It is the site of the beginning of the Industrial Revolution. The smoke billowing out into the sky and the red coking ovens lighting up the night sky with crimson flares. Richard Reynolds at one stage took over complete management of Coalbrookdale itself, though most of his time was spent at nearby Ketley. He encouraged his workers to experiment and in some ways perfected and pioneered coking technologies which speeded up the process of iron smelting. He linked the river with the ovens by a wagon way of wooden rails, pioneering along with people like Stevenson. He was involved in the design of the Telford iron bridge. Also he was one of those who earned a lot of money and was friendly with those Quakers who began to live by honest dealings with money, especially the Lloyds and the Gurneys /Barclays. Richard Reynolds attended Yearly

Meetings in London for forty years and acted as Clerk to some. In 1786 Richard Reynolds was Clerk to Yearly Meeting and signed the Epistle sent out to all meetings in England, Ireland and America. There was only the One Yearly Meeting for all Quakers then:

The account of Friends sufferings brought in this year being chiefly (of) tithes and those of Church rates (and) amount in England and Wales to £4,100 and in Ireland £1243.

Many Elders and heads of families consider the importance of the trust reposed in them and by watchful care over their own conduct be qualified to instruct the beloved youth in the way of piety and virtue, that being examples to them herein, they may with authority rebuke and exhort the unruly and the disorderly walkers and tenderly encourage every appearance of good... 12

Richard Reynolds attended his own Meeting every Sunday. He was concerned about having so much money though he built a fine house for his family and had his children well educated at home. Though he loved horses and the countryside, he never forgot to keep daily patterns simple. He did not hunt or attend races, but did enjoy picnics and organising an annual excursion onto The Wrekin. Workers in the Foundry were cared for and he thought about their welfare and education. He was interested in canals, but objected to men towing the boats as degrading and he set about obtaining an act of Parliament to make a towing path forhorses up the Severn which was not passed. He refused to make cannon balls on one occasion in support of the, by this time, definite Quaker testimony against all wars and the carrying of arms.

In 1791 **Priscilla Hannah Gurney**, of Norwich, came to live with the Reynolds family seeking `*succour from the world, and peace'*. Her father was **Joseph Gurney** of Norwich, the Gay Quaker mentioned already and her mother was **Hannah Barclay** granddaughter of **Robert Barclay**, the Apologist. So this house was well in the circuit of those Quakers who were doing well in their affairs. In 1798 **Elizabeth Gurney** herself visited her sister at the Reynold's home and was also in need of spiritual succour too.The tension between the gay Quakers and the plain Quakers was tearing their lives apart. They were glad to see that a plain Quaker could still live a happy and comfortable life and still be true to God. Elizabeth writes the following in her memoirs:

Sept 4th After tea we went to the Darbys accompanied by our dear friendRichard Reynolds and still dearer Priscilla Gurney.. .we had spent a pleasant evening when my heart began to feel silenced before God and without looking at the others I found myself silenced under his loving hand. I soon found that the rest were in the same state...

It may well have been on this occasion that **Deborah Darby**, the same as comforted **Ann Crowley** and had lunch at the home of **Robert Reynolds in Faringdon** in 1791, felt moved to minister that she felt that *Elizabeth would he a light to the blind, speech to the dumb and feet to the lame..*, certainly Elizabeth did become more open to God's guidance from this time on. She finally married **Joseph Fry** the Plain Quaker in 1800 at the age of twenty and became a Plain Quaker herself. After this she threw herself into prison reform as **Elizabeth Fry.**

I have managed to find the following letter in the Reading Archives and certainly Richard Reynolds addresses Robert Reynolds (born 1740, married Ann, disowned 1811, died 1813) of the Farm Faringdon as his Cousin. I think he must have visited Faringdon at some point in his life and perhaps worshipped with Vale Friends too. I feel quite certain that he was family. It is interesting that Richard Reynolds portrait was in the farm until it was sold in the1960s, also silhouettes and memorabilia such as the cup.

Bristol 11th of 11th Month 1805
Robert Reynolds

Dear Cousin,
I am obliged by thy enquiry after my health which thro' mercy is full

as good as can be reasonably expected considering my age tomorrow (if I live) will compleat myseventieth year - Tho not so old by several years, it is possible thou also may feel the

approach of some Infirmities which I already experience - The best use we can makeof these certain tho' gradual warnings is to obtain thro' faith in Christ Jesus andobedience to the manifestation of his Grace, an assurance of our acceptance with himbefore we are summoned from works to rewards. May this be our experience. Thy nephew S. Allen brought me the hare thou wast so kind as to send me in the 9th month, and I have received the other of the pheasant mentioned in thy favor of the 8th inst., for all which I am much obliged to thee as furnishing the means of obliging my friends which is abundantly more agreeable to me than using them in my own Family. I should be sorry if the scarcity of Game this season makes it a difficulty to thee to fulfil thy kind intention to send some to my friends as usual. I had rather go without it than subject thee to any inconveniency. Some of them are from home at present, so only wish a Hare might be sent to Samson Lloyd at the Bank Birmingham - and to know if thou could send one readily to Wellingborough in Northampton Shire - I hope for thy answer soon as convenient and that thou will be able to inform me of thy own and thy family's health, with love to whom. I am thy affectionate Kinsman,

Richard Reynolds [13]

Addressed to Robert Reynolds Faringdon from Bristol.

Envelope Richard Reynolds to Robert Cousins

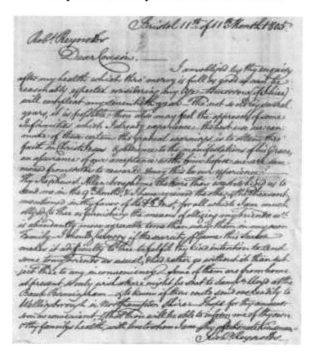

Facsimile of the letter of Richard to Robert Cousins

So the Faringdon Reynolds's are considered as relatives of Richard Reynolds of Coalbrookdale and of The Allen family and also keep in touch with Lloyds of Lloyds Bank in Birmingham. At the beginning of the nineteenth century they are part of the established Quaker world. They are very comfortably off and about to build themselves fine houses and businesses in Faringdon. Though they might have been seen as a bit quaint and perhaps treated as the country cousins, they are, nevertheless, part of the scene. Possibly more in touch withopportunities of the period than more traditional Faringdonians of the time. Yet by the mid nineteenth century most of these Faringdon Quakers were dead or had resigned or been disowned. How this came about I shall attempt to unravel in a subsequent chapter.

Photo of a Richard Reynolds jug in the farmhouse in 1960's

I think, however, that the advice given on the 25th day of ninth month 1764 at a Yearly Meeting in Philadelphia and recorded in The Journal of John Woolman is apposite to the Faringdon situation at the turn of the century. The young Quakers of the eighteen nineties were living in very different circumstances and had a rather different outlook from to that of their Grandparents of the early years of the eighteenth century:

`John Smith of Marlborough (PA),aged upwards of eighty years, a faithful minister and elder, and appearing to be under great exercise of spirit, informed Friends in substance as follows: "That he had been a member of our Society upwards of sixty years, and he well remembered that, in those early times, friends were a plain lowly minded people; and that there was much tenderness and contrition in their meetings. -- that at twenty years from that time, the society increasing in wealth, and in some degree conforming to the fashions of the world, true humility was less apparent, and their meetings in general were not so lively and edifying. --that at the end of forty years, many of them were grown very rich; and many of the society made a specious appearance in the world; that wearing fine costly garments, and using silver and other watches, became customary with them. so the powerful overshadowings of the Holy Ghost was less manifest in the society -that there had been a continued increase in such ways of life, even until the present time, and that the weakness which hath now overspread the society, and the barrenness manifest amongst us, is a matter of great sorrow." He then mentioned the uncertainty of his attending these meetings in future, expecting his dissolution was near; and having tenderly expressed his concern for us, signified that he had seen the true light, that the Lord would bring back his people from these things, into which they were thus degenerated; but that his faithful servants must first go through great and heavy exercises.'[14]

This was prophetic fo, not only in America was the nineteenth century to see further`degeneration' and splits between evangelical Quakers and Quietist Quakers, but in Britain also, numbers were to drop even further before a new awakening occurred. For John Woolman these words were an influence upon him. He was already led spiritually and finally devoted his energy to living the Quaker Way. Everyone mattered to him, native peoples and black slave peoples. He went on to persuade Quakers and others to stop using slaves.

NOTES

[1.]*Vale Minute books 1668* - onwards, Oxfordshire Archives

[2.] VIPONT (Elfrida), *The Story of Quakerism*, Bannisdale,1954, p134

[3.] *First Directory of Faringdon* - copy in Faringdon Library

[4.]*Reynolds papers* lodged in the Berkshire County Archives Reading by Mrs Wattsin 1961. DEx 160 Fl-17.

[5.] WHITTIER (George Greenleaf), `the brewing of soma', first published in theAtlantic monthiy,Vol.29 (1872). Quaker Faith and Practice 1995 20.03

[6.] PUNSHION (John), *Portrait in Grey - a short history of Quakers*, QHS 1984,p 130

[7.] STORY (Thomas) *Extracts of Quaker Journals*, Friends House Library

[8.] VIPONT (Elfrida), *The story of Quakerism*, Bannisdale 1954, p138-140

[9.] CROWLEY(Ann), *Memoirs of Ann Crowley* a diary of extracts, Friends HouseLibrary

[10.]*Vale minutes books* Oxfordshire Archives

[11.] RATHBONE (Hannah Mary*)*, *Letters of Richard Reynolds 1852 Memoirs of the life of Richard Reynolds 1882*
    PRYOR HACK (Mary), *Richard Reynolds*, Headley Bros. 1896

    RAISTRICK (Arthur), *Quakers in Science and Industry*, Bannisdale,1950

[12.] Yearly Meeting records Friends House Library

[13.]Reynolds papers as note 4

[14.]WOOLMAN (John), *A Journal of the lift, gospel labours and ChristianExperiences of that faithful minister John Woolman*, Thomas Hurst 1 840 p.122.

CHAPTER SEVEN

THE VICTORIAN TIMES

Friends are after all the most tolerant people on earth.
John Bright [1]

The century opened with Faringdon and Burford as one Meeting and Uffington as another. I have found very little information about who exactly the Uffington Quakers were. It has to be supposed that they were known by the Faringdon Quakers who accompanied Thomas Shillitoe on his visit to Uffington in 1803. I have no idea if the Thatcher family still worshipped as Quakers, but, later, Mary Ann Reynolds mentions her friend Betty Thatcher of Longcot in a will, so it seems likely that some of the Thatcher family still were Quakers. A branch of the Uffington Thatcher family still worship as Quakers in the United States. I like to think that Reynolds and Thatchers were present when the Meeting mentioned below took place.

There is a little piece about **Uffington Meeting** in the diary of Thomas Shillitoe born in London in 1754. In 1803 he visited Berkshire and Oxfordshire. He went to Warborough where three Quaker families still resided. He writes:

> *Went to Shillingford and Warborough.*
> *'if my feelings are correct the life of religion is at a very low ebb.'*

On to Abingdon he went, where he mentions that only one family of Friends reside who keep up the meeting:

> *After sitting with this family I walked fourteen miles to Farringdon - First Day attended meeting there, which is pretty much made up of one family. I proceeded in the afternoon to Burford - Third Day to Witney and thence back home.*

I had not been long at home before the subject of my having meeting at Uffington near Farringdon became a burden too heavy to bear and on 13th of tenth month 1803 left home and reached Farringdon on the following day. On informing Friends there of the cause of my returning they very kindly proceeded to have the (Ufflngton) meeting house prepared and notice given of a meeting on First day afternoon.. When we reached Uffington many were gathered round the Meeting House and in a short time it was full.

The solid quiet behaviour of the people during the time of silence which continued for a full hour, was commendable and the solemnity felt over the Meeting was more than is often experienced where the company is so large; and principally persons not of our religious persuasion, very much unacquainted with our manner of sitting together for the purpose of divine worship. Whilst I was on my feet addressing the assembly, a circumstance occurred that for a short time broke into the solemnity with which the Meeting was favoured. The main beam of the upper gallery, which was crowded with people, as well as underneath, on a sudden gave a violent crack and broke short off. My feelings were much excited for those who were under the gallery. It was however soon cleared above and below without any of the company sustaining any injury except for fright. The people such as could coming again into the meeting house again and the meeting settling down quietly... The Meeting closed under a precious sense that Holy help had been near to us during our sitting together.

I returned to Farringdon, I hope I may say, thankful to my Divine master who had so bountifully cared for me this day.
[2]

Thomas Shillitoe was a Quietist Quaker trying to follow the ways of the first generation of Quakers. He was not influenced by the evangelical movements of the time. He and Sarah Grubb were of the old stock and great leaders of the quietist traditions. They visited meetings both in England, Ireland and America. Many Friends of the mid-Victorian period were evangelicals. This trend of evangelicalism within Quakerism was, even in England, on the verge of being hardly distinguishable from other denominations such as Methodism or Congregationalism. People were being appointed and paid to do certain jobs. The meetings were often planned beforehand and hymns were sung lustily. This was greatly disliked by such as Thomas Shillitoe who on his deathbed said:

> *The clergy of this country, to a man, every one of them, are antichrist so long as they wear the gowns and receive the pay.* [3]

The ideal of Quaker ministry was, certainly in George Fox's time and even now in Britain Yearly Meeting, that always it should be unpaid and inspirational. In the later nineteenth century though, when some meetings seemed to lack ministry, there was pressure from the Evangelical wing to appoint and pay people to travel in ministry. These people should work full time as *'Home Missioners'* and get regular financial support. This was certainly the custom in some parts of the Americas by then. Quakers such as Thomas Stillitoe were very much against this.

The Uffington Meeting house had been repaired in 1801, but what happened after the incident above I do not know. Those who came seeking Truth could not have been much inspired, for the First Day Meetings did not resume and Meetings were discontinued there. In 1821 the building was sold and turned into a private dwelling which it is to this day. This actual building had been built in 1730, so it had been used for Quaker worship for almost a century. Quakers of the village were mentioned from the beginnings of Quakerism and we still have a member living in the village as I write. I suppose those who had been Quakers became Baptists or Methodists, for the most part, as happened in Faringdon. As I have never traced many Quaker names in Uffington it is difficult to ascertain who changed allegiance and where they went.

An entry in *Kelly's directory* in 1847 describes **Faringdon** as: *having a neat and clean appearance, and is well lighted with gas.*

The centre of the town has not changed much since that time. The population of the town was rising, a census in 1801 was 1,928 but by 1861 it had increased to 3,400. In 1864 the town was linked to the main line at Baulking by rail. So there was a short lived golden age, but the coaching business and its trade folded and the population decreased rather dramatically. This town was still the market centre for the Western Vale. On market days the town was full of carriages and wagons, horses and people. There were Fair times as well with all the fun of the Fair. In a survey taken in 1847 there were one hundred and seventy five traders in the town. Many associated with horses and farming and many more with the things people needed. There were apparently twelve shoemakers and four tailors for example. The town had its own mill for grinding corn. Also at least one maltster. It was only at the beginning of the nineteenth century that the town really became one. Up until then it had been divided by The Brook. The Port, where the main market place and the Church were, was bridged to the western side known as Westbrook. I surmise that on the Westbrook side lived a lot of the non-conformists because that is the side where the Meeting House and the Baptist Chapel were, and where later the Wesleyan Chapel (in Gloucester Street 1837) and the Independent Chapel in 1840 and the Primitive Methodists' Chapel, in 1850, were built. In 1852 the Baptist Chapel was repaired and extended. They are situated on this Westbrook side even today. Only the Anglican Church is on the east side of the town.

According to Robert Phillips, there were three schools in Faringdon in 1854. Somewhere up London Street was a 'ladies school' run by Miss Priscilla Clark and Miss Temperance Kent. Here the girls were probably taught the Three R's, Embroidery, the Bible and some social graces, but no formal education. Along the Stanford Road was the National School, founded in 1823, (British School and later still C of E boys secondary up to 1935), which gave elementary instruction to local boys and girls in reading, writing and arithmetic. The parents paid a small weekly sum for this schooling, but mainly the work was supported by subscriptions from charitable people living locally. In 1854 there were 125 children at this school. In 1853 an additional school was opened in the Westbrook area possibly in Canada Lane. There was also a small boarding school at Sudbury

House. [4]

The National Schools and British schools were the outcome of the monitorial system brought to the fore by Joseph Lancaster, a Quaker by convincement, and Andrew Bell an Episcopalian. The keynote was cheapness so that more children than in previous times could benefit from an education. The more pupils a student teacher or monitor could teach the cheaper it would be. I have not found much evidence that Faringdon Quakers either supported the (British) National school or did not. I feel that they must have done so as usually trades-people in the town would do so. The children who went to the school could have free education and certainly were not asked to pay very much. The Quaker **Thomas Fawkes** was on the committee of the British School for a time as was George Fidel and George Crowdy and Mr Ballard who were Baptists. So it appears to have been run on ecumenical lines!

In 1820 Faringdon Meeting was part of Witney Monthly Meeting and the records show that the following families still belonged to the meeting: **Thomas Giles** (possibly a butcher) and his wife, **Benjamin & Mary and Katharine Collier -De Home, Robert Huntley and Isett** and family, **Richard Reynolds** and **Jane, Ann Elizabeth and Mary Ann Reynolds,James Mary and James Junr., Michael Richard,** and **Elizabeth**. In course of time some of these died or left Faringdon. Robert Huntley was greatly missed when he left. In the mid-century period other members resigned or were disowned by the Society of Friends. Fortunately **Thomas** and **Rebecca Fawkes** were accepted into membership. Rebecca died in 1847 and Thomas devoted himself to the meeting until he himself died in 1875. In the 1851 census he was living at 54 Marlborough Street, aged 49, and listed as a plumber and glazier. His mother Sarah, a widow, aged 70, was listed as a visitor and shoeseller and a Mary Jackson also forms part of the household, aged 26, and is listed as housekeeper. [5]

Thomas Pole, M.D. (1753-1829) must have therefore visited Faringdon and joined in Meeting for worship. He appears to have been quite friendly with **Richard Reynolds** of Faringdon as well as Richard Reynolds of Bristol. Dr. Pole at some stage, possibly afterhe retired to Bristol drew both Richard and James Reynolds's Houses in

Faringdon and also the Meeting house. Both water colour paintings are dated 1823 and are amongst a collection of some fifty pages of works. [6]

Early Nineteenth century miniatures of the Reynolds family
[cameos in private collection]

Thomas Pole's grandparents were born in Wales but settled in Somerset. They were Quakers. His Father emigrated to Burlington, New Jersey and married a Quaker girl. Thomas was born in America. Both parents died whilst he was young and so he was brought up by guardians. When twenty-two years old he came to England to visit his relations and stayed for the rest of his life. His story is well told in *Thomas Pole, M.D. by Edmund T. Wedmore 1908.* He not only practised in medicine himself but lectured too and studied anatomy and chemistry. He corresponded with William Allen and was interested in pharmacy. Always his spiritual life mattered, both his own discipline within the Society' of Friends and the needs of the wider society. He was one of those who established and ran Adult Schools. In 1823 he published a little book *Observations Relative to Infant Schools,* designed to point out the value of such schools for children of the poor, their parents and to Society at large. He was a sort of Froebelian because he had first hand experience of the connection between undernourished children and unhappy, failing, children. He felt children were all pure and teachable given the right start in life. They were born sinless. He supported the work of Joseph Lancaster. He did not live to see the birth of the Quaker Liberal Tradition, but he was a fore-runner. Thomas Pole would not, I think, have agreed with those in the very evangelical Quaker wing who rooted their theology in the concept of original sin. Through the Fall, the image of God in man is totally effaced so that it is impossible for man to please God or obey his law by his own efforts. Only through the sacrifice of Christ can this be brought about in the believer. This theology viewed children as born fallen and sinful.

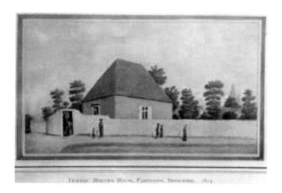

Richard Reynolds always wore black and you can see him in ThisMeeting House picture[original in Friends House, London].

In *the 1851 Census* **Benjamin Collier De Horne** aged 60, of 55

Marlborough Street is listed as a Fund Holder and retired Cheese Factor, his wife Mary is with him and two servants. Round the corner in Westbrook, on the left side, live **Charles Reynolds** aged 72 a farmer with 200 acres who employed 8 labourers. With him live **Margaret,** his wife, aged 66 and his son **Charles** aged 34, unmarried, his daughters **Mary Jane** aged 32 unmarried, and **Mary Ann** aged 26, unmarried (no mention of **Richard**) and **Eliza Sellwood** aged 23 a servant. At 71 Westbrook live **James Reynolds** aged 35 Draper and Mercer employing 4 Assistants, **Michael Richard** aged 34, Landed Proprietor with 3 Assistants and Mary Ann Peck, a widow and Housekeeper. (Appendix Reynolds Family Tree) At 72 Westbrook lived **Jane Reynolds** widow aged 70, a Fundholder and money at use with a cook and housemaid.

Also in the same census on the South side of the Market place lived James Fidel aged 44 a widower and an Auctioneer and Ironmonger with his two sons Albert 11 and Edward 10, and a servant. He was a Baptist who married Ann Reynolds (18…1844), daughter of James senior the draper. More about this as the Victorian era unfolds. [7]

James and Robert Huntley

When Robert Huntley had first been involved with the meeting Faringdon and Burford were one meeting (1797-1818). The fact that Faringdon stood on its own again, by 1818, I think, hinges upon the life of Robert Huntley, the half brother of Joseph Huntley who founded Huntley and Palmer Biscuits in Reading. Thomas Huntley, (1733-) their father, was a most enterprising school master in Burford. He had Joseph (1775 -1849) in his first marriage and Robert (1785-1853) in his second, his first wife having died. The school was for Quaker children who still could not go to Establishment schools. It was called the Hillside Academy and French, Latin, EnglishGrammar and some Commercial Book-Keeping were taught there. The mother of Robert, Hannah Cowdry, was also an enterprising woman. She apparently made delicious biscuits and she sold these to make money for her housekeeping needs in the school or so the story goes. Horses and carts went slowly up the steep hill in Burford past the Academy and there was time to buy these well renowned biscuits on the way. This, it is said, is where her stepson Joseph got his idea from. He actually started out as a teacher, like his Father, teaching in the Sibford Quaker School before he became involved in the biscuit venture.

Plan of Quaker households in Faringdon in the mid nineteenth century.

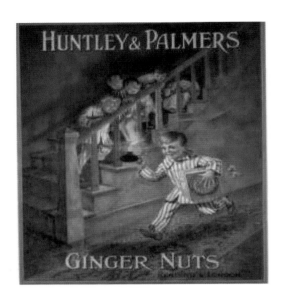

A picture of a biscuit tin, original in Reading Museum

Ginger nuts were one of 150 different types of biscuit manufactured by Huntley & Palmers in Reading at the turn of the century. Packing biscuits by hand provided work for hundreds of women and girls [Reading Museum & Art Gallery].

This may seem a side line to Vale Quakers but they must all have known about how Joseph the school teacher married the daughter of a rich Reading maltster and how he left teaching and moved to live in Reading, made the friendship of Thomas Palmer, who had an Uncle with a Bakery and Biscuit shop in Uxbridge, and together they got a biscuit shop going in Reading. The tins for these biscuits were another sideline but what wonderful tins they were (to be seen in the Museum at Reading today). The labels were printed by a Quakerprinters in Birmingham, White and Pike. The Quaker virtues of honesty and fixed prices helped the business to grow. People soon knew that the ingredients were nothing but the best and that there was no short weight. There was no bargaining. The lovely tins kept the biscuits fresh. I am certain that the Faringdon Quakers ordered their tins of biscuits at Quarterly and Monthly Meetings as the founding Joseph became a seller of his son's biscuits in his middle years.

The next generation of Joseph Huntley and Thomas Palmer were to carry the venture into a major commercial enterprise. As the business developed those who ran it were to feel a tension between Quaker simplicity and the demands of an international business and as with other Quaker foundations the original bonds with Quakerism were in to some extent severed.

As for Thomas Huntley's other son Robert born in 1785, I am not so clear. He was the son of Thomas and his second wife Hannah Cowdry. He obviously was at the Burford school under his father and then he seems to have been apprenticed to some shopkeeper in Faringdon, presumably a Reynolds Quaker, and most likely Robert Reynolds. He eventually married Isett Reynolds whose father, James, was a cheese factor. She also was born in 1785.

They married in 1813 when they were 28 years old *(Robert Huntley [chemist] m. Isett R. Reynolds 1813)* and then they had at least seven children who survived to adulthood. By this time Robert Huntley had become Dr Huntley. He seems to have removed to a vet in Liverpool (*Witney M.M. Extracts of Minutes1677-1854: 1809- Robert Huntley removed from Burford to Liverpool)* to get his medical Certificate and returned to Faringdon after that. So he must have met the Rathbone Quaker family, the family into which the daughter of Richard Reynolds of Coalbrookdale married. They may even have helped Robert Huntley to obtain an indenture. Quakers either got medical training abroad or sometimes, as in Robert's case, got it via a veterinary training. They still could not go to English Universities because of their faith.

Robert missed out on the new provincial Universities that allowed non-conformists to attend. In 1881 even Oxford and Cambridge removed doctrinal tests from their entrance exams and Quakers could go there too. The Witney MM minute reads *'1813 Robert Huntley back from Hardshaw M.M.* His sister Mary Huntley married Benjamin Collier De Horme in 1814, and they lived in Faringdon, as did Robert and Isett.

169

RobertHuntley   ***Isett Rachael Huntley [née Reynolds]***
Probably sent from Australia to Faringdon relatives.

Soon Faringdon PM separated from Burford PM and I suspect that Robert Huntley kept it going for a bit. He went to Monthly Meetings and must have been a useful member. In 1826 Robert and Isett moved to Staines in Middlesex and on the 8th March 1836 he and Isett and the children sailed away to Australia on the Duchess of Northumberland, he working their passage as a ship's surgeon superintendent. By now Robert and Isett were 51 years old. They bought land south of Sydney, 2560 acres at 5 shillings an acre and they called it Faringdon Park. As a comparison with this acreage, Charles Reynolds in Faringdon, Berkshire, farmed 500 acres, which was, by English standards, considered a reasonable size. Robert and Isett had ups and downs, a drought led to bankruptcy, but Robert still continued in medicine. Some of his children left Quakers and joined other denominations. Robert finally moved to be near his eldest son in a suburb of Sydney called Balmain and practised medicine there. He may well have been the first doctor there. He died on 26th November 1853 and Isett died in 1862.

They both had remained as Quakers. There was a meeting house in Sydney by 1836, but by the time Robert and Isett moved into the locality it had been sold. They obviously brought up their children as Quakers but, from the following correspondence their son had with

Witney Monthly Meeting, one can see how difficult being and remaining a Quaker must have been in Australia at that time.

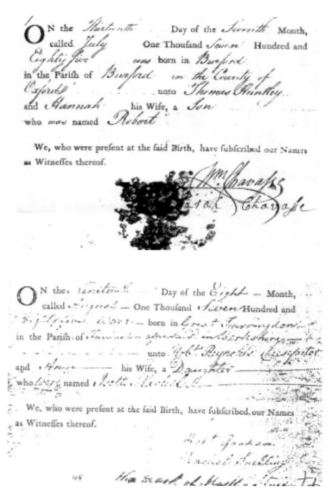

Birth certificates of Robert and Isset Huntley

I imagine that Robert and Isett may well have been buried in part of the general cemetery set aside for Quakers. This is on the site of the present Central RailwayStation in Sydney. I have to thank **Ruth Evans** for helping me with some of this information. She is the great grand-daughter of Robert and Isett and lives in Australia.

The following is from Robert Huntley's son Robert born in Faringdon in 1817 and who left Faringdon in 1826 and who arrived in Australia in 1836 at the age of nineteen. He was therefore 36 when he wanted to get married and wrote to Witney Monthly Meeting just before his Father died.

Monthly Meeting at Charlbury 11th month 14th day 1853A letter from Robert Huntley (Jun) from Australia was read:

I thought you had been informed by my relatives in Faringdon that the Meeting House built by the late John Fowell was sold some years ago and no other built in its place.. there are very few members of our Society residing in Sydney or neighbourhood and most of them are at a distance from each other so that they are not in the habit of meeting together. I am now living with my Father and Mother and we continue to follow the practice of reading the Bible after breakfast as well as in the evening.

There is a subject I am desirous of mentioning - that of my intention of marriage and as there is none of our persuasion here with whom such a conjunction could be performed and if so no properly constituted Meeting where the ceremony of marriage could be solemnized - I shall be compelled to adopt other means of accomplishing this object. In doing so, I assume you and I shall do it with regret being still attached to the principles of Friends in which I have been educated and it would give me great pain to forfeit my membership.

Robert Reynolds Huntley (Junr)

At Witney Monthly Meeting on 2nd 13 1854 this letter was again considered:

Under our consideration and considerable sympathy has been expiated on his behalf in the peculiar situation in which he is

172

placed, with his candour in mentioning the circumstances of his intention of marrying and would recommend him in the event... to keep as near as practicable to the principles of Friends in the solemnization and would ask him to keep us informed

Clerk Robert Sessions to write to him.,. [9]

Robert Sessions of Charlbury was clerk of Witney Monthly Meeting in 1854.

On the 11th month 13th day 1854, Robert Huntley informed Witney Monthly Meeting that *he was married at the Parish church at Balmain on 10th month 13th day1854 adhering in all respects as strictly as possible to the principles of Friends.* (In my letter from the great grand-daughter she refers to Robert marrying in 1853. So there is a little puzzle for someone to sort out if they wish.)

One feels this may have been one of the first properly conducted ecumenical marriages of the time, in Australia or even in the Christian world and that the minister or vicar must have been a far-seeing sort of man. Did they have a long period of silence and a certificate signed and witnessed by all present? If only Witney Monthly Meeting Elders and Overseers had applied this charity to their own members who married 'out', perhaps meetings would have continued to flourish. They however continued to disapprove of such marriages and those members involved were disowned and not allowed to attend Friends' schools.

Of course there was correspondence between the Reynolds family in Faringdon and the Huntleys in Australia and some of this is in the Reading archives. But the departure of Robert Huntley in 1826 soon followed by the deaths of the older generation of Quakers left the meeting in a fragile state. The changes in Victorian society, economic and political, also affected life in Faringdon. Some more Quakers left the meeting, either through marriage or for other reasons and the meeting dwindled. Those left did not keep up with either Monthly Meeting, Quarterly Meeting or Yearly Meeting commitments and gradually only a few went regularly to meeting. They missed out on the evangelical Quaker experiments that were going on elsewhere and the non-conformist spiritual strength of Faringdon and elsewhere in the Vale was to be found in Methodism and Baptism. It was as if the Reynolds Family was worn out. They had served their useful life and just seemed to die out.

There is a letter from a Dehorne in the James Reynolds papers held at Reading Archives. It illustrates the extent to which the Faringdon Quaker families were Interlinked by marriage through the generations:

> Dear Uncle
> Obliged by the kindness to Benjamin and hope that his future
> behaviour will merit a continuance of that..,. [19]

Was this money for school fees or new clothes or a training in some trade or profession? Whatever it was, it shows how the remaining Faringdon Quakers are mostly interrelated in some way.

Or another letter from *Abraham Dehorne to Dear Uncle [Robert Reynolds on the envelope, dated 30t/i April 1835]*and thanking for something.

The family looked after each other and their Quaker employees. The Meeting was becoming irrelevant to their lives. They had become quite wealthy and middle class and there were other denominations flourishing in the town that seemed more available and theologically satisfying. The effort of going to meet strange Quakers in faraway places for Monthly and Quarterly Meetings must have seemed irksome and pointless.

The De Hornes seem to have come from Buckinghamshire but with London connections, though William Penn mentions the name in his travels in Germany. Perhaps it was part of a Flemish or French family that became Quaker and moved to England to the Jordans area and some of them married into the Reynolds family and the fourth generation of English born Dehornes lived in Faringdon. This is pure hypothesis but irresistible. There were Dehornes in Brigg meeting also who travelled in the Quaker Ministry in the eighteenth century and must have passed through Faringdon on their way to

Bristol.

Joseph Besse in his introduction to *The Peace of Europe and other Writings* by William Penn writes:

> *About this time it pleased God to inspire the hearts of two protestant ladies of great quality in Germany with a sense of the follies and vanities of the world and to excite them into an earnest inquiry after the knowledge of himself (Penn). The one was Princess Elizabet, daughter of Frederick the fifth, Prince Paletine of the Rhine, and King of Bohemia, granddaughter to James the First and sister to Prince Rupert etc. and the other Anna Maria De Homes, Countess of Hornes.*

These women appear to have corresponded and Penn wrote a dedication to the exemplary character of Princess Elizabeth in his book *No Cross no Crown*. Perhaps, after her friend Princess Elizabeth died in 1680, Anna Maria De Horne moved to England to the strongly Quaker Buckinghamshire Jordans area or to London.

A letter to Witney Monthly Meeting in 1842 is from Benjamin Collier Dehorne:

> *Dear Friends, Being desirous of attending meetings as I was formally enabled to do and feeling that I am prevented in consequence of your having disowned me. I trust that you may see it right to restore me to membership, and as I have not felt satisfied to attend any other place of worship, I wish to impress upon your minds the unpleasant situation I have been placed in, in consequence.*
>
> > *I am very respectfully your Friend*
> > *Benjamin Collier*
> > *Dehorne*

At a monthly meeting in Faringdon on 3rd month 1844, **William Allbright** and **Frances Gregg** were appointed to visit **'Benjamin Collier Dehorne'** and in the following monthly meeting he was readmitted into membership. By 1846 he was a representative of

Faringdon at Monthly Meeting. Why he was disowned I was unable to trace.

Another family that travelled about was the **Wheeler** family and again there is correspondence about the Wheelers in The Reynolds papers. It is extraordinary that here in this backwater of Quakerism there are ways of keeping in touch with those Quakers who still played on the world stage and lived at the forefront of their times. I do not know if the Wheelers I am referring to were a branch related to the Faringdon butcher - a Quaker, or if they just knew about them and it was something that one gossiped about in letters. You copied good bits from letters and passed them on. Perhaps the Reynolds had met the Wheelers, they may have met at Quarterly or Yearly Meetings, though by this time only a few Faringdon Quakers went to these. This copied piece is in the collection of Reynolds material found at The Farm in the sixties, it has no signature or other reference than the date.

> *17.2.1835*
> *our dear friend Daniel Wheeler and his son Charles are safely arrived in Hobart town their peril has been beyond description, having passed through upwards of twenty violent storms or rather hurricanes, some of them attended by thunder and lightning. They were fifteen weeks on the voyage from Rio Janeiro to the Derwent River in Van Dieman's Land: They cast into the sea every encumbrance on the deck and lightened the top as much as possible. We have now to rejoice with thankfulness that everyone of the crew escaped safe to port. And one of them asking the rest how they were after it was all over, the reply was, there is not an acking finger amongst us - and Daniel Wheeler remarks that the health of himself and his son is as good as when they left England.. .But oh the sweet state of mind of our Dear Lord, he says he is all lighter in the balance than the small dust compared with the love and mercy of his heavenly Father. Daniel's words, [1]'The Lord hath done great things for us whereof we are glad" his counsels also are "faithfulness and Truth".*

Daniel Wheeler was born in 1777 in London and served in the army and navy in his youth. He joined Friends in 1799. He felt called to do some work in Russia and accepted an invitation of the Tsar who desired agricultural help from a Quaker. There he lived for some years draining nearly 6000 acres and bringing half of it under cultivation. In 1832 he felt called to visit the 'antipodes'. He travelled around the country and Quakers realised that his was the true call and got Meeting for Sufferings to buy him a ship. He set sail with his son Charles in the Henry Freeling in 1833. In a terrible storm around the Cape of Good Hope he recorded in his journal that he believed his ship was saved by a phalanx of two hundred whales swimming close to the ship and forming a natural breakwater. He held meetings amongst the convicts of 'Van Deimens Land'(Tasmania) sharing the love of God with them. He did not try to convert these people to his own faith, but he did wish to share his belief in the everlasting love of God for each man woman and child, of whatever colour, status or background. Daniel came back to England and then visited America. He died in New York of pneumonia when in 1840 when he was 69 years old. [11]

Even today the *Quaker book of discipline* includes the following extract:

> *- Last First day, in our little meeting, the Master was pleased to preside, and it was indeed a 'feast of fat things'; and the language which arose in my heart was, 'Take, eat, this is my body'. I never remembered being under such covering, and my desire is, that I may never forget it; and oh! that the fear of the lord may so prevail amongst us, as to entitle us to His Love, which can alone enable us to 'run through a troop, or leap over a wall': and which at this time enableth me to call every country my country, and every man my brother.*
>
> > *Daniel Wheeler written in Ochta near St Petersburg 1819.12*

At the beginning of this century, Burford and Faringdon were one First Meeting and there are some minutes in the *Burford Women's Meeting Book*. In 1791 they met at Milton under Wychwood and appointed Hannah Huntley from Burford to attend the next Monthly Meeting at Faringdon. They met alternately at Burford and Milton, very rarely at Faringdon which seems remiss, but presumably Faringdon women did not make much effort to get to these meetings and got rather left out of the picture. In a meeting in 1813, held at Burford, it is recorded that Ann Reynolds contributed 12/-, Jane Reynolds 12/-, and Mary Reynolds the same. Had they been visiting or been visited and handed the money over then or had they made a supreme effort to ride over the ten or so miles to Burford? On 29th of eighth month 1813 the Women's Meeting was held in Faringdon and again in 1815. In the ninth month of 1817 Ann and Elizabeth Reynolds (daughters of Robert) were appointed to be representatives at Monthly Meeting. So something was happening in Vale circles but not a lot in the way of Quakerly good works it seems to me. Of course the families in both meetings were related.[13]

The times had changed and somehow Vale Quakers or Faringdon Quakers were getting too set in their ways as far as Quaker spiritual life went. Possibly they were very quiet in meeting and had few to minister, perhaps they had lost touch with Quaker roots and replaced that with little to nourish the soul. Perhaps it was the case that the form of worship and the Quaker dress, the lack of concrete Christian symbol and church ritual had in themselves become the symbol and the silence was silence and not any longer deep spiritual prayer of the soul with God. The situation seemed to have returned to the time of quietism mentioned in a previous chapter. Sometimes they were visited by Quakers from other meetings for Sunday worship, but by the mid-century this happened rarely. They were leading busy home lives and had local pressures of non-Quaker worldliness was pressing upon them. It became more difficult and even pointless to keep to strict Quaker discipline, and Monthly Meeting and Quarterly Meeting Elders and Overseers did not seem to deal constructively with the matter. As in the eighteenth century the vigour went out of the meeting. Those who lived their Quakerism and were grounded in its ways died or left and the young ones had no one to talk to deeply about the reasons for worshipping in the Quaker way or of how to bring fresh zeal and Light into worship, no one to explain the Quaker Testimonies of honesty, simplicity, humility and the business methods and structures of the society. The roots were lost and the new trends of spiritual Quaker thought did not get shared with Faringdon Meeting. They might have survived in a Quaker Pastor led community such as the one about to be developed in America.

Looking back at the Faringdon situation I can begin to sympathise with those Quakers in America who looked for a new way of organising the meeting. The Faringdon Quaker families lacked stimulus and purpose I feel. They had probably not read the books their Grandparents read: the early Quaker Journals, the mystical works of Jacob Boehme or followed the observations of the leading Quakers of the day in Yearly Meetings, or read their Quaker Epistles. So they had both lost their Quietist roots and failed to become involved with the Quaker Evangelical movement that was sweeping the country.

The rise of Evangelicalism had a profound effect on mid-Victorian Quakerism. It is, of course, difficult to be sure of the real impact of doctrine upon attitudes and behaviour or the connection between developments in theology and social changes, but some of the consequences of the widespread adoption of evangelical views by Friends seem fairly clear. One of the most important was that it helped to destroy the concept of *the Society of Friends as a Peculiar People, especially called to follow a distinctive way of life in partial isolation from a 'corrupt' environment.* [14]

It is almost possible to surmise that a Quaker evangelical felt closer to a non - Quaker evangelical than to a Quietist Quaker.

This was a bad time for the Society of Friends and the numbers fell to about 13,859 in 1861. This decline levelled out and numbers did increase, but relative to the increase in the general population the Quaker Society remained a very small denomination. Many Evangelicals left Friends and certainly in the Vale of White Horse many became Baptists and possibly Methodists too. I have not followed this last possibility through.

I have not discovered where the Faringdon Quakers were educated. Perhaps they had a tutor at home or went to local non-conformist schools. Those boys born in the late eighteenth century may well have gone to the school in Burford where Robert and Joseph Huntley were educated. As mentioned there was a boarding school in Faringdon in what is now Sudbury House and a ladies school run by Miss Priscilla Clark and Miss Temperence Kent nearby. Rufus Jones lists eighty schools managed by Quakers in the nineteenth century in England. Charlbury within the Monthly Meeting had such a school. Sibford Quaker school was not far away either, and Joseph Huntley taught there before he got involved in biscuits. There were various girls' boarding schools that Bristol Quakers and Birmingham and York Quakers used and which Vale Friends may have sent their daughters to but it is difficult to find records of attendances at those schools which were privately run. The young Quaker men could have gone to Ackworth or Bootham Quaker Boarding schools. [15]

Dissenters were still unable to attend universities though there were now more provincial ones being founded, which were open to all. Certainly the more advanced Mechanics Institutes and Adult Schools included some quite academic and technical courses and indeed some courses in these places were perhaps more advanced in the technical and scientific fields than some traditional university courses. Quakers did attend those. The Bill to permit Dissenters to proceed to degrees was presented to Parliament in 1834. The House of Commons was in favour of it but it failed to pass the House of Lords. It was nearly another forty years before it was finally passed. If the Faringdon children were mainly educated at home or locally they did not get in touch with the ideas of the mainstream Quaker movements of the period. They probably did not feel the need to do so. They were happily occupied in the town with shop keeping and selling real estate. [16]

Not far away Thomas, the son of the Rev Hughes at Uffington, was sent to the school run by the renowned Dr Arnold at Rugby. Arnold developed his ideas around 1828 and they spread to other establishments after his death. In 1857 Thomas Hughes wrote the book *TomBrown's Schooldays* about the school.

The Quietist view, lingering from the late eighteenth century, was rather against too much knowledge. This might interfere with a direct listening to the 'Truth'. Robert Reynolds and James Reynolds of the late eighteenth century may have stuck to the traditional view that the *'light within'* was the teacher.

So perhaps fathers like Charles Reynolds (1779-1852) or his brother James Reynolds (1781-1829), themselves brought up in the Quietist tradition, felt home tuition in reading, writing and book-keeping was enough for their own offspring. After that, experience of life, and listening to God was the teacher. After all it was this sort ofattitudethat had led some Quakers to a *Concern* about the state of Quakerism in the nineteenth century. This centred on the realisation that Quakers did not know their Bibles properly and were living in a *dead sort of way* so far as Christian Faith was concerned. These worries that too many were leaving the Society of Friends because it did not givethem enough spiritual nourishment resulted in the evangelical thrust which put learning the Bible at the forefront of education. This in turn led Quakers to support mission work. For evangelicals the Bible was the central source of a knowledge of God. Whereas for the early Quakers and the Liberal Quakers the source was the '*still small voice'*.

As you will see, from mid-century the torch was not passed on strongly enough to keep the spirit of Quakerism alive in the Vale. No new people were inspired to come to meeting and become members and the old families faded away. All the influences that led to the three strands of Quakerism (Quietist, Evangelical and Liberal) that were exercising, and even in some cases fracturing, London Yearly Meeting, do not appear to have impinged upon the Faringdon Quakers.

There is a beautifully written diary and memoirs of Caroline Westcombe Pumphrey called *Charlbury of our childhood.* She was born in 1844 and died 1925. She describes a closely knit Quaker Meeting in a small town within the same Monthly Meeting as Faringdon. It really is a first-hand peek into social history of Quakers at the time. The old ways giving way to the new - the traditional and the liberal. She visits the other meetings in the Monthly meeting and gives some vivid descriptions of Sundays in Charlbury.

Page 20 In my early days it seemed to me that the grown -ups always read Friends books on Sundays. Our Aunts, especially Aunt Carry, were particular about Sunday reading and

Sunday occupations generally. Certain games like brides, dolls, linguist, etc., never came out on Sunday and there were special Sunday picture books with Bible pictures... and dissections with 'Joseph and his brethren' and 'Daniel and the Lions Den' instead of 'England and Wales'.[17]

She seems to have been given quite a lot of freedom and describes wonderful walks in Wychwood Forest and paddling in the Evenlode stream. Uncle organised picnics in the forest or in hayfields and sometimes these were all day affairs with lunch and tea taken in the open air.

Page 68 Faringdon Monthly Meeting was another pleasant Quaker picnic with its delightful long drive thro' Bampton and over quaint old peaky bridges and streams where there was a tantalizing profusion of white water lilies and water violet. And there we went to the Clump as regularly as to meeting. Jane Reynolds, our hostess, was a quaint old Quaker lady with maids somewhat quainter than herself. It was at Faringdon that Uncle John first 'spoke in Meeting' to use a phrase of the period.'

Charles Reynolds Senior

Uncle John must refer to **John Albright** 1816-1909. He took over the family shop in Charlbury which she describes. It appeared to have a banking section, a drugs section, chocolates, and drapery and groceries. As there is no date in the above extract it is difficult to know if the *Jane Reynolds* mentioned in the above extract is the sister-in-law of Robert Reynolds. His brother Richard might have married Jane as a young girl who could have been a very, very old lady in about *1850*. A Jane Reynolds is mentioned in the Monthly Meeting Burial notes as dying in 1861, aged 79. I think this is the one. She will have really lived with those eighteenth century Quakers, met them and thought like them. If the picnic took place when Caroline was about 12 years old then Jane would have been *a quaint old lady* dressed in plain clothes and Quaker bonnet.

There is a book in a private collection, *The faithful provider,* with a message on the front fly sheet: *'James Reynolds from his Aunt Jane R. 18th October 1837 or 1851*

A story has been passed down by the late Jean Pocock that her Aunts, who lived in the Farmhouse in Faringdon (in the early twentieth century), told about the Quakers going to the White Horse hill for grand picnics led by Charles Reynolds senior (1779 - 1852) or one of his sons. I expect that they probably did. I think that Charles and James junior went hunting as there are papers in the Reading Archives of local Meets of the Old Berkshire Fox Hounds.Below is a Reynolds family crest with a Fox on it. Of course Reynard the Fox is a folk hero and Reynolds might be derived from that. I cannot unravel this idea here.

Hunting was not something that strict Quakers of the time would do and might have been a reason why Charles, who had been so faithful to the Society as a young man, resigned in 1859. His brother Richard was disowned in 1859. So this might have led to Charles and a lot of others in the Faringdon Meeting resigning. I actually think that there were other reasons for these resignations from the Society which involved grave stones! In Charles's case he was married by the 1861 census and this might have been the reason for resignation. The new Book of Discipline came out in 1861 and, influenced by Evangelical Friends, began to break down the barriers that separated

Quakersfrom everyone else and they could relax on Quaker dress and speech. By the 1860's the attitude towards the Arts had begun to relax too and pianos could be found in some Quaker homes. Since 1859 Friends could marry 'out'. Perhaps Witney Monthly Meeting was a bit slow to take these things up or did not wish to do so. The Reynolds Family Tree in the appendix may help in following the different generations and branches of this family.

The Reynolds Crest

There is a record in the Witney MM Extract that *Charles Reynolds is disowned because he marries outside Friends.* This could be Charles senior (1779-1852) who married Margaret, a non - Friend, or their son Charles (1817-1867) who also married 'out'. It is odd because Charles the son of Charles eventually resigned in 1859, which is after his own child was born. Faringdon must have just arranged things as they thought fit. Possibly Charles senior still felt himself a Friend and brought his children up as such. His daughters and sons certainly were buried as Quakers, contributed to funds and were recorded as members and were representatives at business meetings after their resignations! What confusion.

I cannot resist including the following snippet from Caroline

Pumphrey's memoirs. It has the human touch about experience of wearing Quaker bonnets:

> *Page 13 Most Friends wore Friends' bonnets in those days. They took to them as soon as they left school or earlier. They were inconvenient, not to say unwholesome, on account of the weight and non-ventilating properties of the pasteboard, besides the amount people had to wear on the head in the way of lined bonnet caps, oiled silk, etc., to keep lining, pasteboard and silk from getting greasy. One of us was guilty of saying she 'did not like kissing Deborah Beesley in her Friends' bonnet, because the air inside was so close and confined'.*

A wonderful recipe book has been handed down through the Reynolds family. It has *Elizabeth Reynolds 16th Oct 1811* on it. One recipe is for Bugs, perhaps bugs in bonnets!

Quaker bonnets in the 19th century.

Elizabeth Reynold's Bug poison
1½~ pint spirits of turpentine
1/2 a pint of spirits of wine
1/2 an oz camphor, with sufficient quantity of conserve sublimato to render it destructed.

185

(this last instruction I am not sure about.)

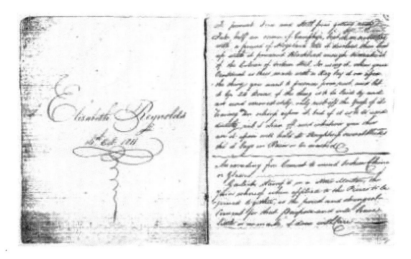

Elizabeth Reynolds's Cookery Book

Ratafia Cream sounds exciting:

> *Take six laurel leaves and boil them in a quart of thick cream, when boiled throw away the leaves and beat the yolks of five eggs with a little cold cream and sugar to your taste then thicken the cream with your (? bat) and set it over the fire again but don't let it boil keep it stirring all the while one way and pour it into china dishes when it is cold its fit for use.*

(I think the ratafia biscuits must have been in the bowls already).

There are heaps of recipes for family illnesses such as colic or piles, coughs and dropsy. Lots of brandy and wine is used, so no thoughts of being teetotal in 1811. The book includes household hints such as how to make polish for mahogany or how to preserve birds. Some of the recipes are anything but simple:

> *A fine cake recommended by friend Cockfield.*
> *Take three pounds of fine flour, 3 pounds of butter well*

washed in rosewater, 3 1/2 pounds of good lump sugar finely powdered 16 eggs well beaten. Break the butter and mix with the flour and other ingredients. Then add a pint of cream, and a gill of brandy and beat and work them well together, then add 5&l/2 pounds of currents, 1 ounce of cinnamon, 1/2 ounce of mace, 2 nutmegs, 1/4 pound of candyd lemon and orange peel, 2 ounces of citron and 1/2 a pound of blanched almonds and mix well together. Rub the inside of a bake pan with butter and put in a moderate oven bake. [18]

The only minutes that I can find about Faringdon Meeting, which also demonstrate the slow decline, are to be found in the *Witney Monthly Meeting Women's Friends Minutes*:

1874 Held at Faringdon. no reps present

14 of 7 1874 Held at Faringdon. Mary Ann Reynolds rep from Faringdon.Meeting with her were Rachel and Caroline Albright of Charlbury. Read anEpistle from Yearly Meeting and one from New England Yearly Meeting.

6 of 8 1875 at Faringdon. . .No Witney Friends present. Faringdon no appointment. [19]

So Caroline and Rachel Albright came all the way from Charlbury to sit with themselves. They may have visited Mary Ann who was probably very ill by then with something, perhaps TB. She died in 1880 aged only 55 years old. Leaving her niece Margaret Tryphena.

In 1876 Caroline and Rachel enter answers to queries which seem to me to be no more than wishful thinking! Where the meeting is held is not recorded, so one assumes it was in Charlbury.

'That Meeting for Worship are held regularly on first day & well attended. A deficiency exists on weekdays. Meetings for Church affairs regularly held and generally well attended'

Another meeting is held in Faringdon 6.13.1876. Again no representatives fromWitney or Faringdon. So Caroline Albright appoints herself to represent them atGeneral meeting at Sibford. She appears to be the only Friend present, and again nodoubt visits Mary Ann. Another such meeting on 6.10 78 and in 6.10.1879.1 think it was an excuse to visit Mary Ann and see what was going on. The meeting was an excuse for oversight.

In 1880 the minute reads:

> *Our meetings for worship are, with one exception, arising from illness and smallness of numbers, regularly held.. .Those on first days are well attended...*

On *11.5.80* they go to Faringdon for the last time. I wonder if this was the funeral of Mary Ann who died on 5.5.1880? The nineteenth century Women's meeting notes are just not to be compared with those of the Vale Women in 1680. If it had been then we should have been told about the niece of Mary Ann and what was to happen to her. The actual holding of *Meetings for Business* had, I fear, become more important than the purpose for holding them. The Friends appear to be unaware of the extra help that was needed by members in the meeting. They are not caring enough. They have perhaps led very sheltered lives and have not the practical common sense of those of earlier days. I am not surprised that someone like Anne Reynolds daughter of James the draper (1781-1829) had married out of the Society.

Looking at the Victorian Baptist records in Faringdon it seems clear that often through the years Quakers became Baptists, or some members of a family belonged to one and some the other denomination. Mostly I think Quakers became Baptists, the strain of running their own meetings for worship and Church Affairs was too much. The Baptist Minister was paid and trained to do that and it was quite clear what the Christianity being taught was. It was quite clear how the Bible was meant to be used and what was expected of a Baptist Christian believer. There would be good clear use and knowledge of the Bible and the Sermon was sound and helpful.

The following family names appear in both Baptist and Quaker records over the years:

Butcher- Langley - Wheeler - Vokin (Voking)- Warmen -Cox - Reynolds -Cole-Fry -Pocock-etc.

Ann Reynolds, daughter of James and sister of James Junior, was proposed for communion, and received Baptism in June *1833.* She married James Fidel (his first wife having died) in 1833 the same year that the Faringdon Baptists agreed to petition the government to abolish Slavery. She must have felt very much at home. Faith into action. Ann died in 1844. In the 1851 census, her sons, Albert and Edward were 11 and 10, so they were born in about 1839 and 1840 respectively. Perhaps two little ones took a toll on her health. Later it is recorded that in 1862 Albert James Fidel died aged 23. Was this polio, cholera or TB or an accident? We have no idea. These times were not easy and many died quite young.

By 1866 Edward Reynolds Fidel was an upholsterer and Chairman who signed letters for the Baptist Church. He became a Deacon and a Trustee. Elizabeth Reynolds, possibly sister of James and Ann was a member too. John and Elizabeth Cox were members. A Thomas Reynolds was a member. In 1859 there were 72 members of the Baptist congregation. Baptists were running shops and businesses in the town with the strength of Quakers a hundred years before. They formed the backbone of the Faringdon Auxiliarv Bible Society with contributions from Wheelers, Reynolds, Fidels and Pococks amongst others. Also they were members of the Faringdon Abstinence Society and The Band of Hope. All these were movements that Quakers in other parts of Berkshire and Oxfordshire were strongly supporting.James Fidel, the late Ann's husband, was a leading light of the Baptists and gave a lecture on April 25th *1851:*

The spot on which this chapel stands has been employed for the purposes of divine worship for nearly three hundred years by Protestant dissenters of the Baptist denomination. The 'interest' must have been founded in very early times, probably in the reign of Henry 8th, About a century ago or more (during the reigns of William and Ann and George 1st) there was a flourishing cause here It is credibly related that several of the most wealthy and respected persons in the neighbourhood attended this chapel (verified by dates on tombs in the churchyard) but from circumstances unknown the cause fell into decay and the place of worship was used for menial purposes. The pews were torn up and thrown to one end of the chapel while the other end was used as a chapel. From this state it was redeemed in 1770 by the assistance of Mr Freeman a Christian friend resident in London. For 60 years it was occasionally supported by students of the Academy Bristol. The present building replaced the old at about this time.. Nearly four years ago some considerable (?and acceptable) sums were made available to the congregation and the place enlarged. [20]

This piece I include in my Quaker story because in fact by 1880 the little meeting of Quakers in Faringdon was about to undergo similar neglect. It is interesting how these things happen. God does indeed work in mysterious ways.

The Faringdon Quaker Burial Notes make sad reading as one after another the Quaker community died out. There are only a couple of tomb stones in the Burial ground and I may have found out why. It seems that Yearly Meeting decided to regulate burials and the size of tomb stones to be used. This tied in with testimonies to simplicity and that Quakers do not test someone by the expense or size of a stone but by the example of their life as a spiritual person. Also the practice of uniform stones, as all are equal before the Lord.

It seems that Yearly Meeting wanted a stone for each person and that the size should be 15 inches long by 20 inches wide. This seemed unacceptable to Faringdon Quakers. I imagine that they had a very full burial ground by this time and that what had been the procedure for a family was to them satisfactory and 'the right and decent thing to do'. They asked to continue with their ways and were not allowed any flexibility. They were very upset by the lack of understanding of their Monthly Meeting. I think all of this upset could have been avoided if Elders and Overseers had been doing a proper job and London Yearly Meeting had listened to the grassroots flock. It is just another example of silly rules and regulations that are man-made taking over from the real teachings of Love and Truth that Early Quakers understood and some Victorian Quakers did not.

On 7th month 13th day 1857, at a Monthly Meeting at Faringdon, James Reynolds and Thomas Fawkes of Faringdon being present: both requested to have gravestones put down over four graves. This meeting consents thereto and appoints them to lay them down according to the directions of Yearly Meeting...

I am not sure what the above means. Possibly James and Thomas were asking for one large stone to be used in a family grave, whereas Monthly Meeting thought they were asking for four little stones.

At a Monthly Meeting held at Charlbury on 9th month 7th day 1857 the following letter from Faringdon was read:

> *Dear Friends*
> *We therefore hope that Friends will accede to our request to place one stone, when required for families in the same grave instead of a number of stones... Jane Reynolds, Mary Ann Whitfield, Margaret Reynolds, Mary Ann Reynolds, James Reynolds signed Clerk Thomas Fawkes.*

Apparently Monthly Meeting saw no reason to alter its decision as expressed and would not allow Faringdon Friends to do what they wished to do.

The Dehorne family particularly objected to having to lay a stone over the grave of each of their children and to the disturbance of it due to a reduction in size. The following minute was received by Monthly Meeting from Faringdon Meeting on First month eleventh day 1858, signed by their presiding clerk Thomas Fawkes:

> *Faringdon PM have again taken into consideration the matter of gravestones fixed on by Monthly Meeting and concludes not to lay any down for the present.*

It was after this that resignations and a lack of Monthly Meeting attendance by Faringdon Friends really set in.

According to the Burial notes that we have, twelve more burials took place up to 1902 as follows:

Mary Ann Whitfield (spinster)	l5~2.	1858
Jane Reynolds (widow)	l0~7	1861 aged 79
Joseph Giles		1867about 68
Margaret Reynolds (spinster)		1867 aged 82
Charles Reynolds (Junior)		1867aged 51
Margaret Jane Reynolds		1873aged 55
Thomas Fawkes		1875 aged 73
Clarissa Louise Harding (a baby)		1877
Richard (Michael) Reynolds		1879 aged 58
Mary Ann Reynolds (spinster)		1880 aged 55
Elizabeth Reynolds (Richard's widow)		1899 aged 76
(not in membership)		
(delivered to undertaker William Collin Sell)		
John Gardner (husband[2] of Tryphena Reynolds Gardner)		
	11. 9.1902aged 81	

So no burial stones and perhaps we now know why. It is sad to note how young Charles Junior and his siblings Richard, Margaret Jane and Mary Ann were when they died. They were nearly all outlived by their Aunt from the previous generation. I do wonder if they died of tuberculosis. It appears to have been an ailing Mary Ann that tried to keep things going until there were no Meetings held on Sundays and the Meeting House was not used for worship.

At a Witney Monthly Meeting for Ministry and Oversight 4th of 4th 1889, the latest report from Yearly Meeting for Ministry and Oversight was considered:

> *The consideration of the report sent up by our subordinate Meetings has brought us into sympathy with many who are seeking faithfully to obey the call of the Lord, and to serve him in the teaching and shepherding of the flock. We have been reminded that the Apostle exhorts us to "Covet earnestly the best gifts" and to seek in the exercise of these that we may "excel in the edifying of the church".[21]*

The subordinate meetings (Preparative Meetings) were by this time

192

not Burford, which closed in 1855, (though it did re-open again in 1891) - not Faringdon which had no Quakers left to worship. Charlbury was just keeping going by then and Witney was about to close for three years. Even Chipping Norton was struggling and closed in 1910. There were no meetings in the western Vale at all any more.

It was Oxford itself that was about to have a new lease of life. Its meeting house had been sold in 1867. The meeting was re-opened again in 1888 after **Charles Edwin Gillett** moved to the town. And in 1891 a Preparative Meeting was established with 18 members. The new growth areas were in Oxford and Swindon, where the new enthusiastic Quakerism of evangelical vigour took over from the Quietism. In both towns, which strictly were outside the Vale, Adult schools were begun and in Oxford there were things happening everyday. Band of Hope, Evangelistic Meetings for worship, The Christian Endeavour Society, The Coal Club. These Quakers were missioners. The meeting soon grew to over 60 with many attenders from all walks of life.

The Manchester Conference of 1895

In 1895 a great Quaker Conference was held in Manchester. Over a thousand Friends gathered in Manchester to discuss the life and work of the Society. The arguments between the Evangelicals and the new Liberal thinkers were aired. In America such arguments had led to splits and the development of the Evangelical and Pastoral Yearly Meetings leaving the traditional and silent 'Conservative' Yearly Meetings. The question was should British Quakerism go the same way. Of course Britain is a relatively small island with a fairly cohesive population compared to the United States and somehow it kept itself as one Yearly Meeting.

The substantial unity of Friends in the Victorian period can be explained in a number of different ways. Bright attributed it to Quaker virtue: *'Friends are, after all, the most tolerant people on earth, and I verily believe our little Church is the only one that could freely discuss and make great reforms without schism and something like dissolution .'* There were, however, more tangible factors which fostered Quaker unity. Certain of these discouraged both schisms and resignations of individuals.

The intense attachment of members to the Society was compounded of many elements. Quakerism was so different from other denominations; it affected life at so many points - especially before 1860 - that to abandon it after a lifetime of sitting through silent meetings, saying 'thee' and 'thou', refusing to pay tithes and wearing a collarless coat, was to threaten one's whole sense of identity. Quakers prized the length of Quaker descent as a nobleman prizes the antiquity of his titles. Even those who left the Society continued to take a pride in their Quaker antecedents. Moreover in the Victorian period, Quaker membership was difficult to obtain, easy to lose, and correspondingly valued.. The Society of Friends, was in a literal sense a society of kinsmen. To leave it was to cut oneself off, to some extent, from one's relatives and friends, and very possibly, one's business associates.[14]

The Quaker Evangelical trend had by the end of the nineteenth century almost run its course in Britain. The doctrine of the Light within became important once again. The Quaker Christian view tended to reject the doctrine of original sin and cherish the notion of the seed of God in the heart of each one. The love of God for each of us was a guiding light. If we listened, we would hear the call and know how to conduct our lives.

The light by which our consciences must be enlightened, the light of obedience to which is our supreme good, must be something purer than this fallible faculty itself. It must be that power within us, if any such power there be, which is one with all wisdom, all goodness, all order and harmony, within us; one with 'the power, not ourselves, which makes for righteousness'; one with 'the eternal will towards all goodness'. It must be a power as all-pervading and immanent in the spirit of man as is the power of gravity (or whatever yet more elementary force gravity may be resolved into) in the outer world he inhabits. It must be the power in which we live and move and have our being - the power and the presence of God.[23]

In America the divisions in Quaker interpretation and practice which had started in the eighteenth century, well before such divisions occurred in Britain, remained and hardened. In large cities there were meetings that followed different traditions and belonged to totally different Yearly Meetings. Over the country as a whole though there was a geographical distribution.

In the late nineteenth century, the rural areas of the Eastern Seaboard area were mainly traditionalist and Quietist, here the insistence on religious experience, the inner light and the mystical was to the fore. These traditions were more in tune with the British Friends of the twentieth century. Those Thatcher Quakers descended from the Uffington, Thatcher family, were of the Quietist Yearly Meeting - the Hicksites, they had followed Elias Hicks (1748-1830). He ministered that life was an awareness of that of God within, and that the whole spiritual life should be given to opening ourselves as listeners to this inward light. So his way sharpened the dualism that is latent within Quakerism by denying human intervention. No teaching or preaching, no study, no Bible. This was quite the opposite of those who were concerned to put some discipline and Christian message back into the meetings. In the Mid-West area of the United States, the Pastoral Tradition was strengthened. So there were Programmed Meetings and paid Pastors, and in the Far West Quakerism was strongly Evangelical with paid pastors, programmed worship and strict Biblical interpretation laid down by the elders.

The amazing thing is that with all this variety of belief, stretching from almost a Unitarian emphasis on the first principle, God, to the almost Trinitarian emphasis on the equality of the Christ as spirit and father and son, yet have the American and the world Quakers remained as one recognisable body. This is another book in itself as to why this is so. Many individuals have sacrificed themselves to build bridges and foster renewed understanding and respect during the twentieth century. Basically none of the main Yearly Meetings have forgotten the centrality of the love of God for each one, the humility of each within the truth, and the importance of each person before God. They somehow remain Friends and hold to their testimonies of Truth, simplicity and peace. They always regard faith and action as one thing, that all life is sacramental.

For many Yearly Meetings, including *London Yearly Meeting [Britain Yearly Meeting today]* this was the beginning of a modernised Society of Friends. Many of the silly and outdated rules and patterns were seen to be so. The Society had become as set in its ways as the established church had seemed in the early days of the seventeenth century. A key figure in the new more relevant Quakerism was John Wilhelm Rowntree (1868 - 1905). He pleaded for a teaching ministry, pointing out that it was becoming increasingly difficult in modern business and professional life to give the same attention to the needs of the ministry that the previous generation had been able to give. He managed to help people see that they could take their past into the future. Out of all this came George Cadbury's inspiration for a Quaker College, Woodbrooke, and various other educational establishments and projects:

> *Yet a religion merely intellectual will never warm the heart with the fire of self- sacrificing love. Let us in our message offer that which is beyond all creeds - tthe evidence in our lives of communion with the spirit of God. The need for positive animating faith in the inward presence of God's spirit has never been greater than now..The church exists to create for each succeeding generation the ideal of Christ in the thought-form of the age, and in the adaptability of Christ's teaching lies one secret of his power. Friends are not bound by a heritage of creeds, and need not break with their great past to put themselves in touch with the present.*[24]

Sadly all this was too late for Vale Quakers who had perhaps failed to carry on the *Light of Quakerism* due to their own weaknesses, but for whom, both Monthly Meeting and Quarterly Meeting had been careless or to put it more strongly, by whom they had been let down. In fact one wonders what was the Committee for Ministry and Oversight doing apart from self perpetuating itself. When Faringdon Quakers had been irritated by regulations about dress and marrying out and the uniformity of tomb stones and when most resigned, no one in the wider structure seemed to care. There was no discussion about individuals who resigned, recorded in Monthly Meeting Minutes apart from that with Benjamin Dehorne in 1842. Was this

Christian charity and love? The early Seekers after Truth would have been very sad to see how things had worked out for Quakers in the Vale.

NOTES

[1.] ISECHEI (Elizabeth), *Victorian Quakers,* Oxford University Press 1970

[2.]SHILLITOE (Thomas), *Journal of the life of Thomas Shillitoe,1754 -1863,* extracts at Friends House library, London

[3.]HODGSON (William), *The Society of Friends in the nineteenth century, Philadelphia /875 Vol I p.314*

[4.] KELLY *Kelly's Directory 1847,* (copy in Faringdon library) *Billings Directory',* (copy in Faringdon library)

PHILIPPS (Robert) *A short History of a Wessex town,1970*

[5.] The census records & Witney Monthly Meeting minutes in Oxfordshire Archives

[6.] WEDMORE (Edmund T),Thomas Pole *M.D..* (Friends House Library) London

[7.]Census records 1851, 1891, copies at Westgate Centre Oxford Monthly Meeting Membership lists

[8]CORLEY (T.A.B.), *Quaker enterprise in Biscuits, Huntley and Palmer of Reading:* Hutchinson 1972

[9.] Oxfordshire Archives, Witney Monthly Meeting minutes of this C 19[th]period. Also information from correspondence with the present family in Australia.

[10.] REYNOLDS papers in private hands

[11.] VIPONT (Elfrida), *The story of Quakerism* p195-6, 208-, Bannisdale press 1954 Letter in Reynolds papers, Reading, Berkshire Archives

[12.]*Quaker Faith and Practice* 1995, 2.04
2.04 Memoirs Daniel Wheeler, 1842 p71

[13.]*Burford Women's Meeting book BOQIYJHV 6 1786-1799, JJV 7 18/3*

[14.]ISECHEI (Elizabeth), *Victorian Quakers* 1970 OUP

[15.] JONES (Rufus M.), Later Periods of Quakerism, p 706 London: Macmillan,1922 (2Vols.)

[16.] CURTIS S.T. & BOULTWOOD M.E.D., *An Introductory History of English Education since 1800.* ch. XV University Tutorial Press 1960

[17.]WESTCOMBE (Caroline Pumphrey), *Memoirs of Caroline Westcombe Pumphrey: Charlbury of our childhood.* William Sessions, York 1990.

[18.] A photocopy of this recipe book is in the Ironbridge Gorge Museum Library, Telford, Salop.

[19.]Oxfordshire Archives *Witney Monthly Meeting Women's Minutes* BOQMXX1 V1 1.

[20.] Baptist records in Faringdon.

[21.] See 14 above page 66.

[22.]Oxfordshire Archives QQM 1x iii1.

[23.]STEPHEN (Caroline), *Quaker Strongholds, Quaker Classics,*

Friends Home Service Committee 1980.

[24.]HERON (Alastair), *Quakers in Britain a century of change, 1895-1995*, Curlew Graphics 1995

CHAPTER EIGHT

THE REYNOLDS FAMILY

Some Family Mysteries Resolved

From left to right: Margaret Jane, Richard, Charles, Mary Ann,
Margaret

There seems to be no doubt that during the eighteenth century the Reynolds family consolidated the wealth they had and that they were really quite comfortably off as the nineteenth century opened. They were in a position to make the most of the development of Faringdon during this later time too. This had happened to many other Quakers in England and America. Quakers had not spent their money on frivolities, had not *'publicly'* drunk it away, had not gone dancing and betting or to the theatres and music halls. Some still lived with simplicity compared to most non-Quakers in their income bracket though others lived rather comfortably and weakened on their Quaker principles. They saw nothing wrong in using their money prudently and wisely and they had quite a bit to use. They placed it in Banks, many of which were in the hands of Quakers and you may be sure that Yearly Meetings and Quarterly Meetings, as in the previous century, provided opportunity to discuss stocks and shares as well as new scientific and technical ventures into which to invest. The Reynolds family were in a position to take advantage of these things.

Mary Ann [left] and Margaret

The Reynolds family were, at the beginning of the nineteenth century, involved in getting the most they could out of the money made in farming. This had branched out into related activities, malting, drapery and cheese making. They also were involved in stocks and shares in roads, railways and other businesses locally and nationally as the century advanced. Members of the family had moved or married away from Faringdon had spread all over the country by now and they wrote to each other and gave advice about money matters and other things. This was the end of the canal age and the time of improving roads, and by the mid-century, the time of railways. The Faringdon Reynolds family did just as other Quakers they knew were doing.

The following are some snippets of letters and instructions found in the farmhouse in Faringdon in the nineteen sixties. As an example Richard Reynolds who died in 1835 left these instructions

> *Memorandum of R.R. wishes that his nephew C. Reynolds Senior should have after his decease what money may be coming from the Radcot Road - Also the dividend arising from the Glamorgan Canal shares during his life and on his decease to be between his daughters Margaret Jane R. and Mary Ann R.*

Also a paper:

> *Faringdon and Burford Turnpike Trust Annual*
> *Statement*
> *1862.* 111

The recently discovered Account book of Richard Reynolds's Legacy is a useful guide to the situation during this period. I think this legacy must have been left by the Richard Reynolds (died 1837?) son of Robert and Mary Reynolds, married to Jane (Aunt Jane 1782 -*1859* or 1861). Though it might have been Richard Reynolds (--1847) son of Robert and Ann married to Elizabeth and brother of the Elizabeth (died 1848) mentioned above. A Richard Reynolds was disowned in 1811. These members of the family, born in the late eighteenth century, died in their seventies which is above the national average of the time. Here we are once more confused by the same name used in each generation and by siblings for their children. Perhaps a glance at the Reynolds family tree in the appendix might clarify things. Disowned or not Richard still leaves money for the Monthly Meeting as his father would have done and as his family had done for over two centuries.

The following extract from Richard Reynolds will is scribbled on the fly sheet of the Account Book of the Legacy:

1 give unto the treasurer for the time being of the Friends eeting House at Faringdon aforesaid the sum of £100 to be used and applied in the repairs of the Meeting House and for the benefit of the poor members attending. the same is his direction.'

Legacy   £100
duty deducted 10

90

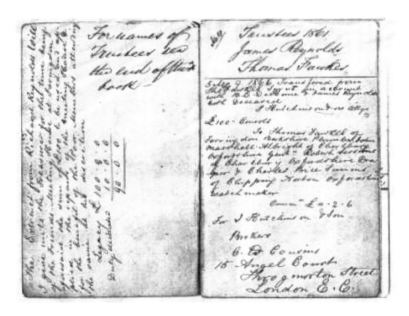

Richard Reynolds's will in Account Book

A scribbled note in this book says *continued from another book now full* and the *balance in December 1853 is fourteen shillings and five pence. Repairs having been undertaken to the tune of six shillings and four pence.* However, dividends are recorded in the following year and the accounts keep going. The accounts are signed by **Robert Sessions** of Charlbury. The Trustees in 1861 are **James Reynolds** (this must be the next generation; again the linen draper who died in 1862) and **Thomas Fawkes**. In 1866 it is transferred still to include Thomas Fawkes plumber of Faringdon (died 1875), James having died, and now also **Marshall Albright** of Charlbury Gent., *Robert* **Sessions** of Charlbury draper, **Charles Price Simms** of Chipping Norton watchmaker. The brokers are **C.D. Cousins** of 15 Angel Court, Throgmorton London E.C. [2]

During the time of the book entries, money was given to **James Wheeler** in 1854, to **J Harris** and **C. Green** several times (are these grave diggers?), and to **Thomas Fawkes.** They bought bracing irons in 1854. Money was donated to a local poor Friend from time to time, and to cleaning the Meeting House, up to 1875. Sometimes money was sent to build up stock which stood at £138 in 1884. This takes us up to four years before **Mary Ann Reynolds** died. She was the last of the Quaker Reynolds in Faringdon. Bits and pieces were paid out after this and repairs done on the Meeting House in 1904. The receipt book ends with a balance of £63.8.7 in 1908 and is signed in 1909.

After this the book presumably moved from monthly meeting clerk until **Thackwell Smith** of Charlbury had it. He was Clerk from time to time and related to the Gillett bankers of Banbury. Finally it has come to light in the attic of **Reg (Gillett) Smith** a descendant of Thackwell and who considered himself a birthright member of Witney Monthly Meeting, but did not come to worship. He died in 1997 and his ashes were interred beside the Thackwell grave at Charlbury Quaker Burial ground. So this account book was found amongst his possessions and is now in the Oxfordshire Archives. [2]

I spend some time on this little book because it is at least evidence that the Vale Quakers or the Reynolds family were still in and out of their meeting and in a small way sticking to good business practice.

Elizabeth Reynolds's (1770-1848) accounts (held in Reading Archives) are full of bits and pieces of shares in this and that, for example, she gets £55. 2.0 from shares invested in Bristol Gas. She gets £600 from Robert Huntley's share in grass from grounds in Coxwell and Faringdon. She gets £5 16.13.4 from Robert Reynolds Legacy (see below). She gets rent from cottages from Thomas

Franks and Jane Reynolds £14 and £9 respectively.When she died in 1848 as a spinster her household furniture was sold at the Crown in Faringdon and included all sorts of things - listed under rooms: bedrooms, dining, kitchen, pantry, passage and staircase and other - an oak tent bed and divinity furniture, breakfast and tea service, pair of decanters. I have no idea where she was living before she died. I suppose as an unmarried daughter she lived in the house of her father Robert, and inherited some of the family fortune. But there were all the new houses around Broomsgrove, built by the family. Today these are listed buildings...No 1, No7, No 41, No 43, No 45. Perhaps Elizabeth had lived in one of these.

Elizabeth Reynolds's sampler [private collection] photo Coalbrookdale

As a matter of interest there were some books in the Sale ofElizabeth's effects including *Sacred History 2 Vols., Spectator* 8 *Vols., Annotations of the Bible, Encyclopaedia and Solicitude Memoirs.* Some of these things she will have inherited. It is clear that none of her family needed these things themselves. The whole lot eventually made £110.15.06. Her nephew-in-law, James Fidel was the Auctioneer. This was the Elizabeth who was daughter of Robert the Cheese Factor and Malster and had become sister-in-law to Robert Huntley the half-brother of the biscuit manufacturer.

Shop and homes, now Ferndale School

Elizabeth also in her will writes to Mr James Reynolds, her nephew:

> *I give you the ware house near to your dwelling house on the site of which you are about to build your expensive shop.*[3]

There is also a document of probate in the Reading archives (F3) of a James Reynolds (brother of the Elizabeth mentioned above) who died in 1829:

> *a draper who gives all goods plate lunch china pictures beers and liquors to various people including* **Daniel Rutter** *of Witney. He gives all the freehold copyfold and leasehold, including lands at Kingston Lisle, Baulking and Great Coxwell, and Faringdon and elsewhere, to his brother* **Charles Reynolds** *(yeoman in Faringdon).To suffer and permit his wife to carry on trades and business until his*

youngest is twenty one or until my said wife sees fit. The proceeds of the above to provide for his wife and the education of his children. 3

The business referred to above must have been the cheese factor and malting business. This was possibly, more or less, on the site of the present building known as *Top Goddards* until it recently became a restaurant, *Rats' Castle.*This is an early to mid-nineteenth century grade two listed building. It is a two storied stucco fronted building, stucco on brick, with a gabled end to the street, *number 1 Broomsgrove.* The inside of the building is galleried around the first floor with an oblong top light over a coved ceiling. The original mahogany shelving and the counters are still intact, with banks of pigeon holes and drawers for the goods along the walls.

The building today, exterior and interior

Exterior   **Haberdashery shelves**

Next to it is the Ferndale school again an early nineteenth century listed building with stucco re-facing and of three stories, which was built for a member of the Reynolds family. The garden at the back extended right down to the Westbrook and used to have a wonderful copper beech tree until well into the second half of the twentieth century, so I am told. It is possible that the land upon which the

Congregationalists built their community room behind the present site was part of the Reynolds gardens.

If you look at a map of the Congregational and now the Roman Catholic development you see a scribbled note *'James Reynolds land'* (Records of Faringdon Congregational Church at the Oxfordshire Records Office). Further along the road are more listed buildings, Nos. 43 and 45 Broomsgrove. Also at the end the Farmhouse, a seventeenth century and early nineteenth century rubble stone with a projecting eighteenth century staircase and a block and hip roof. All these fine buildings were built or modified by the last of Reynolds's family that were born Quaker and buried as Quakers, but some of whom were disowned or resigned in the C19[th].

Looking upwards to the glass roof lights.   *Notice of draper's shop sale*

I do not think we shall ever quite get the exact story about the rather fine drapers shop now listed as No I Broomsgrove. It seems that when James senior died there was a bit of an argument between his brother Charles, as sole trustee and Uncle of James's son, and the son James himself. There are papers in the Reading archives which take the matter to a Special Court for the Manor of Faringdon in 1848 after Aunt Elizabeth had died. The will was somehow over-ruled and a codicil inserted which was agreed by Charles Reynolds, Mr and Mrs Myers and Michael Richard Reynolds. So James got ownership of his warehouse or shop as Aunt Elizabeth had desired in her codicil.

James Reynolds junr. and his brother, Michael Richard thus inherited their father James's business of the cheese factor and malting or eventually they did. The sons built the new shop.

Picture of Robert and James Reynolds's house [painted by DrPole]

I think that both sides of the family looked after each other in wills and in other ways and so it is quite complicated. Faringdon was growing and I think quite a bit of land was sold to various people, especially the lands in what is now Tuckers Bellway developments and the area around the railway line some of which might well have originally been part of the Reynolds farmlands. Oxford Colleges owned quite a bit of it too, but may have rented it out for locals to use for grazing and general farming. All this area to the South of the town, as it is today, was perhaps to the West of the town when theplace was smaller, west of the brook. As the town grew they could sell land to builders or even get houses built to rent. All this area got built on by the twentieth century.

Charles Reynolds 1825 [private collection; part of family picture]

Charles's pig [private collection]

There are documents in private hands which show that a lot of land was sold in 1855 previously owned by the late Charles Reynolds. He died in 1852 and his son may have decided to concentrate on investments rather than on farming. This son, also Charles, got married in 1855. The Sale was at the Crown Hotel and the auctioneer was his Cousin Anne's husband, James Fidel:

> *An unusually valuable Estate adjoining the town -56 acres of very productive Agricultural land. 12 lots have road frontages and eminently adapted for building purposes.70 acres of tithe free arable land South side of Sands, yards and cattle sheds, land at Great Coxwell.A valuable orchard at West End of Faringdon being the lower portion of the homestead of the late Charles Reynolds. Adjoining a field called Adams Mead. Together with an excellent enclosed fruit garden. Substantial stable and cattle pens thereon. The whole containing about one acre altogether with a right of carriage road and driftway there to along the road to be set out from the street or highway opposite the Baptist chapel. Reserve figure £350.*

> *March Marlborough Street, drawing room, 20 x15, Dining room 20 x15, Parlour, 5 beds, dressing, water closet, etc. Coach house and stabling in occ. John Hoskins (MRR £700)*

> *House occupied by Mr Francis Smith Boot and shoe maker Res. £200. 4*

I think though that gradually as the century wore on these Quaker Faringdon families got more involved in money and stocks and shares and left farming and running shops and business behind. The men died off and the women lived on the inheritance. By the time the town wanted to build the Corn Exchange in 1862 to meet the increasing pressures of the railway age the Quakers were not involved in raising subscriptions. A Mr Wheeler gave desks and stands costing £74, but though he was most likely the son or grandson of the Quaker Wheelers, he was by now a Baptist. Lord Radnor contributed £40 to this venture incidentally.

The railway was built and some of that is on land that belonged to the Reynolds farm. There are maps showing the railway and who owned fields and some of them are marked as Reynolds land.

In the 1861 census **James Reynolds (Junior)** was living at 56 Block Green (this was Westbrook) aged 48, Draper, with his brother **Michael Richard Reynolds** Landed Proprietor plus three assistants and a Housekeeper. Next door at 57 was **Harry Liddiard**, a Cheese Factor plus wife. Along the road was **Margaret Reynolds** widow and Fundholder aged 76 with **Charles** married aged 44, retired farmer, and **Margaret Jane** and **Mary Ann** and a servant. These people were also listed in Monthly Meeting membership lists. There is no mention of Charles's wife or of the baby Margaret Tryphena who was born in 1857.

There are some letters in private hands that rather show both James and his brotherMichael Richard were not very strong men. In 1848 a letter from Elizabeth Myerswho was married to a farmer in Henley in Arden (She is daughter of RichardReynolds who died in 1847):

> *My Dear Reynolds,*
> *We are very sorry to hear that Mike has been so poorly but pleased he is getting better. Please tell him with our love to come here for a little change we will nurse him and if possible put him right again.*

June 1850 E. Reynolds (wife of Richard) to James

> *Writes as acting executor to her sister Elizabeth (died 1948) wants her painting. Aunt Reynolds (Jane) has gone to Yearly Meeting Best wishes to Michael and brother Charles and family, Your Affectionate Aunt Elizabeth*

15th November 1850, Elizabeth to James:

> *Further request, now urgent as Mr Myers (her daughter's husband) has entered into an engagement to take a medical practice in London at Christmas next and wish him to pay £200 on Monday week next and the whole of the remainder by the end of January. £185. Cannot sacrifice the interest of my children's education, of my grandoms and putting them forward in life. Wants to know if the house Mr Wilson vacated*

has been since let

1853 Letter from James to Mike..:

Hoping he is well I have been in the shop (I am happy to tell you...)

1859 Letter from Caroline Boldy - Cirencester 9th month 2nd. 1859:

To my Dear Cousin, (envelope to Michael Reynolds)
I hope thy brother will return home strengthened and refreshed by his excursion and with our united love

30th April 1860 from Richard of Faringdon to his Cousin James R. of Faringdon:

Asks to borrow 16/- as he is to take part in court on Wednesday next. Has had doctor attending him and his wife for 12 weeks... [3]

James died in 1862 (Annual Monitor 1862, I think).

James (1812-1862) was said to be benevolent and of unselfish character endeared to all manner of people and although he rarely spoke of his religious experience the firmness of his Faith in Christ was exemplified in his life. He had for many years suffered from a severe disease of the lungs which he bore with patience and resignment died aged 50.

Margaret, the widowed mother of Charles, the mother of Charles Junr., his brother and two sisters, died 10th August 1867. Charles her son also died in 1867 shortly after his mother.

Following the lives of this family has been a fascination and I have been fortunate to get information bit by bit. It has almost been like a game moving from clue to clue.

The next clues are to be found in the deeds held by the owner of the restaurant called The Rats Castle. This was the shop,newly built by

James Reynolds in 1848 or just after. His Aunt Elizabeth referred to it as an *expensive shop.* James junior had not married and on his death the shop business seems to have been inherited by his Uncle Charles's wife, Margaret Reynolds and eventually her children. She divided her real estate and chattels equally between her children Charles (1816-1867), Mary Jane (1818-1873) and Mary Anne (1825-1880) and bits and pieces to her brother in law's children too. Margaret's son Charles died at about this time. Her other son Richard (1821-1879) does not get mentioned!. So the two daughters, Margaret Jane and Mary Ann are left to manage the estate on behalf of their little niece, Margaret Tryphena, their brother Charles's daughter. One has to assume that by this time the estate includes money from sale of farm land for building development around the town, or for other purposes, as well as some share in the drapery business too and much also in stocks and shares.

It is impossible to unravel the intricacies of the two closely knit Reynolds families. In 1867 James who had inherited the shop was dead. He died in 1862, leaving no children. His brother Michael Richard (died?) also had no children. So they must have left things to their cousins. They were the Charles Reynolds family. The mystery is why Richard, Charles's brother who married an Elizabeth (1825-80) never gets mentioned as inheriting anything. He was disowned by the society perhaps for marrying 'out'. He may have been the Richard Reynolds who was a taxidermist and has a specimen in the Swindon museum. Anyway Charles (1816-1867) being the oldest son, a retired farmer in the 1861 census, married by this time but no wife is listed which is strange. He was then living with his mother and two spinster sisters at 82 Block Green. This is now called Broomsgrove. Perhaps this was the farm, now called Reynolds House. This farm has always been the family farm. He inherited a sizeable amount of wealth when his mother died in 1867, but he died almost at the same time, also in 1867. He left all he inherited *to his sister Margaret Jane Reynolds, spinster, to hold for the benefit of his daughter Margaret Tryphena until she is 21.*

Margaret Tryphena Reynolds

So who was this daughter of Charles Reynolds who seems to have no mother in the census? I have traced her and she was a person called **Margaret Tryphena Reynolds,** born in 1856. In the 1871 census the two sisters Margaret Jane and Mary Anne lived at the Farmhouse aged 53 and 46 with a servant. There is no mention of a child living with them. No mention of the child who must have been 15 years old. Was she back with her unknown mother by then or at a Dame school in another town? Who was the mother?I have eventually traced the mystery mother and she was a Quaker lady called **Tryphena (Williams) (Reynolds) Gardner**, but more about her later on.

There are many things in a family collection that bring Margaret Tryphena to life. A Birthday book, for example, in which are the signatures of the Quakers *Thomas Fawkes*and *Richard Reynolds* from Faringdon meeting, and Monthly Meeting Friends too from Charlbury *Rachel and John Aibright, Caroline Westcombe Pumphrey, , Charles Sessions, Edward and Lydia Sessions and Thackwell Smith*. So this child must have met these people either socially or at Quaker gatherings. She may have been considered a birthright member of the Society of Friends.

The Farm house in the early 1990s:
Jean Pocock [left] with Juliet Dyer

216

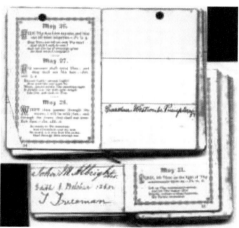

Pages from the Birthday book given to *M.T. Reynolds from her Aunt Mary Ann Reynolds 1874 (* Margaret Tryphena was then 18 years old)

When Margaret Jane died in 1873 she in turn left all to her sister Mary Ann Reynolds (a spinster). According to the material in the deeds at the old drapery shop (now the Rats Castle), Mary Anne appears to have made her will in 1875 and she appointed a William Sell as her sole executor. She gave her brother Richard £100 as an annuity for life and £50 to his wife Elizabeth, so she at least looked after her brother, although he died a year before she did in the end.

Mary Ann Reynolds gave Mary Thatcher widow of William residing in Longcot an annuity of £13 and thence after her decease to Mary wife of Charles Davis. To James Crewe an annuity of£13. She gave and devised to the said William Sell all her real estate and chattels to assign according to and during the natural life of her niece Margaret Tryphena Reynolds. Mary Ann died in 1880.

Her obituary reads as follows:

Mary Ann 1824-1880, daughter of Charles (1778-1852) and Margaret, a family related to the philanthropist Richard Reynolds, only surviving member of the Society of Friends in Faringdon. Meek and quiet, warm and a faithful friend of the Meeting for Worship with one or two others has died after a long and lingering painful illness at the age of 55. Annual Monitor 1880

When Mary Ann died in 1880 the legacy was divided into three parts: Frederick William Cox, betrothed to Margaret Tryphena, Margaret Tryphena Reynolds, and William Collins Sell. It refers to the draper's shop formerly being occupied by James and Michael Richard Reynolds and now occupied by William John and William Collins Sell. So these latter must have been keeping the business going for the ailing Mary Ann.

Notes on the will mention a marriage between Margaret Tryphena Reynolds and William Cox. [5] Notes in the material in the Rat's Castle deeds

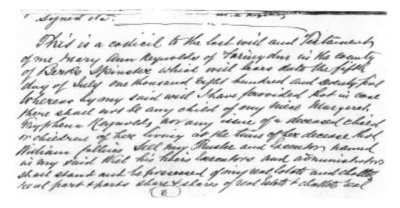

Part of Mary Anne's will 1875. She mentions 'my niece Margaret Tryphena Reynolds'.

How it all worked I am not sure but the actual shop seems to have been given by Elizabeth (died 1848) to her nephew James linen draper thence via Cox and Sell to Goddards in 1920. Certainly William Sell is listed as a Draper in the 1891 census living with his wife Sophia at 216 Southampton Street which may well have adjoined the Broomsgrove land and complex.

The story of Charles and Tryphena

The time has come to attempt to disentangle the romance of the period, so far as the Reynolds family were concerned. Again I have to thank the late Jean Pocock for introducing me to the melodramatic tale. From scrutinising purposefully such material as deeds and wills, I think 1 have nearly moved the story out of myth and into reality. Truth is stranger than fiction and indeed this seems to be so in the following case history.

It appears that Charles junior (1817 - 1867), the Quaker farmer, fell in love with a fairground gypsy girl. Fairs were an important feature of Faringdon life in those days. Quakers were not to dance or go to dances, yet if they lived in the town where the fair came they were likely to know all about it. They must have seen it, smelt it and heard it and been tempted, certainly as children, to partake of it. There were the coconut shies, the roundabouts and the stalls selling lovely things. The Morris men and the fairground fun. Certainly the Buckland family were travelling showmen who came to Faringdon and had a Dancing Booth in those days, according to their descendant Jim Heyward who is himself still connected with Travelling Show people [1995]. He has a record of an Aunt called Tryphena Butler who died in 1869.1 wonder then is this connected to the same family from which our 'Quaker' Tryphena came? It is possible that Charles when a young man could not find a Quaker girl to marry. His father Charles was perhaps strict about that side of things, even if he had been disowned, and would not let his son marry 'out'.

The young Charles saw this sensuous gypsy child dancing and somehow got a fixation on the girl. She was too young perhaps to marry and he waited until she was legally old enough. His father died in 1852 and so Charles Junior became head of the family. How the wedding was arranged we do not know but the marriage certificate states that Charles Reynolds married Tryphena Williams at the parish church of Thatcham near Newbury on December 6th 1855. Three years after his father had died.

Charles and Tryphena Marriage Certificate

The Quaker minutes have nothing on the subject and yet in 1859

Charles resigned from Quakers, Richard, his brother, was disowned, also his sister Margaret Jane disowned. His cousin Richard Michael resigned. Why this upheaval, there is no answer. It just could be that the Quakers found out about his marrying in a church and so he had to leave the society (or it was the tomb stone argument mentioned in the previous chapter). The young wife was of full age, so over twenty one. She died in 1911, some 55 years later. Her father was a rat catcher. So where the family myth about the Romany bit is or the Dancing gypsy bit, I just do not know. The photos of her granddaughter do show a woman of dark romany complexion. Perhaps too young to cope with the Quaker family and the older husband and the middle class life, she seems to have run away at some point after a baby, Margaret Tryphena, was born in November 1856. Where she ran to I do not know. Perhaps back to her home in Thatcham or perhaps back to the travelling life of the Travelling Fair. If she was a dancer, then she could earn her living that way. Perhaps she and the baby went to live, she as a servant or maid, in a household away from Faringdon.

Margaret Tryphena Birth Certificate

The young mother apparently ran away from Faringdon and from Charles. She may have run away back home to Thatcham with the baby. However Charles's daughter, and Mary Ann's niece, mentioned

221

in the deeds at the old drapery shop and the wills of Mary Ann Reynolds, 5th day of July 1875, was called Margaret Tryphena Reynolds and was born in 1856.

The child may later have been brought up at The Farm by the two unmarried Aunts. Perhaps she attended the Dame School up the London road or was taught at home by the Aunts. Little books saying love from Aunty Mary Ann are still intact. Also exercise books, beautifully written. Charles died in 1867, when the child was eleven. Did he die of illness or sadness? We don't know if her real mother had anything to do with the bringing up of her daughter or not. As mentioned above, the Birthday Book was signed by many Friends who belonged to Faringdon local Meeting and to Witney Monthly Meeting. She knew about Quakers. Margaret Tryphena Reynolds came of age in 1877 and should have inherited the family fortune. In the 1881 census she was living at 166 Broomsgrove Place aged 24 (just before her 25th birthday) and listed as a landowner. Living with her was Betsy Thatcher a cousin aged 29 and farmer's daughter. So when Aunty Mary Anne died her best friend must have organised a companion for the niece.

By this time Frederick William Cox, a Buscot farmer must have begun courting her. He succeeded in winning her hand because she married him. The wedding dress was of blue velvet and is still in a private collection. Frederick Cox, being the Victorian husband, would thus inherit also the Reynolds fortune, if by then it was still a fortune, that is.

In the 1891 census Margaret Tryphena *Reynolds* had become Margaret *T. Cox* married to Frederick William Cox. They lived at 157 Broomsgrove Place with their children, Ethel Wynne (5) and Charles Reynolds (3). So Margaret had her first child when she was about thirty. Those children might have been brought up as Baptists but there are no records of baptism of any of this family that I can unearth. I wonder if somehow Margaret Tryphena thought she was a Quaker but with no Meeting in Faringdon she just let it rest?

A lot of the above is pure guesswork but there are enough facts to be able to draw some conclusions. The wills, the deeds and some

Quaker and Baptist entries help to give reality and truth to the story. The mother gets mentioned in a memo attached to notes when the Linen drapers shop (Top Goddards or now Rats Castle) was being sold by Cox and Sell to Goddard in 1920:

> "Under settlement an annuity of £15 payable to Tryphena Gardner on death of her daughter, M.T. Cox (Margaret Tryphena (Reynolds) Cox)."[Then scribbled in pencil " When did she die?][Scribbled reply in a different hand]Tryphena Gardner died 28th August1911. 5(5)

This must be the Tryphena *Reynolds Gardner* whose membership is listed under Charlbury Preparative Meeting in 1906/7/8 up to 1911 as living at Farm Villa, Faringdon.

What a life this woman had? Perhaps brought up as a dancing Romany travelling fairground girl, if indeed she was, with a Father a rat catcher. She then found herself marrying Charles Reynolds and perhaps becoming a Quaker at the request of Charles's sisters. He was no longer in membership by then. Then she had a child and ran away from Charles. She was still in her early twenties, not divorced and unable to marry anyone else. How did she earn her living one wonders, or did Charles send her money and how did she look after the baby? She was widowed at a young age when Charles died in 1867. Perhaps she went into service in Swindon and left the baby with her own mother. At some point she met a John Gardner and they married. Perhaps that is when she became a Quaker. He himself was buried at Faringdon as a Quaker in 1902 aged 81 years, though not listed in local Quaker records. There is a Certificate of burial held in Quaker Archives at Oxford for him but not for Tryphena.

One last possible reference to Tryphena (Williams) Reynolds Gardner's family is from The Faringdon Advertiser 12th November 1887. *In the year of 1887 Charles Feltham and Alfred Jones were summoned for trespassing in pursuit of game. They stated the dog took a hare of own accord There was reference to Feltham's son in law, Williams who 'travels the country shows'. They were each fined £1.*

Could this Williams be a brother of Charles's Gypsy dancer Tryphena, or even her elderly father or Uncle? One can visualise what a trial all this affair must have been to the Faringdon Reynolds family if so.

All there is about the 'Romany' wife of Charles Reynolds is her membership record *Tryphena (Reynolds) Gardner of Farm Villa, Faringdon who died in 1911*. This is listed in *Berks Oxon Quarterly Meeting 1908-1953*. She is part of Charlbury Meeting as Faringdon Meeting was closed. Did her daughter then probably living at The Farm look after her in her old age? Had her daughter died as might be concluded from the odd note above on the Rat's Castle Deeds? Had she finally made it up with Charles's sisters before they died? Was she living away from Faringdon when her daughter seemed to be left alone as in 1881 census? Finally Tryphena 'the gypsy dancer'died and as yet I have no record of where she was buried. She died according to the memo, mentioned above, on 28th August 1911. She was possibly 81.1 have not found a Quaker Certificate of Burial. Did her daughter or granddaughter not know about Quaker procedure and just make arrangements with a non-conformist church in the town of Faringdon? The records of burials in the town of that period have not been well kept. There appears to be no record of burials in the non-conformist burial ground of that period and I could find no stone.

The life of Charles Reynolds's and Tryphena Gardner's daughter is equally lacking in factual material and yet must have been unusual - as a babe brought up by rather old fashioned maiden Aunts in a Quaker home, or with a young mother who was running away from the very 'peculiar Quaker household'!' The Aunts were elderly and sickly. We do not know if Margaret Typhena lived sometimes in one household and sometimes in another. Her father died and she was almost like an orphan and an heiress of the Reynolds fortune or part of it. Did she go to a Dame school in Swindon as a boarder? We still have a few of her school books neatly written. It is unlikely that she could have been a Quaker. If when she was born, both her parents had been Quakers then she was a birth right Quaker, but her Father was disowned in 1859. Her Aunt Mary Ann always remained faithful to Quakers and may have had influence about spiritual matters.

I have been unable to find information about the period after Charles got married but he may have lived for a time with his new wife in Thatcham and perhaps have been considered by his sisters as mistaken and as having let the family down. There is no record of Margaret Tryphena,daughter of Charles, becoming a Baptist though I think her husband was and the wedding may have been a Baptist wedding. There are no records of Margaret Tryphena Cox as a Quaker, so that is not clear either. She knew about Quakers and that her Aunts were Quakers. There seems to be no record in local material of her death or burial place. (I have not written to the Office of National Statistics.) It is possible that her husband died and that she joined her daughter, Ethyl Wynne, in The Farmhouse, perhaps up to the 1930's. She was the one to tell Jean Pocock about her mother and the dancing Fairground gypsy. Jean talked to me about happy memories of visiting her Aunts in The Farmhouse. These must have been Margaret Tryphena and her daughter. I shall mention a little more about her daughter in later material.

If this had all happened in the more settled times of the 1830's when Robert Huntley and Elizabeth and Jane Reynolds had been around, perhaps the outcome would have been very different. Perhaps Tryphena could have come to live with the family before marriage and become a Quaker. The marriage could have been more orderly and the child brought up in one place. When her father died she could have been sent to a Quaker Boarding School and then perhaps she would have known how to keep an eye on her estate.

So it was that the Reynolds Quaker family of Faringdon after over three hundred years died out. The strict rules about marrying a member of the Society of Friends and possibly illness seemed to have contributed to the final situation. There were no males to carry on the line. The farm house was still in the hands of the daughter and granddaughter of Charles Reynolds until they both had died and the farm was sold in the 1960's.

NOTES

1. *Reynolds papers*. Berkshire Archives.

2. *Witney Monthly Meeting.* .Oxfordshire Archives

3. *Reynolds Papers* . Berkshire Archives

4. Family letters and press cuttings in private hands - *Annual Monitor 1864 James Reynolds and 1880 Mary Ann Reynolds*

5. In private hands. *Deeds of the property now called' The Rats Castle'*

CHAPTER NINE

THE FIRST HALF OF THE TWENTIETH CENTURY

'You cannot foster harmony by the apparatus of discord, nor cherish goodwill by the equipment of hate. But it is by harmony and goodwill that human security can be obtained...' [1]

It may be that the last century finished on a rather sad note for the Vale Quakers. That early promise that had been so bright had almost gone, but it was not quite extinguished. Those Quakers and Enquirers, living in the Vale, were indeed scattered but they could and did get to Abingdon, Oxford and Swindon for worship. To begin with they travelled on horseback or in carriages to Sunday Meetings for Worship and also by train to Monthly Meeting. Soon those who could afford to do so travelled by car.

The following was inserted into the introduction of a list of Members of **Berks and Oxon Quarterly Meeting for 1906-7;**

Although we recognise the children of our members as objects of our care and partakers of the outward privileges of Christian fellowship, we would earnestly remind all, that such recognition cannot constitute them members of the Lord's spiritual israel. Nothing can effect this but the power of the Holy Spirit working repentance towards God, and faith towards our Lord Jesus Christ~ therefore let the words of our Divine Master have their due place with us all...'Ye must he born again'...May all our members become such on the ground of true Convincement and be prepared in their several places to bring forth fruit unto God. [2]

So these, to some of us at the end of the twentieth century, rather traditional Christian ideas and phraseologies were still used by, and acceptable, to most Quakers, at the start of the century. Soon though the more liberal ideas of the 1895 Manchester Conference, mentioned in chapter seven, were to change understanding of the Truth By the end of the century the above quotation does sound rather strange and stilted to most Quakers though the idea of children being' free' to grow into faith would he acceptable.

In **Witney Monthly Meeting** Ministerswere still appointed and usually sat at the `front' of the meeting room on a special `ministers' bench' or even on a raised bench. Charlbury had one of these and the one at Burford is still there. I am sure that Faringdon had had one too. The ministers in 1906 were **John Marshall Albright** (Charlbury), **Caroline Westcombe Pumphrey** (Charlbury), and **Gertrude Mary Gillett** (Oxford). There were appointed Elders but no Overseers and no one from Faringdon or Witney was appointed.

Abingdon Meeting House was at Vineyard in 1906 and was busy with an Adult school for men and a separate one for women, a Junior (Sunday) school, a mission meeting, Missionary Helpers Union, Christian Endeavour, Girl Guides, Mothers' Meeting, Band of Hope, Temperance Meeting with **John Smallbone** as Clerk. There were 27 members (eleven married couples), 10 men and 23 children.

What a contrast to **Faringdon Meeting** which was gone. From time to time in the next years some who lived in the Vale did come to worship at Abingdon. Arthur Bissell does mention that a Monthly Meeting was held at Faringdon in 1922, but I could not see this from the Monthly Meeting Minute Book. Some may even have gone over to Faringdon to try to keep an eye on the derelict building there. Today Abingdon has lost its Meeting House but has a thriving Preparative Meeting which meets regularly on First day for worship in rented accommodation. [3]

BurfordMeeting had 20 members (3 married couples) 6 men and 5 children. It had been closed in 1854 and re-opened again in 1891. It was again closed in 1921 and those Friends who lived there went to

Charlbury Meeting. Burford got going again in the same lovely old Meeting House in 1956 and hasn't looked back since and has a new extension in keeping with the old but providing twentieth century amenities.

Charlbury Friends had their own meetings in their meeting house and a mission meeting at Fawler and various other activities. Their Clerk was **Thackwell Gillett Smith**. They had 14 members (5 couples), 6 men and 4 children. Charlbury continued until 1957 when the Burford Friends, got their own meeting going again and stayed in Burford. The Charlbury Meeting house was nearly sold but Roger Warner and his mother insisted it was only rented out and not sold. After some thirty odd years it opened again for worship in 1987 and it has flourished since still in the same old Meeting House but with a new extension to meet the demands of the twentieth century. [4]

On the 1906/7 Charlbury list was Tryphena (Reynolds) Gardner of Farm Villa, Faringdon, Berks. So either she became a Friend when she married Charles Reynolds or later after he died (see previous chapter). Anyway she has the honour of carrying the Faringdon Reynolds' family into its, chronological, fourth century of Quakerism. She died in 1911, but no trace of the burial place. Her daughter is not recorded as a Baptist but her granddaughter, Ethyl Wynne (Cox) Watts, though she knew of her Quaker origin, became a Baptist.

Chipping Norton had 11 members (1 married couple) 3 men and I child.

Oxford meeting was renting 40 Canal Street Jericho, as they could no longer afford to keep up the Meeting House at Nelson Street. They in fact eventually sold that in 1921. The meeting moved about until it finally, in 1946, settled at 43 St Giles, not far from the original Meeting House built so long ago in 1687. Their Clerk in 1906 was **Henry Gillett** and they too were very evangelical with adult schools mission meetings, Gospel meetings and two Junior First Day meetings 10.30 and 2.30. There were 50 members (6 couples) 23 men and 14 children.

Witney meeting was still at Wood Green where they had a considerable property and a burial ground. They had 50 members (11 couples) 30 children and had lots of things going on - Adult schools, mission work, Junior First day, Mothers meeting, Band of Hope, Cottage meeting in the winter and Young Peoples Meeting at 8pm on Fifth day (Thursday). They had Meeting for Worship on First day and 6th day (Friday) at 8pm.

It is interesting that these meetings were so evangelical when elsewhere there had been the great change in the thinking about where Quakerism stood with regard to spiritual matters. That seed sown in 1895 at the Manchester Conference, for acceptance of a more liberal argument incorporating mystical traditions to explain the mystery of God rather than the evangelical and Biblical interpretations, had not it seems come to influence Witney Quakers. [5]

Think rather of high noon of Summer, or stillness of a snow - covered country, how the heat or lightness everywhere gives an intense sense of overflowing and abounding in life, making a quietness of rapture rather than fear. Such, only of a deeper and far more intimate kind, is the atmosphere of waiting souls. It may be that words will spring out of those depths, it may be that vocal prayer or praise shall flow forth at the bidding of him whose presence makes worship a communion, but whether there be speech or silence matters not. Gradually, as mind and soul and even body grow still, sinking deeper and deeper into the life of God, the pettiness, the tangles, the failures of outer life begin to be seen in their true proportions, and the sense of the divine infilling, uplifting, redeeming Love becomes real and illuminating. Things are seen and known that are hidden to the ordinary facilities. This state is not merely one of quiescence; the soul is alive, active, vigorous, yet so still that it hardly knows how intense is its own vital action. [6]

Returning to the early twentieth century in Oxford and Swindon Meetings, the development of more fundamentalist evangelical Quakerism can be seen to take hold as they built themselves up. This had come out of the evangelical era of the nineteenth century and seemed particularly right in the overpopulated industrial cities. The Abolition of Slavery and the Reform Acts to regulate employment and society, and the Elementary Education Act of 1870 had influenced Christian outreach and vision. Quakers felt that they were 'doing' their Christianity and could throw themselves into doing something to change things for the better. Poverty was rife and the needs for health education and better housing were obvious. Those who followed the evangelical path felt that the people needed help and it became a mission to set up adult schools adjacent to the meeting houses and to help people to read the Bible and live by Christian moral standards. Temperance Societies were founded and supported as alcohol was seen as the demon.

Meantime also other Quakers were in touch with the latest scientific and philosophical ideas. Since the admission of non-conformists to civil rights in 1828 and other relaxations, Quakers could now go to Established Universities and were involved in banking, industry, medicine and the professions and many were well and widely read and travelled. The theory of Evolution, of Rational Deduction, the latest about the Historical Jesus coming in from archaeologists was all considered. Many of these younger Quakers could not see going back to fundamental Christianity as a choice or as a possibility. Yet for a time they did not get their way at the grass roots level.

Report of the Mission Committee of Witney Monthly Meeting 1st day 5th Month 1900.

Our different Meetings have been visited as under:
Abingdon frequently by C.E. Gillett, Alice Liddell and R. Buckingham etc.
Burford Charlbury Chipping Norton Oxford and Witney have all been visited too.
Villages were visited - Hailey Fields, Ramsdon, Crawley, Minster Lovell. . .Leafield Appleford . . .Chilson distributing gospel, temperance and peace tracts, books, (Woolman and Bunyan) - sold 23 Bibles and 158 Testaments, 80 Gospels. Held Cottage Meetings in various villages... Several meetings were held at Faringdon with worsening attendance... [7]

The Baptists were still going strong in Faringdon and in their records I have found the grand - daughter of Charles Reynolds mentioned in the last chapter, Ethyl Wvnne (Cox) Watts. She inherited something from her parents no doubt. She married a Mr Watts and went to South Africa. There were no children and the marriage ended. She came home again. In the Baptist records there is a Mr H. Watts, who goes to Maritzburg S. A. in 1911. A Mrs H.Watts joins the Baptists in 1914. Now, according to the late Jean Pocock, Ethyl Wynne did marry a (Harry?) Watts who took her to South Africa, just before the First World War. He was working for Crosse and Blackwell Soups out there. The marriage did not go well and Ethyl came home (Mrs Harry Watts). In the Baptist records a Mrs. E. Watts was a member in 1962. This must have been the granddaughter of Charles and Tryphena. Some older residents ofFaringdon remember an organist at the chapel called Mrs Watts. She was a smallish and swarthy lady, those who remember serving her at Carter's Grocer's shop say. She and her mother Margaret Tryphena lived in the Farmhouse where the Reynolds family had lived since records can be traced, in fact, back to the sixteenth century.

In Mrs Watts's attic and around the house were so many Quaker treasures; papers, letters, maps, books, tracts and portraits. Much of this material was finally placed either in the Reading Archives or the Ironbridge Museum at Coalbrookdale Shropshire. The extraordinary thing is that all this material lay around in the attic of the farm house, through most of this century and before that, telling us so much about Quakers in the Vale. Ethyl Wynne (Auntie Winnie) knew about it and eventually in 1961 she showed the Reading Archivist round her house and some papers and letters were deposited there. But, not being a Quaker, it probably held no particular spiritual or historical significance to her and some of the material had been badly neglected.

The Quakers in Witney Monthly Meeting could not be expected to know that there were precious documents in the attic of the Faringdon Farmhouse. Some of it lodged there since the mid seventeenth century. Most evangelicals were not bothered about the past or in getting involved in the analysis of it. They just wanted to go to meeting and worship, deal with the business of the day and involve themselves in `good works', that was more than enough. After all they were doing what they expected to do. Why should anyone have known that there on the doorstep was a treasure trove of Quaker material awaiting analysis? Most never thought about Vale Quakers as such in any case.

I have been unable to trace the burial date or whereabouts of Charles Reynolds's daughter, Margaret Tryphena Cox, but it must have occurred in the thirties or forties, and she must lie in the Nonconformist Burial Ground at Canada Lane, Faringdon. Likewise Ethyl Wynne, his granddaughter, died in 1969 and must also be buried or cremated. I have tried to find out where but with no result. It is a matter of paying to get the records from the Office of National Statistics and also looking at other material.

The following is an extract from a Tract, written by the now mature Caroline Westcombe Pumphrey. I quoted from her diary in chapter seven when she was a child in Charlbury. This Tract was taken and reprinted from an article by her in the *Quaker Weekly Journal of the Friend - 21st Nov. 1902*. I notice that the journal has gone all modern with the dates. Perhaps this journal was now in the hands of the Liberal Quakers?

A Minister's Needs
The first thing is to know God and so to know him that we must make others know him too... The preacher must not only know about God but as Dr. Parker says he must be a man who is "passing the Gospel through his own soul". To be widely effective a preacher must know something (experientially) of what he preaches... I think one should preach God's Truth as nearly as one knows it, which is I hope a little ahead of one's own experience...A message is useful onlyso far as it is understood...

This was a time when London Yearly Meeting was still anguishing about the way worship should be conducted and what exactly the ministry in the *Silent Tradition* should be. At a meeting of *Yearly Meeting Ministry and Oversight in 1903:*

Minute l0...the question has been raised whether under present

233

circumstances a free and unprofessional ministry can be maintained. It is felt that upon an affirmative answer to this question the continuance of the Society of Friends largely depends.

On the one hand no branch of the church can afford to neglect its evangelists; and on the other hand no branch of the church can afford to neglect any part of the message spiritually committed to it. The true way to present our principles to the world is by act rather than by word. A Meeting held in the power and life is better witness than much exposition of principles.

In 1909 at a *Quarterly Meeting of Berks and Oxon* at Banbury - a two day affair on the 26th and 27th of April Minute XI - the following was read:

A Testimony on behalf of our late dear friend John Allbright has now been read and has afresh reminded us of the loss our Quarterly Meeting has sustained: for 94 years a member and for fifty years a member amongst us. Born in 1815, eighteen days before the battle of Waterloo...

At another *Quarterly meeting* in 1912 at Reading:

Min 1 The special subject for our consideration this evening is `National Service and International Peace`. Reminded `All war is contrary to the mind of Christ', but that is not enough to say we object to war on principle. It would have more weight if we could say `It is my conviction that all war is contrary to his mind'... If we think that military service is not for us we have to show the world that we are prepared to serve our country in other ways...

At a   Quarterly Meeting in 1915 there was a report about the *Friends' Ambulance Unit...Started in October 1914 at Dunkirk ...a Typhoid Hospital was set up capable of taking 200 cases at a time...*Later that year Q M set up a committee for the assistance of aliens' families and provided clothing and coal as they were being held in awful conditions. Also help for feeding the babies.

In 1916 a special minute refusing to agree to Compulsory Military

Service was read out from Yearly Meeting. It asked meetings to support those who were deciding to be Conscientious Objectors. Indeed some of the privations these men underwent were similar to those of the early Quakers. They were before their time and paved the way for others. Over 1100 Members and Attenders applied for exemption as Conscientious Objectors and some of these lived in Witney Monthly Meeting.

Swindon Meeting

I have decided to include a little bit about Swindon Meeting as Swindon had become larger than Faringdon, due to the Rail Engineering business and Vale people were beginning to go there for all sorts of reasons. Some went there for work or education, others because they needed a hospital or nursing home and yet others because the shopping had more to offer. This trend has continued through the twentieth century as Swindon has attracted new commerce to the town and more houses. Today a purpose-built pedestrianised shopping centre, modern sports and leisure facilities and state of the art museums and Art Gallery all add to the attraction.

In 1892 **William Clark Eddington** arrived in the town, from a branch of the Clark Shoe Quaker family of Somerset. Shortly after that **Mr and Mrs Dorcura** arrived. In 1892 **Richard Cadbury** of the Birmingham Quaker family arrived in the town. Later in the year another Quaker from an old Quaker family arrived, **Edgar Sessions**. On September 18th 1892 a recording of a Quaker Meeting for Worship was registered. [10]

A Meeting for Worship was held at Mrs Dorcura's at 11 am - after the style of Friends this being the first meeting held in Swindon.

Norman Penny, a leading Quaker of the day, joined them for worship. He was a member of Nailsworth and Gloucester Monthly Meeting and in 1900 he became Librarian at Friends House London. So it was that meetings began to be held every third Sunday in each others' homes.

In 1892 Richard Cadbury is recorded as having read a short paper on *the necessity and duty of Friends letting their Light shine.* He also mentioned that an offer had been made by a Friend to pay the rent of premises and to provide chairs. Tucked in the minute book is a letter from George Cadbury.

Cadbury Bros.   Bournville   9th month 30 1892

Dear Richard,
I am very much interested to hear of your starting a meeting. I shall be glad to help you with cash for hire of a room...
George Cadbury [11]

This was the George who with his brother Richard had taken over the cocoa business in Birmingham from their Strict Quaker father, in 1861. They were particularly interested in the Adult School movement and in the welfare of their workforce. Each working day began with a Meeting for Worship and there was a regular weekly half holiday. They joined in their workers sports and knew their families well. By 1900 the business was re-sited at Bournville on the then outskirts of the city and employed thousands. They made chocolate and sent it all over the world. The Bournville village was an important development in town planning towards a clean healthy environment for working people. George Cadbury gave his former family home to the Quakers to use as a College in 1903 - Woodbrooke.   The Richard who came to Swindon and set up a printing company with William Clark Eddington was the son of George Cadbury's brother Richard. He had been born in 1868, the youngest, and his Mother died ten days later. So a caring uncle is showing an interest in his nephew.

On 7th month 27 1893 the following letter was sent to Gloucester and Nailsworth Monthly Meeting:

Dear Friends
The question how to provide a Friends Meeting and how to further promote Friends work in Swindon have been much in our minds. The time now seems to be ripening for a more special effort in this direction but we feel we need both of advice and help before taking any active measure...

Yours sincerely, Richard Cadbury (Junr), GW Docura, Edgar Sessions, Frederick John Hunt

By October 1893 Swindon Friends found a house at the corner of Prospect and North Streets. They obtained their chairs and set up an Allowed Meeting with plans for Mission work and adult Education. **John Bellows** was interested in the meeting and one day **Mary Hughes**, daughter, or was in granddaughter, of Tom Hughes, author of *Tom Brown's Schooldays*, came with him to Swindon meeting. She eventually went to work with the poor in Whitechapel and became a member of the Society of Friends in 1918. Shortly after this (1895) the Printing Works of Eddington and Cadbury closed and the regular Meetings came to an end. Richard Cadbury's father had died in 1899 and Richard left the Swindon meeting.

The Quaker outreach in Swindon was so valued and needed that it continued. Bible classes for men, women and children. There were 31 members of this Evangelical Quaker venture before long. Somehow they kept going with new people joining the Meeting as the founders left. In 1899 they booked a Temperance Hall and held a Meeting for Worship - *no singing at the first meeting*. God must have been working in mysterious ways because in 1901 a new Meeting House had been built and Swindon became a Preparative Meeting with its first Clerk **Ada Mary Warner**.

In Preparative Meeting January 1926 the meeting received reports from both Gloucester and Nailsworth Monthly Meeting and Witney Monthly Meeting and there was a proposal that they should transfer to Witney. This must have happened for in the Swindon P.M. minutes of August 1926 they were in Witney Monthly Meeting. They still had a busy outreach programme with Girl Guides using the building and a Boys' Club and the Adult Schools too.

I think the last minute I shall refer to brings us nicely back into the twentieth century:

29.8 1926
A letter was read stating that a Wireless pole is being erected by members of the Boys' Club and asking that meeting should help in

purchasing a wireless set. We ask the Clerk to reply giving reasons the meeting cannot comply with this request and pointing out that individual Friends may be approached in any waythe club may think fit.

This demonstrates the Quaker Business Method in action. The minute is Quakerly in tone, one is not given the reasons why they could not comply. It could be the connection with wireless as a military tool or the feeling that this modern contraption was not Godly enough for the meeting as a worshipping body to support. However they compromise and see a way out of the dilemma. They are interested in the needs of the Club and wish to remain on good terms with them. The Club can still get help from individuals and no doubt they did and no doubt they did get their wireless set. However purists of Quaker Business method might feel that somewhere in all this is a watering down of Authority and Truth

By the nineteen twenties the Quakers in Britain were a very much more Liberal Society, they had worked on their Testimony to Peace during the war. They backed the idea and the implementation of The League of Nations. Many Quakers had first-hand experience of the problems and needs of people from all walks of life. They needed better education and health care. They needed better conditions in the workplace. They needed better homes, indoor sanitation and running water. So many Quakers threw themselves into socialism and joined the Labour Party. The weekly journal of The Friend cost two pence and had a certainty about what was believed. The quotation on the front cover was:

`In Essentials Unity, in non-essentials Liberty, in all things Charity'   Vol. LIX 18: 19:*

In our life as a Religious Society we have found it true that the spirit of man can thereby learn of God...This which is within us has sometimes been called "the seed", because this term reminds us that wonderful growths can come from the tiniest germs of life...   [12]

London Yearly Meeting itself was still active and well-ordered and those who still lived in the Vale and who were Quakers must have kept in touch.

A new *Book of Discipline* was produced in 1922 and **Blair Neatby** gave a report about it to Oxon and Berks General Meeting:

Many have thought that where there is no creed there is no belief - This book has shown us more clearly than before that this is not so. It is a record of experience not a statement of Dogma. George Fox had the conviction of the living Christ in the soul of every man and Quakerism flowed from this conviction. George Fox proved `the power of life' and his successors have proved through nine generations of revolutionary thought that this is so, and this is one of the great lessons to be drawn from this volume.

Everyone was then cautioned that the book needs to be read as a whole because many extracts are different approaches by different minds to the same Truth...

The first advice of London Yearly Meeting adopted in 1931 reads:

Take heed, Dear Friends, to the promptings of love and truth in your hearts, which are the Leadings of God. Resist not his strivings within you. It is his light that shows us our darkness and leads to true repentance. The love of God draws us to him, a redemptive love shown forth by Jesus Christ in his life on the cross. He is the Way, the Truth and the Life. As his disciples we are called to live in the life and power of the Holy Spirit. [13]

More about Faringdon Meeting House

I am still uncertain about what was happening to the Faringdon Meeting House in the early part of the twentieth century. In the 1891 census someone was living there. At the beginning of the century the Mission group must have held some meetings there, but without any response. It may also have been used as a store and often left to itself the Burial Ground must have been a haven for wild life and become somewhat overgrown.

From time to time there were snippets in Witney Monthly Meeting minutes.On 13th of 111928 A.B. Gillett had received an application from Mr Baker, Wheelwright, to use the Meeting House as a store. The Meeting decided to refuse this request. In 1932 there was an application by the Faringdon Boy Scouts to use the Meeting House and in 1933 Henry Gillett reported that an agreement for letting had been executed and ten shillings received. I think this letting was to The Faringdon Boy Scouts. In 1937 a Samuel Walter reported on the condition of the property that it was, in the main, satisfactory and he had seen to small repairs. Again in 1938 he reported that the Meeting house was in good structural condition. However in 1939, just as the country was embarking on the Second World War, he reported that someforms were badly attacked by wood worm and should be destroyed.

Forms were welcomed for use at Burford Meeting House and Monthly meetingauthorised the transfer of those forms which might be of use to Burford. [14]

In 1941 Samuel Walter and Basil Stratton reported serious dry rot in the floor and an estimate for a concrete floor by A.E. Baker and Sons for £16.10 was accepted and the job done. The Boy Scouts still used the meeting house twice a week and on other nights occasionally. It was agreed that the Burial Ground might be used by the Boy Scouts, for growing Vegetables. In 1946 the Boy Scouts helped with repairs to the building.

I have had an interesting Ghost story from Jack Bungey now of Stanford in the Vale. He used to live at no 3 Cottage Lane with his brother. This is beside the old Bakehouse and overlooks the Quaker Burial ground. He claims that at about the time when the Boy Scouts were `Digging for Victory' in the Burial Ground his brother was haunted by the ghost of a Quaker lady. I think it possible that the idea was put into his head by a Boy Scout who had found bones. Of course Faringdon townsfolk are fond of mixing up Quakers with Roundheads and anyone dressed in black and white collars and bonnets tends to be confused with Quakers, even in a ghostly dream. Most old buildings in the town centre are `haunted' with Cavaliers and Roundheads. However for those readers who like a little snippet, I throw this one in. Certainly there must have been a lot of disturbance in the old Burial Ground and somehow there are only two or three tomb stones now in the area. For me that is a mystery. Perhaps theyare under the top soil somewhere. Though I do mention the problem Faringdon had with London Yearly Meeting via Witney Monthly Meeting in chapter seven regarding tomb stones.

Once again Friends were involved in Conscientious Objection and Peace work during the Second World War:

There appears to be no other way to resist tyranny than by violence, and men cry out that they have no alternative but to match destruction with more destruction and slaughter with more slaughter... Yet there is another way. There is a right way to do things, a way that is not just our own but is based on principles which are always right... Right is Right and Wrong is Wrong and behind is the Authority we call God. It is only when we acknowledge the authority of God that there exist standards which are unchangeable... Our trouble is that we have shut out and ignored God.

Statement by the Peace Committee 1943

The Society of Friends had once again had a difficult time during the Second World War and taken a stand to support those who wished to be *Conscientious Objectors*. *The Friends Ambulance Unit* had worked throughout the war and at home many Quakers threw themselves in to all sorts of relief work and connected activities. After the war there was so much to do in war starved Europe, helping refugees to survive in the camps and then to get to some safe haven either back home or elsewhere.

I am sure that some Vale people became *Conscientious Objectors* and certainly there were quite a few in Witney Monthly Meeting who did. This time it was not so straightforward because there were so many areas where social conscience played a part. Was working in the Land Army or in a hospital, for example, War Work? Again Friends formed *The Friends Ambulance Unit* and involved themselves in Relief work. Once again Quakers, who up to the war, were still mainly nurtured in Quaker families, met those from other denominations or from none and were forced to re- think their priorities. Also many who had never had anything to do with Quakers before, but were interested in Pacifism and liked the Silent tradition of worship began to come to meetings.

However at last the War was over and quite a few Quakers thought they could see that the ideas of the Welfare State and the Labour government policies would equate with their ideas of fairness for all and that everyone would have a chance of living in a better way. This equated with their ideas of the sort of world that a Christian should have. Everyone was valuable and those who had least should be helped by those who had most to give.

Back to the *Monthly Meeting Minutes*, this time 1949. The meeting was informed that the Faringdon Meeting House was in bad repair with damage to windows and the door. The inference being that in some way the Boy Scouts had neglected their tenancy. In fact I rather think that Monthly Meeting had neglected their obligations. Anyway the roof needed repair. The District Commissioner for the Girl Guides wanted to rent the premises for a Guide group and this seems to have been agreed for £8 a year. The repairs were completed at a cost of £85. 11.9 and some internal repairs costing £30.12 and £7. It was proposed that the Scouts should contribute £15 towards all of this. Gas fittings were also included at a cost of £ 3.17.6. This time the agreements with tenants included a clause that *the Meeting House could he used byMonthly Meeting at any lime with Six month's notice on either side.*

In 1947 the Nobel Peace Prize was awarded jointly to the *American Friends Service Committee* and the *Friends Service Council of London and Ireland Yearly Meetings.* John Gunnar declared:

`It is the silent help from the nameless to the nameless which is theircontribution to the promotion of brotherhood among nations. They have revealed to us that strength which is founded on faith in the victory of spirit over force' Oslo 10th Dec 1947.*

Anyone who had lived through these war years, be they Quaker or non-Quaker, was changed. Britain was changed and the nature of the Society of Friends and the wider Society had too. Many people, who could see for themselves the awfulness of war and the suffering and pointlessness of Hiroshima and the Concentration Camps of Europe and Japan, felt disillusioned and came to the Society of Friends where they felt their pacifism could be upheld. Others wanted to feel that God existed but then wondered how could God allow such devastation and hatred and suffering to happen. They wanted to worship in peace, to try to make sense of it all. They came to Quakers as cautious seekers and whilst some found *the still small voice* others did not. Some brought a stronger universalism into the midst of worship and others brought various forms of humanism and agnosticism into the life of the meetings. It was all very complicated. These pressures were going to make a difference to the Society ofFriends and soon *The Weekly Journal of The Friend* was unable to put the confident motto on its front because we were no longer united in essentials.

`If we want to get somewhere we would be well advised to learn to swim rather than float. The swimmer is intensely active and is going somewhere, the floater yields to the flow of the water and savoursbeing where he is. He too is going somewhere, but that is the concern of the current that carries him. His major decision is whether to trust the tide. If he does not he must guide himself by his swimming strokes.*

We were perhaps losing our way and this was painful to those who thought they knew what Quakerism was, but at the same time we were trying to find our way with a new generation and coping with a rapidly changing set of circumstances. A hundred years ago the Society did not open its doors to those who might have needed it and nearly shrivelled away and died. This was not going to happen in the fifty years to come.

NOTES

[I.] *All Friends Conference 1920*: this conference took place in London at thesuggestion of New England at which it was proposed to consider the implications ofthe Peace Testimony, more than a thousand Friends attended, representing alltraditions. It was the first world gathering of Quakers.

[2.]*Yearly Meeting Minute* read at Berks and Oxon Quarterly Meeting in 1861. Faringdon Baptist records

[3.] Notes in an uncatalogued box under the care of Oxfordshire Archives

[4.] Conversation with Roger Warner of Burford in 1990's. To confirm what happenedsee Witney Monthly Meeting minutes for the period in the Oxfordshire Archives

[5.]See previous chapter about The Manchester Conference

[6.] FRY (Joan Mary), *Swarthmore Lecture 1910*

[7.] 1 think this means that the first numeral refers to the day. If not, then they met on5th January1900. Some Friends still avoided 'pagan' words for days and months. Iwonder if Alice Liddel is anything to do with the child of the book *Alice inWoderland!*

[8.] Faringdon Baptist records

[9.] Subject Guide to British Conscientious Objectors during World Wars I and II andthe Peace Movement 1914-1945, this is a full list of materials held in the library atFriends House, London

[10.]*Berks and Oxon Quarterly Meeting minutes 1 XI,* Swindon Quaker records arehoused in the Oxfordshire Archives because it belongs to a Monthly Meeting that ismostly in that area now.

[11.] Taken from papers that are in the Oxfordshire Swindon materials.

[12.] Copies of the Friend are in the Library at Friends House, London.

[13.] Taken from *Christian Faith and Practice* replaced in 1995 by Quaker Faith andPractice. QFP 1.02 Take heed dear Friends, to the promptings of love and truth inyour hearts. Trust them as leadings of God whose light shows us our darkness andbrings us new life'

[14.]*Witney Monthly Meeting minutes of 1939*. Oxfordshire Archives.

[15.] Hoare (Edward), *Deepening the spiritual life of the meeting*, Publication of theFriends General Conference 1995. This concept of being led is discussed in a book*When the well runs dry* by Thomas Green, a Jesuit. This theme is also one that Julianof Norwich understands - *All shall be well*.

CHAPTER TEN

VALE QUAKERS IN THE SECOND HALF OF THE TWENTIETH CENTURY

Part I: The Charney Years

When we read George Fox and are shaken by a power and a passion which we have apparently lost, what we should seek is not an impossible return to the historical moment which fostered such convictions but to see it in terms of our own very different, though also chaotic, times what the centrality of Christ can mean to us now.'

Lorna M. Marsden 1985 [1]

I think this has been the most difficult chapter to write. There is so much material, all the records for all levels of Quaker business and spiritual growth are readily available and I myself have had first-hand experience of some of the major considerations and outcomes. So although the history is generally in chronological order and covers the fifty years of the Vale Quakers in sequence there are some topics that seem best dealt with as one piece over a longer period.

Friends began to use the term **Concern** from the earliest days of Quakerism, when an individual or group became aware that God was asking them to do something. If theybrought this to the Meeting, then, if the Meeting felt it was indeed from God, it would support it. Today this term has often been confused with *being concerned about*

247

some matter and is sometimes not connected with spiritual *inner conviction*. Quaker Home Service has had to remind us about 'testing concern', both as an individual and as a gathered meeting, and about giving ourselves more time to lay the matter before God. We require experience of the Quaker method to 'Know' whether or not the concern is a calling from God.

'To be called by the living God to some action, some witness, some change of direction is indeed a high calling. We cannot merit it. But we can prepare ourselves for being open to such a call if and when it comes by seeking always to 'walk in the light and by taking the risk of being vulnerable to God.' 2

Many times I have been in situations where the above is not understood or even known about, even within Quaker circles, in Britain Yearly Meeting. Too often decisions have been made with emotion and haste and with a lack of seeking God's guidance. This has caused much unnecessary sadness and pain in many Quaker hearts over the past half century. It has also led to huge miscalculations about the balance that was needed between central work and grass-roots Quakerism. This has in turn led to too much time spent on putting our own affairs in order instead of answering the condition of the times by providing a spiritual home to needy people.

In 1952 Quakers celebrated their tercentenary. Most of the main gathering took place in the North West Fox Country where the movement had started when George Fox had climbed Pendle Hill in 1652 and wrote the following in his Journal:

As we went I spied a great hill called Pendle Hill, and I went on the top of it with much ado, it was so steep; but I was moved of the Lord to go atop of it; and when I came atop of it I saw Lancashire sea; and there atop of the hill I was moved to sound the day of the Lord; (to sound may mean to seek) and the Lord let me see a-top of the hill in what places he had a great people to be gathered.[3]
After this George Fox did indeed find his thirsting, seeking people and he and others gathered them into the Quaker movement. This book has been about the development of these Quaker people in the

Vale since that time.

This final chapter is about the life of Quakers in the Vale of White Horse after three hundred years. Several meetings up and down the land were celebrating their tercentenaries. Maurice Creasey when Director of Studies at Woodbrooke (Quaker) College, Birmingham, was asked to address such a gathering at Alton, Hampshire and he spoke about the Prospect for Quakerism. First though he wished to remind his listeners of certain paradoxes and ironies of the Quaker story:

The first of these concerns the remarkable way in which our central affirmation that 'every man is enlightened by the divine light of Christ' holds together historically particular emphasis upon Christ and the universal concern with 'every man'. The tension between the two, and the difficulty of maintaining it, go far, as I see it, to afford a clue both to the meaning of Quaker history and to the wide diversities of understanding and emphasis among us today.

Then there is the striking contrast between on the one hand, our characteristic way of worship - described by most Friends as 'mystical', 'contemplative','interiorised' - and on the other, our distinctive public image as a practical,outgoing, even pragmatic, people...

(He goes on to say) *I mean that the answer to the question of the 'prospect for Quakerism - indeed the answer to the question whether Quakerism has any prospect at all - depends upon two things. The first is whether Friends can discern the 'condition' of the contemporary world. The second is whether we can speak relevantly and credibly to it.*[4]

I strongly commend this little pamphlet, which is in the bookshelf at Faringdon Meeting House and on other Quaker bookshelves, because Maurice Creasey puts so well the contrast of a Society that is broad and one that is narrow. It seems to me that London Yearly Meeting mis-understood his meaning or did not want to listen. In the final years of the century London Yearly Meeting tried to include everyone to be *all things to all men* and was for many Friends in danger of being nothing to anyone. It was so determined to avoid the narrow mindedness of the eighteenth and nineteenth centuries that conditions of membership were widened to include non-believers and humanists and those with dual membership. Almost anyone that felt at home amidst the Quakers was welcomed. It was so broadminded that far too many Attenders and newcomers could not find out what indeed the Society of Friends did believe. [5]

Many hours of business time was taken up with attempting to find unity when the ground for it was often non-existent before the process was begun. By the mid-eighties some Elders, in some meetings, had almost lost their role and rather avoided disciplining, which to them seemed out of place. They hoped awkward people would calm down or leave the Quaker group alone. There was the feeling that if meeting was helping the individual then everyone else in the group should be tolerant and cope with the situation. They rather confined themselves to *the right ordering of the Meeting for worship* in the meeting which they attended themselves. How could you effect discipline if the body to which you belonged had no common core and no commonly accepted principles? I am over stating the case, of course, because things have arisen out of all this that are very healthy and forward looking for the Society of Friends in Britain and we do have the Book of Discipline. But it still seems to me that these attitudes and lack of leadership in the Society of Friends have been open to abuse both from within and from without at too many times. Maurice Creasy had this to say:

It seems to me that, when all is said and done, there really are, as Jesus told us long ago, only two `ways' through life, the `broad' and the 'narrow'. The former the way of self-assertion, domination, self-centredness, appetite - leads as it has ever led to destruction, disintegration, alienation. The latter - the way of self-spending, of compassionate service, of concern for others - leads us as it has ever led, to `life `, to wholeness, to authentic existence .[see note 4]

Elfrida Vipont Foulds addressed a gathering of Quakers in Lancaster Town Hall onAugust 15th 1952:

"So be faithful, and live in that which thinketh not the time long."

{George Fox} For in this century of Quakerism that is opening before us we are called to be like George Fox, "Stiff as a tree and pure as a bell, to be like Margaret Fell, like one of our North Country yellow lilies pushing up through the snow to tell us the Spring is here; like Edward Burrough, our strength must be `bended after God."   [6]

The front cover of The Friend, August 1952
[reproduced by permission]

I am not sure that we listened to this advice as a Yearly Meeting.

Charney Manor

Now once again there were enough active Quakers actually living in the Vale to form a worshipping group. They sometimes met in each other's homes and also at Charney Manor. This beautiful Manor

251

House had been bought by **Henry and Lucy Gillett** in 1948 and given to the Society of Friends as a place of peace and recreation and for educational purposes. As the management of the Manor came under Witney Monthly Meeting and as Oxford Friends were the most involved they felt obliged to go over on a Sunday to the Manor and support the staff there with worship. Often a course being run at the Manor involved a Meeting for Worship on a Sunday morning and outside Friends were welcomed. These Friends became emotionally involved in the venture and were also often on committees supporting the work of Charney Manor and the upkeep of it too. So gradually some began to feel more at home meeting for worship there than in Oxford or elsewhere in the Vale itself.

It was an amazing thing that, here in the very village where three centuries before Quakerism had flowered and where, under the guidance of the Bunce household, Jane and Joan Bunce and Oliver Sanson had all found the Truth that eventually led them to Quakerism, once again the light flourished. The Manor house that stood there then was now a stronghold of Quakerism. The wonderful concept taken from the Journal of George Fox was often to be quoted over the following years and once again Quakers were visible in the Vale of White Horse:

Be patterns, be examples in all countries, places, islands, nations wherever you come; that your carriage and life may preach among all sorts of people and to them, then you will come to walk cheerfully over the world, answering that of God in everyone, whereby in them ye may be a blessing and make the witness of God in them bless you

A letter written to ministers whilst George Fox was in 1656s in Launceston prison. It was written down for him by Ann Downer (Whitehead) who was daughter of a Charlbury vicar but became a convinced Quaker. [7]

The Friends that supported Charney Manor and came regularly to meeting on Sunday began to see themselves as a regular Meeting and as several of them had children, the children came too, and someone looked after them during worship. The group gathered and not only added weight to worship at the Manor, but also organised things for their own nurture.

In 1953 the Charney group held a Meeting for Worship at the Faringdon Meeting House, the same one built so long ago. This was well attended. An interest in holding more such meetings was shown by those who came. Afterwards more meetings were held there. This was all reported at a Monthly Meeting at Charney in June 1953. It was just as well that this had begun to happen because a month later Mrs Reeves of Ivy Cottage, Faringdon applied to be allowed to run a small private school at the Meeting House. The meeting felt that they could not accede to this application as they had already agreed to the Girl Guides' exclusive use of it. Also they wished for local Friends to be able to use it too. [8]

Mrs Reeves went ahead with her idea of a school and finally bought the large house next to the old Quaker Draper's shop in Broomsgrove. This is also a listed house and I think must have been a Quaker Reynolds's residence too. She writes an interesting description of the building when she took it over:

When we bought the house it looked very different, both on the exterior and the interior. I was surprised that the iron railings had survived the war, when most were requisitioned and melted down for armaments. There was a very fine portico over the front door, domed with fluted pillars on each side. However it was badly affected by dry rot, and had to be demolished. There was a very large garden, about forty fruit trees, an extremely fine and large copper beech tree, paths, flower beds and grass areas.

The garden stretched down to Southampton Street at the bottom. Inside there was a substantial cellar with cupboards, a wired off area where presumably wine was kept, and a sink, where the unfortunate servants would have to work. The staircase is particularly fine, being a spiral with twisted banisters, and the main spiral being one continuous beam... Looking at the building from the front, the room on the left had a fine fireplace with tiled ornamented surround and there was a recessed semi-circular china display shelf...the room on the right had a fine marble fireplace...
[9]

Left - Ferndale in the 1990s built by the Reynolds family in the C19[th].
Right - the Draper's shop and Reynolds House about 1890
Both Grade II listed today

Mrs Reeves had over 135 pupils at her school by the time she sold it, due to ill health, in 1979. Now the school is much larger, called Ferndale School, and has bought the building next door for expansion, also I think built by the Reynolds Quakers in the previous century.

It is extraordinary that the meeting house had virtually been unattended by local Friends for well over half a century, and at a time when selling the Meeting House might have seemed like a sensible option, along came someone who wanted to run a small school there and might have even bought the place. At this very time, a space of about eight weeks, the Vale Quaker spirit was back and in no way could the place be sold. This was a watershed time - June and July 1953.

Mrs Reeves also describes the `Quaker Building' at that time. She was then the District Commissioner for the Girl Guides and was particularly anxious to find a suitable headquarters for the local Company. She writes as follows:

The Quaker building at that time, the late 1940's, was completely derelict. The door stood ajar, all sorts of litter such as leaves, general rubbish, even carcasses of dead birds abounded. The roof was in a poor state, with several places where the rain had come in. Certainly no one used the building for any purpose. I made enquiries and discovered that it belonged to the Quakers who lived in Oxford. I discovered an address, which I don't remember, and went over to see a lady and gentleman who I understood were the trustees. They agreed to let me have the building at a peppercorn rent and they would repair the roof if we undertook other ongoing repairs.

You will appreciate that this is nearly fifty years ago.. .The building appeared to be in two parts, with a semi partition - I understood that men and women did not sit together! - I know it was very cold - I have a feeling we had a portable paraffin stove. The floor was rough. There were no toilet facilities and we put an elsan into a small shed at the back. The garden was very overgrown and the grass was waist high but I do not remember that there were many tomb stones, which, I think, were leaning against the surrounding walls, rather than marking graves. [9]

This is a wonderful description of the meeting house at the time, mid-twentieth century. The partition in the Meeting House is interesting and may have been something added by the Scouts in their time. However Charlbury Meeting House still has its partition which was so that women and men could have separate Business meetings. So this may well have been the one that Faringdon might have had. Men and women always worshipped together, though in some cases, in the very early times, women and men sat separately within the meeting room. This practice was for some meetings mere custom, and in others had practical implications. If the meeting was raided by the authorities, the men liked to be nearest to the door so as to offer women and children some protection. As we know Faringdon did get raided in this way in the seventeenth century.

In fact a permanent transfer of Vale Quakers to the Faringdon site did not occur for almost another thirty years, because the Friends who met at Charney were quite happy to continue meeting there. Geographically most Friends came from the Wantage side of the Vale and The Manor was central for everyone. I even note that in

255

1955 a Reynolds, Alfred Reynolds of Manor Farm and later of Goosey Wick Farm, Charney Bassett was a member of the Charney Meeting. I wonder if he was any relation to the Quaker family that we have been meeting throughout this story. [The present owners of Goosey Wick Farm know nothing about him or even of his ever having lived at the farm!]

Richard Reiss was asked to inspect the Faringdon property and have a talk with the then tenants. He reported back that the Meeting House had not been used for some time by the Girl Guides, though they wished to retain the tenancy. They would be willing to sub-let to any other organisation that could make good use of the premises.

Early in 1960 a Faringdon Builder Henry Higgs, who owned most of the land around the Meeting House, negotiated for the purchase of the Meeting House and the land. He had an architect draw up plans for conversion of the building into a dwelling house. The story is that Monthly Meeting or the Management Trustees agreed a Sale and a price, though there seems to be no correspondence on the issue. The Charity Commission had to give final permission as all Friends properties came under London Yearly Meeting, as part of Friends Charitable Trusts Ltd., by then. They refused to give permission because the price was too low. This was not a businesslike affair and the Monthly Meeting, without meaning to, does seem to have got a bit confused. So one way and another, and, after water had gone under several bridges, the meeting house was not sold.

At Oxford on 9th July 1960, Witney Monthly Meeting, Mm. 20:

Our Treasurer has received a letter from the Roman Catholic Priest at Buckland/Faringdon asking whether we would sell the Friends Meeting House at Faringdon for their use as a chapel. We refer the matter to the Management Committee.

At the next Monthly Meeting at Burford it was reported that the Meeting House in Abingdon had been sold for £2500. Then attention was turned to the letter from PC Venables of Buckland /Faringdon. It was decided that as the Faringdon Meeting House was at present let to the Girl Guides, it was not available for sale.

It is another oddity that Monthly Meeting did not also sell Faringdon Meeting House when the Abingdon one went, but there were those who met at Charney who still liked to feel all was not lost at the lovely old place in Faringdon. The Roman Catholics finally found a home in Faringdon at the Congregational Chapel in Marlborough Street, which had a church room at the back on land, quite possibly, originally, purchased from the Victorian Quakers. The Reynolds had owned a lot of land around there originally.

In 1964, since it was now meeting regularly on every First Day, it was recommended that **Charney** officially became a **Particular Meeting (Allowed Meeting)**. This was agreed and minuted on 8th May 1965. In July 1966 Charney Friends `expressed a wish to hold their own Preparative Meetings'. The Monthly Meeting was happy to know that they wished to assume this responsibility and were glad to give their approval on 9th July 1966. Meantime Faringdon Meeting House itself was still under the care of Monthly Meeting.

In the tabular statement of 1965 **Charlbury and Burford** were one meeting with 45 members, **Charney** with 13 members, **East Garston** with 18 members, **Swindon** with 34 members and **Witney** with 11 members and **Oxford** with 264 members /attenders. Many Friends at these meetings lived in the Vale area. Soon, though, Witney Preparative Meeting was discontinued and subsequently the Meeting House was sold. 'Witney' Monthly Meeting wondered if it should change the Monthly Meeting name. However this did not happen because of the many legal and financial adjustments to Trusts and Investments that it would have entailed. So it was decided to defer the decision. This idea has not been tabled again and the Monthly Meeting continues to be `Witney'.

The *Witnev Gazette* in July 20th and November 2nd 1978 wrote about the Witney Meeting. Only one member was left, Nina Steane who lived at the Coggs (the original Anabaptist settlement). She put an advert into the paper asking more Quakers to come and to save the 250 year old meeting House at Woodgreen in Witney. It now had a gaping hole in the roof and damp creeping up the walls. There were squatters in the adjacent cottage. Nobody came and so Monthly

Meeting sold it. The burial ground was kept. it was sold to private developers and three flats and two new houses were built with access to the burial ground through an archway. The shell of the original is still there with original doors and sash windows. Happily, less than twenty years after Witney Preparative Meeting closed, Witney Friends began meeting regularly in St Mary's Church Winchester room and in each others' homes. They have formed as a Notified Meeting under the care of the Monthly Meeting. So the `Witney' title of Monthly Meeting is once again perfectly in order. The Meeting House and Adult School at Wood Green are no longer available for Quaker use and only the Burial Ground remains.

It should be mentioned that during the fifties and sixties a Friend, Tom Williams, who had a love of the old Meeting House in Faringdon used to cycle over from time to time from his home in West Hanny to check on the premises. So always there was this thread of concern and responsibility that some Quaker or other continued linking the past to the present and ensuring that when needed the Quaker spiritual life could resume.In July 1966 the first proper Minute book of Charney Preparative Meeting was kept. The following minute received from Witney Monthly Meeting is the first entry:

`Charney Friends have expressed the desire to hold their own Preparative Meetings. We are happy to know that they are ready to assume responsibility and are glad to give our approval. The Clerk is asked to inform Quarterly Meeting of this change.'

The meeting wished to express thanks for the care they had had as an Allowed Meeting under Oxford. They then agreed to hold Preparative Meetings on the first Sunday of the month. The clerk was **David Saunderson** and the Assistant Clerk was **Jill Morgan.** Later that year they decided to study `No time like the present', a study book for preparation for the World Conference of Friends in 1969 in Carolina USA. At this time the Vietnam war was raging and Charney Friends were very concerned about this. In December they agreed to a collection for the relief work in Vietnam at a Carol Service to be held on 23rd December at the Manor. In the following year they were concerned about the `proper understanding of the difference between unilateral and multilateral disarmament and how to educate the wider public on these matters' (15 11 67). They were members of the Monthly Meeting Peace Committee and supported activities to promote discussion about Peace and Disarmament.

This was the period when **Margaret and Harold Douglas** became Wardens of Charney Manor and they also worked with the Charney Preparative Meeting. It was a very happy time for both parties, it seems to me. The meeting was advertised in the Wantage Herald, the Didcot Advertiser, the Wallingford Gazette (being aware of also advertising Wallingford Meeting) and in the Oxford Times. Geraldine Barker arrived from Woodbridge Meeting. She came from an old Quaker family. By 1970 children's classes were held on the first Sunday of each month and one can imagine that they could have a lovely time playing in the garden whilst the adults had PM after Meeting for Worship. Bring and share lunches in the Manor garden, especially in the Summer, must have been idyllic. The Meeting joined the Wantage Christian Aid Week and also sent a subscription in support of the Swindon Branch of the United Nations.

In December 1970 the following minute was made. *We wish to record our heartfeltthanks to Harold and Margaret for all they have done for the further life of thismeeting during their three year wardenship of the Manor. Our very best wishes for the future go with them when they leave at the end of this year.*

Henry and Jeanette Hughes became Wardens of Charney. About this time **MaryWilkinson (Guillernard)** took over management of Literature, as she was on the Quaker Home Service Literature sub Committee. So the Charney Library was built up to what it is today. People were encouraged to give good books to the library and new ones were also bought. A proper card index was set up too. The following books were bought by the meeting:

The Silent Room
Your First Time in a Quaker Meeting
Introducing Quakers (6 copies)
QHS pamphlets and Posters

Some of these were specifically for the PM but also for the Manor Library. CertainlyCharney PM Friends could and did use the Manor Library. So this was a good example of the way the two bodies supported and enhanced each other. All a very positive and friendly relationship. In this year there was a first record of marriage.This was between David Saunderson and Margaret E. Jack at St Andrew's Church, Headington.

The meeting continued thinking about ways of holding their Children's classes regularly and about how to publicise themselves. In 1972 the Meeting helped with the collection to re-settle Ugandan Refugees in Wantage and Faringdon and became involved in collection and delivery of clothing for the refugees. They also supported the Greenham Common Women. In fact some of the women came to Charney Manor to refresh themselves from time to time.

In about 1973 **Dennis and Betty Compton** became Wardens and **Margaret Collin** became Clerk of Charney P.M. Her husband had been on the staff at Friends School, Ackworth in Yorkshire before retiring to Tubney. They all worked happily together and the Wardens became part of the meeting too. In that year the little meeting sent £20 to the Bray D'oyly Housing Association, £35 to the Leprosy Mission, £5 to Poole Meeting House Development Fund, £32 to the Royal National Institute for the Deaf

At a General Meeting held at Charney Manor in July, Oxford Friends helped Charney Friends with provision of food for General Meeting tea. Friends would bring their own food for their lunch when there was an all day meeting, but the custom was, and is, for the host meeting to provide tea.

In 1974 the Meeting considered the memorandum sent by the Constitution Review Committee of London Yearly Meeting `the *Financial expression of the Society's concerns.'* The Charney Preparative Meeting minute about this reads: `*We were all rather at sea in the discussion and we look forward to being enlightened by a speaker at our next Monthly Meeting.*

I think in some respects this has been the case ever since, that too many Friends have been upset and confused by decisions made by Central Committees at Friends House in London. The Quota system was set up to help Friends to contribute fairly towards Central Work. The responsibility for collecting this money fell to Monthly Meetings. Some helped poor Preparative Meetings out of MM reserves and others left the PMs to find their allotted amount themselves. This had caused no end of pain and difficulty, especially as the quota went up every year. Thus the Quota System was to be replaced by a more flexible scheme of trusting each individual to give freely to Central Work. Many Friends had never liked the Quota system as it smacked of Tithes.

However central work snowballed for one reason and another and extra staff were therefore employed at Friends House for central work. By the eighties it became clear that the giving to central work by individual Friends was not keeping pace with inflation and the enlarged central work-needs. Also it became clear that Friends House, built in 1935, and a listed Building, opposite Euston Station, needed a complete overhaul costing millions of pounds. None of this was easy and everyone had different views about what went wrong. It did, in my opinion, go wrong, because since that time we have had a painful process of cutting down on central work and on the number of staff employed. For me the most painful bit about this is that George Fox was particularly adamant that paid priests to do Gods work was against theSpirit. Here we were in the twentieth century coping with a situation that never should have arisen. Yet in today's society, changing as quickly as it has, it was not surprising that we got ourselves into a bit of a mess. The miracle was that we did not get into too much of a mess thanks, to some wonderful individual Friends, and non-Friends alike, who have devoted their care and love and time to the Society, for little financial reward, and for not nearly enough recognition, understanding or thanks.

It is sobering to realise that this problem of mushrooming central bodies was beginning to cause worry for some Friends a century before:

The growth of a large official staff at Friends House also raises

the question as to whether the Society which has rejected the authority of a professional Ministry is placing too much responsibility for initiative in the hands of a Centralised body of Administrators.
[10]

It was no wonder that Charney Friends sometimes felt at sea with these documents from central committees though, because many newly joined Friends could not possibly be expected to understand what had gone before and why they were being asked to consider some of these detailed pros and cons of this and that. They wereoften making momentous decisions about their personal worship life and life style,discovering a whole new world of the Silent Tradition; and their whole energy andpurpose was involved in that. So little wonder that the business side of Quakerism was too much to take in all at once. Besides this was an era in Britain as a whole in which stress was laid on the individual and their fulfilment of personal needs. It has even been suggested that religion has, for some, become so personal that the idea of the collective voice or need of a worshipping community seems old fashioned and unnecessary.

The fact was and is that some people tend to come to Meeting on a Sunday, to satisfy their personal spiritual need, and they don't want to worry about the wider aspects of financing and organising a Movement. They really have not got the time or wish to become involved in the business side of running the whole Society of Friends. Many come from worshipping traditions where the clergy do all that. I do not have statistics but I think it is fair to say that since the Second World War the Quaker community in Britain has attracted enough people, who do not have a Quaker background, to swing the balance so that in most meetings they far outnumber those who do come from a Quaker background. This has good points and is also wonderful, but it leaves gaps in the understanding of Quaker practice. It has become abundantly clear that with no trained clergy or leaders the strength and health of the Society of Friends in Britain has been and is vulnerable.

The other thing that has happened is that now most Members and Attenders work in non-Quaker establishments, so that Quaker business and worship has to be squashed into weekends and evenings. Very few have been educated in Quaker Schools. These schools are boarding schools and fee paying. Only those few who live near enough can be `daily boarders'. These schools have become for some Quakers an anathema and the whole question of privilege and the rightness of sending one's child away to board comes up. There are very few whole Quaker families that come to Meeting for Worship. A mother might be a Friend but not her husband or partner, for example. Whereas in the first half of the century more Quakers had been educated in a Friends' school and nurtured into the Faith and its business ways, more had been brought up in a Quaker home and gone regularly to Meetings for Worship and Business. Moreearned their living in a Quaker establishment or family business and could therefore be released to go to meetings, at Friends House, during the working week. Also, before the Second World War, many wives and mothers who belonged to the Society of Friends, as in the wider society generally, did not work outside the home and were therefore available to do local oversight, hospital visiting, to go to mid-week meetings and spend time keeping the wheels of the Society moving along reasonably well.

The "peculiar mission" of a Friends school is to educate for goodness, not by requiring its members to live certain truths, but enabling them to live their lives in ways that reveal Truth to themselves and through themselves to others. A Friends school therefore, should bring each, in the words of George Fox, to the "teacher within". [11]

Very few members or attenders in the Vale or in Witney Monthly Meeting itself have been educated in one of the Quaker schools. Several members, though, sit on Quaker School Committees such as Sibford Friends School Committee and help in various ways. Others also attend General Meetings of other Quaker schools too such as Ackworth in Yorkshire and Leighton Park in Reading. Most Quaker Parents send their children to local State and Independent schools and support these in many ways. Children can go to Quaker Summer School, usually now held in the Easter holidays, and lasting for several days. Usually these are held in a Friends school such as Sibford.

It was partly as a result of the changes of society and family patterns that the central work became overheated. Friends wanted the outreach work done by someone, they wanted Peace Work to go ahead, they wanted Social Action to be supported in lots of areas - prison reform - education - housing - green issues and so on, but they could no longer find time to do it themselves. So staff were recruited at Friends House in London to oversee all these demands. At the same time these things going on in London became remote and removed from the local grasp.

The above potted description is all too generalised and inadequate, very much my overview of something that is complicated and many layered. My written thoughts are full of sweeping statements about things that I only know a fraction about. However it is based on my experience in meetings and in reading letters and articles from Friends in various Quaker publications. Always the spiritual life of the Society has come first and individual Friends have sacrificed themselves for the whole.

It is easy to look back over a period and to be critical, but very different when you are subjectively involved in daily decision making. Things could not have gone on the same, evolution does inevitably occur and the running of the Society of Friends had to change to keep abreast of a changing world. Those who liked it as it was regret that changes have to be made. But with faith and love, patience and courage, change has to be and has been undertaken. This has all intermixed within a background of rapid national and global technological and social upheaval.

Returning to the Vale Quakers a Witney Monthly Meeting minute was read inFebruary 1975:

`We feel that the disposal of Faringdon Meeting House at this time might beregretted in the future. In these uncertain times the continued use of Charney Manor cannot he taken for granted, and Friends in Charney Meeting who live in Faringdon feel that it might be possible to re-establish the Meeting there with the cooperation of other Friends in the neighbourhood who at present worship at other *meetings.*

'We realise that to put the meeting house into good shape and to maintain it would involve considerable expense and that any scheme for retention and use would have to be undertaken with a due sense of responsibility. We hope however that Monthly Meeting will be prepared to appoint a suitable number of Friends to examine with local Friends the possibility of such a scheme before any further action is taken to dispose of the premises' mm.18.

So here we were once again some ten years on since the last crisis, with Faringdon premises hanging on by the skin of its teeth, Charney Friends meeting at Charney Manor and also from time to time holding meetings at Faringdon. But in 1976 things changed. The Charney Manor venture ran into financial and other difficulties and Charney Preparative Meeting felt that their own future there might be coming to an end.

At Oxford 13.3. 1976 the following minute was received from Charney Preparative Meeting:

In view of the possibility of the Manor being closed we feel it desirable to consider what other arrangements may be made for our Meetings for Worship, if and when this happens. We assume that the Manor will only be available until the end of September... We understand that Faringdon Meeting House is to be re-roofed and the building re-glazed and that an attractive estimate for this work has been received. We hope therefore that if the Manor House closes, further restoration of the Friends Meeting House will be undertaken to enable us to use it for Meeting for Worship... Dennis Compton, Clerk

The Monthly Meeting listened with sympathy to this statement and was prepared to consider it again in September if necessary.

During the winter Charney Friends began to feel a bit embarrassed when the Warden of the Manor had no guests or programme and yet had to heat up the Solar for their worship. They had started worshipping there originally to support the religious and spiritual life of the Manor on a Sunday and now they felt like a bit of an anachronism. Some members, especially those living in Faringdon began to think the time had come to move to Faringdon. If they did it would be their own premises they would be running and they could concentrate on that and leave to others the worry of Charney Manor and its future. At about this time the management of the Manor transferred to London Yearly Meeting too, which made the Charney Friends feel less secure.

Meanwhile a Boys' Club, the Marlborough Boys club, used to meet regularly in the meeting House at Faringdon. It had been set up by the Social Services for youngsters who were refused membership of Scouts and other clubs. This was just the sort of scheme Friends liked to support. In April 1977 The Charney Friends provided the money to pay for materials to redecorate the building. The Boys did this in their own way and really made the place their own according to David Saunderson. When the Charney Friends, as they still sometimes did, held a meeting for worship there it was not very comfortable or altogether as they could have wished. However the place was serving a purpose and that was acceptable. There was a lean-to, pull-chain, lavatory just outside the side door and at some stage electric lighting had replaced the gas lighting. I have to assume that the Reynolds family put gas lighting in the meeting house when it came to Faringdon in the previous century. I gather from chattering topeople that in 1977 the Burial Ground was still a bit of a jungle.

By May of 1977 Friends Home Service Committee in London together with the Finance Committee of Meeting for Sufferings had come up with some ideas and planned to keep the Manor open until at least the Autumn of 1977. Later in the same year Witney Monthly Meeting was released from the task of managing the Manor. But Charney PM still continued to meet there.

In September Mary Guillemard expressed concern in a letter about the small attendances at Monthly Meetings and this was opened up at Monthly Meeting. I put this in as it has been a concern of many about Quaker work. It is what happens when you have many new people joining the Society for spiritual nurture and who are indeed often in need of nurture and when you have not enough personnel to cope with all the mundane things that keep the thing working properly. Also added to this is the time and energy needed to explain things to newcomers adequately and care for them properly. 1 think **Alastair Heron** in his book *Quakers in Britain* very nicely explains the century of change that Quakers have undergone since the 1895 conference:

page 126 After the war Quakers made a fresh start, along with everyone else,and during the 1950's resumed familiar ways and events enlivened by the experiences of newcomers. But unsettling times were just ahead. During what became known as `the swinging sixties' many aspects of life in Britain wereexposed to new pressures. To this churches and other religious bodies were no exception.. It would appear that London Yearly Meeting still held a distinctive Quaker Christian position as the decade neared its end...

page 133 In sum: by the end of the 1960's Quakers in Britain entered a `post- liberal `phase in their corporate theological position, mainly by relaxing the basis upon which newcomers became members. By 1993 sixty per cent of the total membership of Britain Yearly Meeting had joined on that basis. [12]

Other churches of course faced the same things, nothing for British Christians was quite the same after **A. T John Rohinson's Honest to God (SCM,1963)**or The Second Vatican Council with Pope John Paul. Quakers not having a credal statement and being open to the spirit, not having a hierarchy of theological servants, were perhaps more vulnerable than most to too great a swing, too quickly. This has led to divisions within the Society, sometimes coming to the surface, but often, in my view, being pushed away. Quite a few old time Quakers have either resigned because they cannot agree with the latest interpretations about God and Spirit or they have just melted away and not gone to meeting any more. They are sleepers and sometimes get struck off the membership list, by those who have not taken in the whole picture of the century of change and its effect on some Quakers.

In May 1977 Charney Friends agreed to hold a special Meeting for worship in Faringdon Meeting House on Friday 17th June 8.30 to 9.15. In August it was reported that the meeting was held in June and a second one was also held in July. It was agreed to hold one on the first Friday of each month in future. They also agreed to put up a notice board and the clerk was asked to find out what legal requirements were for this to be done. By November the nameplate had been organised at a cost of £12.50 plus Vat. Alex Kerr agreed to organise a sanding machine to deal with the floor of the Meeting House and to organise a party to varnish the same. Young Friends came to help with this the following April and Mary Guillemard and others provided them with food.

Faringdon Preparative Meeting once again

When the Manor closed for the Winter, Charney Friends asked Monthly Meeting to help them to meet at Faringdon once again. Now life at the Manor was perhaps sometimes not too easy for the meeting and it was again the feeling of being a nuisance if the wardens had to arrange heating in the solar on a Sunday when otherwise the place would have been shut.

In July 1978 some Friends, I think fearing another difficult winter at Charney, suggested that *perhaps the meeting should now meet at Faringdon rather than at Charney Manor*. They decided to think about this. In September of that year it was reported by **Albert Hudspeth** that the Marlborough Boys Club appeared to be in better order but still the meeting felt the lease should be terminated. By October of that year **Barbara Humphry** agreed to serve on Faringdon and District Council of Churches. Some Friends were definitely feeling a pull to Faringdon as the Quaker home in the Vale whilst others were still prepared to keep things going at Charney.

In June the following year, by which time the Boys' Club had almost ceased, it was decided to meet every third Sunday at Faringdon for worship for an experimental period of six months. The Friday worship there was still continuing, I think. Monthly Meeting informed Charney PM that in future they should take over responsibility for paying their own electricity bills for Faringdon Meeting House.

Witney Monthly Meeting asked Faringdon Meeting to think about taking action to support the Peace Tax Campaign:

We have not found it easy to separate the complicated issues involved.. .to see clearly the motives fuelling the campaign or the possible consequences of its adoption by the Society of Friends. After a lengthy discussion we recognise that we are not wholly in unity on the proper course to follow… because of this we are not able to make a wholehearted recommendation to Monthly Meeting to give immediate support to the campaign. We hope that this will not be seen as indifference to the matter, but rather as an expression of doubt as to whether the Peace Campaign is the right way forward for the Society corporately. (see Faringdon minutes)

In September new curtains were purchased for the Meeting House. This was a sign that some were definitely making their home there now. It was available throughout the week whereas at Charney a programme of the centre was going on and the place was firstly for those on the Retreat or learning course. After another winter of uncertainty everyone was convinced that Faringdon Meeting House should be the permanent home for Charney Meeting. So it was that by 18th December 1979 Friends met at Faringdon for worship every Sunday. **Barbara and Phillip Humphry** were thanked for keeping the meeting clean and warm, Friends were deeply grateful for that. Arrangements had been made for the hire of a local playgroup building on the Infant School site in Canada Lane for the holding of a Quaker Children's class.

PART 2: Faringdon Preparative Meeting Once More

Treat one another charitably, in complete selflessness, gentleness and patience. Do all you can to preserve the unity of the Spirit through the peace that binds you together. There is one body and one spirit - just as you were called into one hope when you were called... Ephesians 4 2-4

I cannot begin to cover the remaining years with a completeness that someone looking back on it will be able to do. I cannot be objective about some of the matters that arose in London Yearly Meeting either. All I can do is to briefly cover the unfolding of the Vale Seekers in a patchy way. Some might say, "Well, don't try." That is not possible for me. I have found the first hand seventeenth century material, that has come to me about Vale Quakers, so useful that even an incomplete view of these last years of the century may also be useful for someone in the year 2300 too. At least it shows that someone bothered and was enthusiastic about it all.

I came to Witney Monthly Meeting in 1987 and worshipped at Charlbury Meeting. In 1995 I moved to Faringdon with my Anglican husband and I joined Faringdon Meeting as the only Quaker member living in Faringdon. I have already explained why I undertook this whole task in the introduction. Fools rush in where angels fear to tread, and that is probably what I am doing. I hope that in mentioning such recent history I shall not offend anyone as that is not my intention. I know, and any reader of this material should realise, this is but a fraction of the whole story. Each person involved has their own experience and could write a very different and valuable version. 1 did write to everyone in Faringdon Meeting and some of their verbal and written views are part of what you will read.

In April 1980, Charney Meeting ran a successful Work camp with six campers and seven others to tidy up the Faringdon Meeting

Burial Ground and do repairs to internal woodwork. This was a great help. The Minister of the United Church offered his church for the Quaker Peace Caravan's Dramatic Presentation, when they came as invited by Charney Friends. Later that year the Peace Caravan did come and it was informative and enjoyable.

In April 1980, Charney Meeting ran a successful Work camp with six campers and seven others to tidy up the Faringdon Meeting Burial Ground and do repairs to internal woodwork. This was a great help. The Minister of the United Church offered his church for the Quaker Peace Caravan's Dramatic Presentation, when they came as invited by Charney Friends. Later that year the Peace Caravan did come and it was informative and enjoyable.

Faringdon Meeting House 1995 [far left, the Children's Room]. The C17th/C18th building still in use.

In May 1980, Charney Preparative Meeting decided that they could not manage to do the supporting of Charney Manor in the way that they had and the following minute was made:

The Clerk is asked to inform Quaker Home Service that its meeting does not expect to be responsible for holding Meeting for Worship at the Manor on the occasion of the Enquirers Weekend next month.

271

However, if required, membersof meeting will support a meeting for worship with their presence.

The umbilical cord was severed. After this when there were Enquirers Weekends atCharney, run by Quaker Home Service, they came to Faringdon or Oxford for worship on a Sunday. Thus they could experience the Quaker worship in a proper Meeting House. The worship at the Manor was also encouraged but Faringdon Meeting House was now an entity in itself. It was again the local place of worship in the Vale.

Quakers were back in the old Meeting House in Faringdon once again. The only problem being the accommodation for a children's class. Friends met regularly at Faringdon now and so it seemed natural to lay down Charney Meeting and once more to call themselves **Faringdon Preparative Meeting**. The Manor survived as a Retreat and Conference Centre and was and is a powerful though quiet Quaker presence in the Vale today and very successful. A half hour Meeting for Worship, open to all, is held at the Manor at eight pm almost every Wednesday of the year.

In September 1980, the film `*The War Game'* was shown in the Faringdon Meeting House. Seventy people came to it and the **Earingdon Peace Group** was formed, It had been an informal group before this but certainly this was the time when it became formal. Sometimes individual Quakers belonged to this group, but mainly they came to things when especially interested. Always most Faringdon Friends lived out of Faringdon and so few joined the Faringdon Peace branch, but the Meeting always have been glad about it. I do not think anybody joined Friends from the Peace group. Sometimes their members might come to Sunday worship but very rarely. However it has been a comfortable arrangement and the group meets regularly in the Children's Room. Many speakers of national interest in the Peace world have addressed this group over the years.

The Twentieth Century Vale Quakers have always been supportive of peace initiatives and when Oxford Friends thought of opening a Peace Centre on the ground floor of No 42, St Giles in February

1986, Faringdon Friends were `excited' *by the proposal'*. It was finally set up in 1987. Often since then Faringdon Friends have sat on the Quaker Centre's Committee of Management and helped on a voluntary basis with outreach there. On and off the nature and purposes of this centre have been discussed.

`In the period from January to June 1996 for example the centre had 2000 people coming in to look for and buy things: Quaker books and also environmentally friendly goods. 165 people enquired about Quakerism and spiritual matters. The downside was that there had been no outreach into schools or into the university from the centre or any publicity about Quakerism at events such as 'The Green Fair.' (a report from the Peace Centre to monthly Meeting 13.10.96)

A thorough review of the activities and working practices of this centre was undertaken in 1997. Obviously it serves the Oxford city mostly because of its situation, but it is also part of the wider Monthly Meeting, too.

Back we go in time to the development of Faringdon Meeting itself. In the *Yearly Meeting Book of Meetings* the 1981 entry read as follows:

Faringdon (Charney PM) FMH Lechlade Road Faringdon
Sunday 11am and First Friday 8pm (There were 19 members, 7 men and 12 women, 6 Attenders and 12 children.)

By February 1981 members felt settled in Faringdon and ready to commit themselves to restoration and extension of the property. They wanted to modify the entrance porch, improve the gateway, build a children's room, have adequate lavatories and hand wash basins and a kitchen with sink and cooker. So they arranged to meet an architect Hugh Creighton to provide plans and do the restoration work. These plans were duly supplied in March with the extension to be added on to the old building as an integral part of it. However as the months passed it became clear that ownership of the boundary wall on the South West side, needed for the extension project, was in doubt and in the end Hugh Creighton appears to have been asked to do a notice Board and new gateway and the porch. In July 1981

273

Faringdon Meeting forwarded the following minute to Monthly Meeting:

Now that we are settled and meeting regularly at Faringdon we feel it would be wise for our official name to be changed from Charney P.M. to Faringdon P.M.

The above minute must have been endorsed for at the next Monthly Meeting the representatives were **Alex Kerr** and **Marjorie Stevenson Jones** from Faringdon. The clerks who have served the meeting since it started again are as follows:

Christine Marns	**1982-83**
Dennis Compton	**1983-84**
Arthur Lockett	**1984-87**
David Saunderson	**1989-92**
Nick Chadwick	**1993-96**
David Saunderson	**1997--**

So about one hundred years after it had closed down here was the spirit alive and well. An active little meeting again serving Quakers who lived locally in the Vale of White Horse, very much in touch with Monthly Meeting and Central Work too. In almost two decades of its existence the members of the meeting have served on Monthly Meeting Committees, General Meeting Committees and Central Yearly Meeting Committees including, Quaker Home Service, Quaker Peace and Service, Quaker Social Responsibility and Education, The Library Committee at Friends House and on Meeting for Sufferings. In the Preparative Meetings one can see how they grappled with all the business at all levels. Often individuals were involved in all tiers of the Yearly Meeting and could really guide the meeting with insight. Such involvement and active service had not been the case since the Reynolds and Huntleys served in the late eighteenth and very early nineteenth centuries.

All this was such a contrast to the state of affairs in the Victorian times, when business affairs often seemed to be a one man band or one woman band. The telephone, the word processor, the motor car have played their part and it is just much easier to communicate and keep in touch than it was. We have Quaker journals published weekly, monthly and quarterly and Faringdon gets all these regularly. In fact sometimes they complain of being *snowed under with paper work.*

In April 1982 **Janie Cottis** was welcomed into membership and she with her husband, **John Cottis**,have stayed and served the meeting ever since. Also **Clare Pomposo** was born to **Sarah**, her third child and another new grand-daughter for **Mary and George Guillemard**. Vale Quakers mostly seem to have come to the area from elsewhere. One Friend in fact has, in her lifetime, been directly involved with starting five new meetings, which seems to me to echo **Joan Vokins** of those faraway early days. This particular Friend has regularly attended Yearly Meetings as have most other members of Faringdon meeting.

Attenders over the years have been a considerable help to the meeting. Some have never got around to joining because of home pressures and the feeling that they just like to come and `be'. Some do belong to Quaker fringe groups such as the Quaker Friends Fellowship of Healing. Most seem to like the freedom to worship in peace and the opportunity to think about things out of personal experience. If they come from another tradition they welcome the liberal attitudes prevalent in Quakerism today. Some of those who have worshipped for years in the meeting are true Seekers and like to leave it like that. Some don't want to analyse their belief and having been unsettled enough in some other tradition before they can take years to decide to actually join this 'new' tradition. Some talk about a feeling of having come home when they are in Silent Worship but they do not wish to become members. Perhaps `once bitten twice shy'.

Some of those who did not become members of Faringdon Meeting just liked coming because of its `lack of pomp and ceremony'. They liked to come and relax in a retreat situation and they did not want to get involved in the busy side of the operation,the 'Church Affairs' side. They were honest good people who come to worship and feared that membership must necessitate responsibility for the running of the Meeting. Though this is not the case, it is a fact that too many 'active' members seem to be too busy and are too busy. Whilst some people joined The Society of Friends because of the Peace work Quakers are involved in, others hesitated to join because they felt uncertain about their attitude to the Peace Testimony. Again though there is no obligation to accept Conscientious Objection and the Peace Testimony as a principle of being a Member there are some in the Society that seem to infer that this is the case. We do not have creedal statements and we are seekers. There are corporate testimonies that, as members, we know will be upheld and which we know a majority of members will see as part of their Quakerism. We do have Advices and Queries. At the same time we should be tolerant of those who may hold a very personal view.

This is a quotation from a letter that shall remain anonymous:

However the few times I did attend Faringdon were always helpful. The meetings were quiet, perhaps two or three people would speak. A short bible reading or thought was shared. More comfortable seating would have been appreciated. Afterwards the other Friends were welcoming and friendly when we had coffee afterwards. I went away feeling better than when 1 had arrived. It provided a precious time of reflection and renewal amidst the modern day hectic family life. The old meeting house had a lovely peaceful atmosphere, it was the distance and the lack of enthusiasm from the family that stopped me attending more often. (This letter will be stored, uncatalogued in archives)

Publicity about this new Meeting was a major concern at this time and many things were tried. Advertisements were placed in local papers, notices were placed in the villages around such as Uffington and West Challow and Charney Bassett, all Quaker centres in the times past. Copies of *Your First Time in a Quaker Meeting* and *What Quakers Believe* were procured from Friends House and widely distributed.

The Society of Friends has a special department in Friends House, London, to deal with publicity. This is usually referred to as **Outreach**, because evangelism has connotations that modern Quakers dislike. This Committee, a subsection of Quaker Home

Service [now Quaker Life], produces pamphlets about Quaker worship which are available to order and also publishes books about Quaker worship and Quaker life. Mostly this Central department links up with Preparative Meetings, but from time to time Monthly Meeting itself thinks about ways of reaching those who might like the Quaker Meeting. [This Committee is now under Quaker Life which replaced Quaker Home Service at the turn of the century]

Dennis and Betty Compton decided to move to a home suitable to their age in 1985 and this necessitated their leaving Faringdon Meeting. They had served the meeting since 1973 and were to be sadly missed. Dennis however worked on various projects and amongst these was a set of notes on a Re-Reading of the New Testament. He eventually presented Faringdon Meeting with his unpublished *Thoughts on the Epistles of Paul 1994.* Apart from anything else, these notes make one re-read the Bible with renewed interest, whether or not you agree with Dennis. Certainly I do not think Robert Barclay (1648 -1690) was as critical of Paul as Dennis is, but then he did not have the further critical information that is available for academics today upon which to rest his `argument'. Then Quakers, in general, had a more reverent attitude toward Christ and to the Bible than they do today.

> *I Corinthians chapter 13 v.1' If I speak in the tongues of men and of angels and have not Love, I am a noisy gong or a clashing cymbal.' Little enough need be said about this chapter - perhaps the best known of the whole Bible. Chock full of good teaching, it gets to the heart of the matter. When Paul gets away from his obsession with Christ he talks real spiritual discernment and power. Verse 12 of course is the one which shows his real understanding of the human situation.' For now we see through a glass darkly; but then face to face: now I know in part; but then shall I know as also I am known.*
> [5]

> *or Romans chapter 8 v31' What then shall we say to this? If God is for us who isagainst us. He who did not spare his own Son but gave him up for us all, will he not also give us all things with Him? v 34...who is at the right hand of God, who*

intercedes for us? [It is Christ Jesus who intercedes for us]
`Paul's peroration is superb. From verse 31 to the end he
demonstrates his true preaching skill. Imagine these verses
declaimed on a soap - box at Speakers' Corner. He'd rival
Weatherhead and Soper, let alone Spurgeon. I gladly endorse
his final assertion, in vv 38-39, except for the last five words.
[God in Christ Jesus our Lord] As I don't share Paul's views
about Jesus [that Jesus is God] I find them quite superfluous.'
[13]

These theological worries have been with Quakers since the
beginning. They have been with mankind since the beginning for
that matter. The mixing of myth into cult and cult into doctrine that
entangles mankind in `his' search for God. Are Christians
worshipping God in a Christ-like manner or are they worshipping
Christ in a Godly way? In the twentieth century, just what
relationship is Christ to God? Is the Trinitarian view one that Jesus
taught? Where is mankind in all this? What about the other World
religions in relationship to Christianity when, as Quakers, we believe
that there is `*that of God in all believers'*? And to what extent have
we been misinformed over the centuries by `*coloured' translations,*
teachings and interpretations of the `Truth'?

These sorts of questions are unacceptable to many of those
committed to established Christian Churches and certain other World
Faiths too. They still see one path to salvation or perfection. Those
who stray are sinners or much misguided. So still the Society of
Friends in Britain is heretical in that it cannot draw up a creedal
statement of belief. It almost encourages members to follow
different paths to God / to spiritual truth. Perhaps this is why many
Quakers find the Gospel of Thomas a refreshing insight into the
teachings of Jesus of Nazareth:

> *Jesus said:*
> *If those who guide your Being say to you:*
> *"Behold the Kingdom is in the heaven,"*
> *Then the birds of the sky will precede you~*
> *If they say to you: "It is in the sea,"*
> *Then fish will precede you.*

But the Kingdom is in your centre
and is about you.
When you know your Selves
then you will be known,
and you will be aware that you are
the sons of the Living Father.
But if you do not know yourselves
then you are in poverty,
and you are in poverty.   [14]

Much of the worry about the decline in numbers and so on reached a peak in the nineties and on June 10 1995 at Burford, the meeting was addressed by Harvey Gillman from Quaker Home Service:

`We are addressing that of God in those we meet and being addressed in return. The light in one is reflected in the light in another. The seed, the voice, the Christ within us is thus affirmed. Outreach is a process of liberation.. .we should think of outreach as conversing not converting,....it is making available a visible option, so that people can make choices...*

After the talk those gathered that afternoon broke up into small groups and considered such questions as What brought us to Friends? What is our ministry as individuals, as a meeting? What do we have to offer the community? What do we tell newcomers? In their reflections together at the end of the afternoon they wondered why it was we tended to hide our Quaker identity... *Our apparent simplicity is very complicated.*

Jumping back in time again to Faringdon in the eighties the garden needed attention yet again. Albert Hudspeth and his Assistant Wendy Playfoot brought some children from his school in Swindon (Park School) and planted some £50 worth of plants in the Meeting House Garden. Indeed even now the garden is mostly grass with a beautiful border of matured shrubs and plants. It is also a wild life sanctuary as there are several types of snail which thrushes love. Thrushes sadly today are an endangered species as they love eating insects and modern farming methods have taken their food away. They are safe in the Faringdon Meeting House garden. Butterflies love the garden too and there are various shrubs and flowers that they like.

Margaret Saunderson and others spent many hours developing the borders and planting for beauty and usefulness. Some pick the plums in season and make jam. Although the garden is a garden it was also a Burial Ground that is now full. There can be no interments. Ashes may still be scattered. So the garden is there for pleasure and peace. Children can play there after Sunday Meeting and Friends can sit there and eat their *Bring and Share* food too. Most Friends are happy to be cremated and at present there are no tomb stones, apart from two or three in the path from previous times. Some plants have been quietly planted in memory of loved ones who have died.

Lettings continued on and off. The Workers Educational Association class met in theMeeting House regularly on a Thursday morning for ten week courses. The whole matter of lettings was gone into. Local Authority rates might not remain on the low scale for `churches if too much revenue was received. In fact it was unlikely that such a thing would happen anyway at Faringdon meeting. As already stated the access to the Meeting House was not easy and parking nearby impossible. There is parking about two hundred yards away behind the Faringdon Library.

I have to mention benches again. Perhaps this shifting around of old benches from one Meeting to another, on the one hand, demonstrates care for each other and care of small things, or perhaps, on the other hand, it demonstrates an inward centring on the needs of one's own Meeting! One could devise a game with benches moving from Meeting to Meeting like trains and the winner is the one who manages to keep them and use them in their Meeting House the longest. Anyway on the 8th of February 1987 Charlbury Friends asked for the return of their benches, lent to Faringdon originally via Burford P.M. in 1980. Faringdon rather needed these benches (which in fact may have been the ones taken from Faringdon to Charlbury years ago) but managed to part with a few.

In fact I happen to know that Charlbury was given some very nice benches from a redundant Methodist chapel in the nearby village of Finstock in about 1990. I actually found these more comfortable than the Quaker ones. The Quaker ones were supposedly specially designed for sitting firmly and comfortably in silent meeting for hours. Perhaps Quakers were smaller in the nineteenth century. I found the support part cut my back to the quick at Charlbury meeting and I find the same with those remaining at Faringdon! In fact one Friend at Faringdon usually sat on her own canvas chair and was immensely comfortable and still in worship.

In the 1980's Mr Higgs tried once more to negotiate with the local Friends a swap of the Burial ground for some land he had adjacent to the road. This was refused and eventually a hairdresser's shop and flats were built. It is a pity that the Monthly Meeting could not have negotiated for that land, as by then Faringdon Meeting was back in its own premises and could have made use of that land for extension and car parking. It would have made lettings more convenient and facilitated easier access for everyone, including disabled and elderly. But the garden (burial ground) area would also perhaps have been made smaller if some swapping of land had taken place too. This would have taken away something very precious to Friends and also to wild life.

None of this happened and the entrance to the Meeting House, as it is now in 1998, is thus rather narrow and the steps leading up to the gateway are picturesque but inconvenient. The old Meeting House is almost hidden behind the south west wall. This may have been desirable in the past but is a drawback today because newcomers find difficulty in locating it.

One Friend who has moved away now wrote the following:

(In 1970's) I often tell the story of the miracle that restored Faringdon Meeting House to use, which came about because I worked in the Faringdon Information Bureau. At that time we were the only Quaker family living in Faringdon. [This lady's husband was a watch repairer.] We had no idea there was a Meeting House in Faringdon - not only that but it was actually at the top of the road in which we lived, Gloucester Street. Imagine my surprise when a Social Worker came into the Bureau one morning... and asked who owned the building... she   told me that it was once a Friends

Interior of Faringdon Meeting House showing benches

House & The story goes on from there with this lady asking Monthly Meeting about it..

(This account will be stored uncatalogued at Oxon Quaker archives.)

In July 1983 the **Monthly Meeting Managing Trustees** thought that the plan for an extension drawn up by Hugh Creighton was too ambitious. It was designed to include a Children's room and modern facilities as an extension to the original building. They suggested a portakabin as an alternative provided planning permission might be obtained. The meeting found out that planning permission would be granted. They began to wonder if they would be wiser to invest in a meeting place in Grove or Wantage where most members lived. Everyone felt rather depressed and uncertain. In August of that year they agreed to start a children's meeting in a tent in the garden. In the winter they would find somewhere to rent again. The Architect was told that the meeting could not find the necessary money to go ahead with the permanentextension.

Money Matters

As with so many other Preparative Meetings up and down the country Faringdon haddifficulty meeting its Monthly Meeting /Yearly Meeting Quota. In 1982 it had been £451 and now in 1983 it was £515. In some other Monthly Meetings, if a Preparative meeting could not meet the demand, then MM picked up the difference for Yearly Meeting. In Witney MM this was not the case. The following minute was made:

Ask our Clerk to forward matters which cause us some disquiet and on which we feel remedial action should be taken:

a) The custom of Witney MM of devolving upon its constituent Meetings the duty of collecting the Yearly Meeting Quota on a per capita basis, a duty elsewhere carried out by MM directly, by means of contribution schedules.
b) The lack of prior consultation by central Finance with Monthly Meetings before setting budgets and deciding the total amount needed by Yearly Meeting. An arbitrary nation-wide `per capita' demand makes no allowance for either the variation in capacity to pay or the different local calls on MM's available resources...
c) The lack of opportunity at MM for Friends to influence either the amount of money demanded of them or to a large extent the uses to which it is put....

In other words Faringdon Friends felt Central Committees must *cut their cloth according to their coat* and trim their budget accordingly. This sort of demand was coming from all over the country. Many Friends were now unemployed, especially in the old heavy industrial areas of the North. Many meetings now had members who could not spend their family income solely on Quakers because not all members of the family belonged. There were people joining who were ill or unable to work but needed the support of the meeting. Many buildings needed updating to meet new fire and safety regulations and the needs of the late twentieth century. So in no way could the quota just go up each year. This all tied up with what I mentionedabove about the relationship between Central Committees and grass roots LocalMeetings not quite seeing eye to eye.

On Christmas Eve in 1984 the Vale Friends and children gathered for a candlelit meeting for worship and in January they had a Christmas party when the children acted a little play. This was a custom continued from the Charney Meeting and was always a happy time. Sometimes Faringdon Council of Churches was invited too but they were usually busy in their own churches at that time of year. By September of that year a semi- temporary building had been erected as illustrated. David Saunderson designed it and it is still in use today. Russell Spinage a local builder did the job at a cost of about £9,190 which included some work on the old building as well. It all came to more than had been expected as is often the case with oldbuildings. Preparative Meeting met some of this cost and Monthly Meeting helped out as did individual Friends. Including all the internal work, the total amount came to £10,516. The costs were met as follows: Witney MM £7,282, Bancroft Trust £2,000, Faringdon Meeting £1,230.

Finally the children's room was carpeted and had chairs and cupboards. Margaret Saunderson offered to make the curtains. Oxford meeting gave the meeting some chairs and books. The only thing was that the children had scattered during the Summer holidays. However soon activities were being offered to the children. From then onwards, so long as children were coming to meeting, there were frequent entries in the minutes about the concerns for, and plans about, the children's work, who is going to do it and what they are going to do.

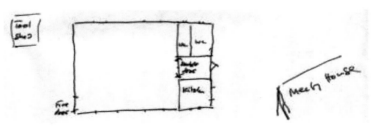

The children's room

8th June 1986 Min.3The children's meeting is attended occasionally by five children. Usually they do not all come together on the same Sunday. It has been suggested that having the meeting on the first and third Sundays of the month would help to ensure all come more often together...

7th May 1989 Min. 2 Arrangements for children during Meeting for Worship,The practice of maintaining a rota for friends willing to be responsible for the children's class has fallen into disuse...

2 Feb 1992   Care of the children during Meeting for Worship. We agree to form a rota of members willing to share responsibility for children during Sunday Meetings for Worship.

In fact the original children of the meeting were older now and did not wish to come to Faringdon on Sundays. Most lived in Wantage and wanted to do things with their friends there. Monthly Meeting was beginning to be aware of this problem and a **Monthly Meeting Children and Young Persons Group** was set up in 1993 by which time Faringdon, more or less, had no children coming to meeting. However **Susan Jappie** represented Faringdon on that group. If a youngster was so inclined, they could go to National Quaker gatherings such as Young Friends or Junior Yearly Meeting and the Link weekends. But this new group at Monthly Meeting level was offering activities within the Monthly Meeting. Eventually there were no children coming to Faringdon meeting which was very sad. The lovely room was there, the garden was there and in the cupboard were suitable books and games.

At about this time the whole country had been horrified by shocking disclosures about child sexual abuse, sometimes on a wider scale than had been imagined. Social Services up and down the country were so shattered by the impact of the wide scale nature of this child abuse that the Government was forced to introduce a new Children's Act: *Safeguarding our children from harm.* This had such a widespread power that the Religious Society of Friends and all Churches had to look at their procedures for looking after children on Sundays and at other gatherings. The Witney Monthly Meeting Children and Young Persons Groupwas involved with this aspect of child care and spent much time in their respective Preparative Meetings working out procedures for the care of children and young people in their midst. FaringdonPreparative Meeting also had to work out its own plans for safeguarding our children from harm. Then if someone came to meeting with children we had a procedure to follow. At the same time Faringdon PM looked into the whole safety of the Meeting House, checking that the latest fire extinguishers were in place, first aid kit was intact and electrical equipment was safe. This was necessary for outside users as well as ourselves.

Before the events mentioned above happened, **Barbara Humphry** was leaving the district and so after fourteen years' service on the Christian Aid Committee of the local Council of Churches she was warmly thanked. **Albert Huspeth** took her place until he went to teach in Cyprus. Since then Faringdon Friends have belonged to this ecumenical body as best they could. Other Preparative Meetings in the Witney Monthly Meeting have been able to have a much more active role than Faringdon, perhaps because they had members living in the actual village or town. However Faringdon Meeting has continued to belong to this local group and has been most understandingly included in planned happenings when possible. This body became **Churches Together in Britain and Ireland**.

By the nineties no Friends actually lived in Faringdon. This made taking part in Faringdon Church events properly almost impossible. Sometimes someone got to a planning meeting and usually they did not. The Churches Together in and around Faringdon bent over backwards to include the Society of Friends but we really must have seemed a 'peculiar lot'. Indeed some of the events planned by the Churches did seem strange to modern Quakers. The carrying of the cross through Faringdon on Good Friday was not seen as something Quakers could join in with. The symbolic meaning of the cross was, to many Quakers, seen as an internal struggle for each 'sufferer' or 'seeker' rather than an outward symbol. The United Services and Christian Aid work were much easier for Quakers to handle theologically. Sometimes the churches were invited to share in a Meeting for Worship at the Meeting House but not very often. Most of the Faringdon Friends who were involved in ecumenical outreach did so in their own town and village which was not in Faringdon. Certainly Friends in Wantage were involved in things in their town.

Some of those who had recently left Anglican or Roman Catholic churches and joined Quakers were not ready to cope with ecumenism. Faringdon Meeting seemed not to have any who held dual membership and could feel comfortable in different religious settings. In Marlborough PM there were several who held dual membership with Quakers and other Denominations and so relationships were easy. In fact once a month before Meeting for Worship they sang hymns.

In 1993 the Faringdon meeting responded to a query about their relationship with other churches:

Faringdon meeting is a member of Churches Together in and around Faringdon.In the past we used to have a regular representative at meetings, but this has become increasingly difficult in recent years, as we no longer have members living in Faringdon. We still try to send representatives to the meetings, but this is on an ad hoc basis...some of our members living in Wantage play a part in ecumenical activities there.

Since 1993 London Yearly Meeting has become a member of Churches Together in Britain and Ireland. This replaced The Council of Churches. Quakers had Observer status of The Council of Churches because they would not be bound by the creedal statement. This new body devised a special category so that Quakers could belong on a non - creedal basis. This meant that they understand us to be *a Christian Church and to accept the substance of the statement that we could work in the spirit of the basis*. Traditionally we have never insisted on members being bound by words.

Words must not become barriers between us, for no one of us can ever adequately understand or express the truth about God...1995 Book of Discipline.[15]

The Basis for belonging to Churches Together that Quakers will not be bound to is as follows:

287

The Council of Churches Together in Britain and Ireland uphold a fellowship of churches in the United Kingdom of Great Britain and the Republic of Ireland which confess the Lord Jesus Christ as Godand Saviour according to the Scriptures and therefore seek to fulfil their common calling to the glory of the one God, Father, Son and Holy Spirit. [16]

The idea of the Holy Trinity has from the beginning of Quakerism caused problems and is part of what has caused us to be dissenters or heretics. Quakers always insisted that religion should be concerned with example and spiritual experience rather than with doctrine. They always avoided emphasis of the idea of The Trinity in their explanations about God. The wording in this Basis quoted above brought in a lot of theological ideas that a substantial minority of Friends around the country found difficult to live with. They even felt it was dishonest to suggest that the Society of Friends *could work in the spirit of the Basis*. Many more Quakers were certain that we were happily in tune with the Basis and this was confirmed at Yearly Meeting in 1997. Our Book of Discipline called *Quaker Faith and Practice - a book of Christian discipline - revised in 1994/5* bore this out.

`Vale' Quakers considered some documents prepared by various Central Committees for the *World Council of Churches* and also for the *Churches Together in Britain and Ireland.* They also discussed some material called, *Who Are We: Questions on Quaker identity... tradition and today -Experience and tomorrow'.* Some members found this interesting and others did not. None of the members felt drawn to Christian evangelism or to Christian Fundamentalism as some Yearly Meetings seem to have been. Most Vale Quakers today are probably Seekers and open to the Light. Most Vale Members are Christian in the widest sense and accept the recently revised Book of Discipline *Quaker Faith and Practice*. They are content to belong to the *.Faringdon and District Churches Together.*

I have already mentioned the problem of financing central work. In 1980 *Young Friends* had initiated a thorough look at the moral basis of Friends investments and finances. They were concerned that money should be invested and used ethically. So the Yearly Meeting divested itself of excessive capital reserves. Some looking back feel this was all done rather too speedily and has caused some problems since, others support the idea and the action. The thrust has been that we should pay our way from our own current resources. It took a further eight years to do away with the *Quota System* and replace it with a *Common Fund*. Financing central work was reorganised and this led to a period of straitened circumstances that no-one liked. Capital Funds had been spent, hence less income from that, and Friends were not contributing so well under the voluntary scheme. Membership was not the same as before the war and quite a number of members worked in the Caring Professions, which did not pay very highly. Relatively more members were in the retirement category and living on fixed incomes. This trend has continued.

So inevitably cuts on work and staff had to be undertaken. One such piece of work that Quaker Peace and Service felt they must cut was funding and organising the *Prisoner Befriending Scheme*. This service had been started by an Oxford Friend, **Dorothy Birtles**, and had been taken over by Quaker Peace and Service. After several years QPS decided that they could no longer do this work. The matter came before Monthly Meeting via Oxford PM and it was not long before Monthly Meeting felt that they should take this important work over. Which they did in 1993. They saw this devolvement of Central Work as a way forward for the Yearly Meeting. Thus a more streamlined Central Office could concentrate properly on less. This Prisoner Befriending scheme was to serve the whole Yearly Meeting. The decision wasreviewed in 1997.

`*8th March 1997 Mm 6.. It gives recognition to the work as part of the corporatework of BYM, and keeps before Friends our concern as Quakers for the humanetreatment of prisoners...There are now over 420 Befrienders writing to prisoners. ..We agree to continue to take responsibility for oversight of the Quaker Scheme for Befriending Prisoners for a further three years, until July2000, and to review our involvement again before that date...*

To go back a bit. In 1985 London Yearly Meeting felt that it was time the Book of Discipline was revised. The first *Book of Discipline* had been issued in 1737 and from time to time since then revisions had been issued. In 1921 it was called *Christian life, Faith and thought*. By 1967 it was called *Christian Faith and Practice* and included a separate book called *Church Government*. These sorts of words were not easy for some in the late eighties and the Review Committee gave all Meetings and individuals an opportunity to discuss the revision and put forward ideas.

In February 1987 Faringdon Preparative Meeting responded (Mm 7):

We have received a letter from the committee currently revising the Book of Discipline, asking for any views, we have on Advices and Queries...

In 1994 Faringdon Friends decided to have a discussion group on the draft Book of Discipline at Charney Manor and in March they wrote fairly detailed minutes on their thoughts. These were forwarded to the Recording Clerk in London:

(Mm 4 May 1994) We are very grateful to the Book of Discipline Committee for their work in introducing this draft, and we are delighted with the result.We are pleased with the way Church Government and Christian Faith and Practice have been combined into a single sequence.

We are not happy with the statement that a testimony "has a purpose, and that is to get people to change, to turn to God." We would prefer the extract toconsist of the first paragraph only (this was Christian Faith and Practice 20.17).

In the published version the paragraph 20.17 reads: *Testimonies are not imposed on members of the Society of Friends but they are reaffirmed corporately and re-expressed sufficiently often to be both a challenge and a way of living to most Friends.*

Faringdon also wanted to know *why no reference had been made to dual membership. Some guidelines on this difficult matter would he helpful.* Dual membership was allowed in a few meetings that is that a person could remain a member of their church and also be a Quaker. Marlborough PM had several such members who also attended their church and took Holy Communion there. Some 'purists' found this difficult to accept theologically. Where was the Quaker integrity of simplicity and avoidance of creeds and ceremony in such a situation?

I myself find dual membership problematical. Perhaps I am intolerant and lacking in imagination in some way, but whilst I love going to evensong and will go and be blessed in church alongside my Anglican husband, I just could not be confirmed into the 'church' or take Holy Communion. I would feel that I was not being true to the sufferings of the first Quakers, to people like Joan Vokins.

In the published version there are some bits about dual membership in the chapter ten'Belonging to a Quaker Meeting':

10.31 Friends are not about building walls but about taking them down. For us as rural Friends, living many miles away from each other and a QuakerMeeting, having dual membership is a way of acknowledging our involvement of where we live: with local activities including Christian ones.
Members ofNorth Northumberland Meeting 1994. (also 10.31)

So it would appear that Faringdon Quakers were listened to and had influence within the whole Yearly Meeting.

Finally in 1994 the new book of Quaker Discipline was published. Now called *Quaker Faith and Practice: A book of Christian discipline of the Yearly Meeting of the Society of Friends in Britain.* The London Yearly Meeting was now to be called '**Britain Yearly Meeting**'. People living in far flung parts of the country had become more than a little tired of London being in the title of the Yearly Meeting to which they belonged. It seemed easy to change the name and much better than alienating Friends which might have led to splits into different Yearly Meetings.

Some were not too happy with the new title `Quaker Faith and Practice' feeling that the Christian basis was not prominent and indeed there were far fewer overtly Christian references inside the covers than in previous editions. Some Friends had pressed quite hard for no Christian reference to be made on the cover feeling that such a reference was too exclusive. They must have been pleased with the inside which dealt with new material tenderly and omitted some fairly traditional Christian language. Spiritual thoughts suitable for considerations about Feminist Values and homosexual needs were now included. For example in the 1960 edition of the Books of Discipline, *Christian Faith and Practice* and *Church Government*, there had been a chapter called *Marriage and the Home*. In the changing world of the nineties this was seen as rather limited and was replaced with a chapter called *Close Relationships*.

> *We affirm the love of God for all people, whatever their sexual orientation, and our conviction that sexuality is an important part of human beings as created by God, so to reject people on the grounds of their sexual [orientation] is a denial of God's creation...We realise that our sexual nature can be a cause of great pain as well as great joy. It is up to each one of us to recognise this pain,...to reach out to others as best we can and to reflect on our own shortcomings in loving others... We need to overcome our fear of what is strange and different, becausewe are all vulnerable, we all need love.., from Wandsworth PM 1989*   [17]

When understanding Quaker marriage, it is still considered to be the work of the Lord to join in marriage and we are witnesses to that in a Meeting for Marriage. May I again quote the same passage as I did in an earlier chapter which is included in the latest Book of Quaker Discipline:

> *We marry none; it is the Lord's work.*
> *George Fox*

> *Never marry but for love, but see that thou lovest what is lovely. He that minds the body not the soul has not the better part of that relation, and will consequently [lack] the noblest comfort of a married life.*
> *.[William Penn Advice to his son 1693]*   [19]

Traditionalists were happy to find their favourite passages still in the Book of Discipline. This nostalgia is rather like that of the Anglicans and the new prayer book, missing old familiar phrases. On pages 665 to 667 in the 1995 Quaker Faith and Practice there is an index of `Well-loved phrases'. Many of these have been quoted in this book about Vale Quakers. Just reading them through gives Quakers today a taste of Quakers of times gone by. It helps them to realise that the Society of Friends is still grounded in its heritage, which is Christian, but open to new light from wherever this may come. Our minutes are still peppered with both Biblical and old Quaker language because we do still read the old journals and the Quaker works of people like Barclay, Fox, Woolman, Rufus Jones and so on. We possibly remain a `Peculiar People' but it is to be hoped that we also remain *useful people*. We hope that we are as, *Children of Light*, both pleasing and useful to God.

The total number of the Society of Friends dropped slightly in this second half of the twentieth century and moved around the 17,000 level with Attenders making up a further 10,000. In 1895 the membership had fallen to 16,476 and in 1994 it was 17,351. Numbers are not important to Quakers as each individual is more important than the whole, yet for someone like myself it is disquieting to realise that at a time when generally people `out there' are seeking for a spiritual centre and simply not finding it. The Society of Friends is not attracting them or they do not find us. At a time when some people are finding spiritual nourishment in Celtic, Medieval or Eastern mysticism then why don't numbers of them come to the Quakers? They have not been reached by us. Are we hiding our *light under a bushel*, so distrustful of evangelism that we are unavailable to some who need us, or is it that we have nothing to offer most people? We did answer a need in the seventeenth century when we appealed to all conditions of women and men, so why not now?

In the early nineties the Faringdon Meeting began to get smaller. Some Friends left the district for one reason or another, other Friends sadly died. Those who remained therefore had more responsibility individually to keep the meeting going. In the tabular statement for Witney Monthly Meeting in 1990 was as follows:

Abingdon	35 members	10 Attenders	and 14 children
Burford	43 members	14 Attenders	and 15 children
Charlbury	22 members	25 Attenders	and 17 children
Faringdon	22 members	6 Attenders	and 0 children
Headington	16 members	7 Attenders	and 4 children
Marlborough	20 members	17 Attenders	and 3 children
Oxford	197 Members	138 Attenders	and 75 children
Swindon	35 members1	14 Attenders	and 13 children

Looking at these figures one can see that Oxford is the busiest and biggest meeting in the Monthly meeting now and has been throughout the twentieth century. Swindon, Abingdon and Faringdon each have a few people from the Vale towns and villages attending. Friends can now choose where they wish to go and so sometimes they do not necessarily go to the meeting near where they live. Some like the active Oxford Meetings at 9.30 and 11 a m, where the Quaker Centre is situated and where there is a lot of outreach going on, more space and more special interest groups. Others prefer the smaller meetings where there seems to be more peace and where they may feel their support is needed. This of course means that those worshipping at a specific Preparative Meeting may only meet on a Sunday morning and do not therefore find it easy to know much about the daily lives and needs of each other.

Such a contrast to the early nineteenth century when the Faringdon Quakers all seemed to be related and literally lived in each other's pockets. Now, too, we live in the midst of change and people come and go as their jobs and circumstances dictate. So, though a meeting such as Faringdon may have twenty members and several Attenders at any one time, it has over a couple of decades had almost twice that number contributing to the spiritual life and serving the business needs.

At a meeting in February 1993 Vale Quakers at Faringdon responded to a draft document from the *Pastoral Care Group of Meeting for Sufferings*, as follows:

`As a small meeting, we are conscious of a lack of continuity in *ourrelationships, leading to lack of depth. We need more opportunities to meet, forwhatever purpose. We doubt ourselves too much, by sharing our experiences with each other we may enable ourselves to work through our problems incoping with the meeting's activity such as the care and nurturing of our children. We do however recognise that some sort of mechanism at local level is needed for drawing out our skills further...*

This comment above was the result of so much that individuals have faced in the pastdecades. Each was discerning God's voice and yet using words very carefully. `God'language was not used overtly very much in business minutes by the nineties. This was the case at all levels by now in London Yearly Meeting. It was even the case in many Meetings for Worship. Membership of the society had become less rigorous than it used to be though it was still seen as a discipleship.

Membership is still seen as a discipleship, a discipline within a broadlyChristian perspective' and our Quaker tradition, where the way we live is as important as the beliefs we affirm.[20]

Yet some Friends have been admitted who are not interested in a Christian perspective and empathise with other world religions, especially Buddhism, or call themselves `post Christian', a small minority are `Humanists'. Choice of words in what one says in ministry or in Business meetings amongst Friends has to be selective. For anyone of the older generation who has been nurtured in another era there is a need for listening to the message in a Meeting for Worship and then if called to minister to add an extra dimension of the here and now, and then uttering with care. The feminist movement has also influenced language as has race awareness within Quaker circles as elsewhere in the wider community. Always Quakers have to be alert to the right use of language and try to avoid hurting one another. They should strive to upholdeach individual's dignity.

I think that a knowledge of philosophy and linguistics has influenced the way Quakersconduct their worship. They are more objective perhaps than they used to be. At one level the Ministry remains open to the Spirit and that which is voiced is a result of *Trusting in the Lord* that the right words will come. But at another level Friends are conscious that there is a human listener at the other end who has feelings and values and might get `the wrong end of the stick'. This has even led the Society of Friends back to a sort of Quietism. One is not certain that the idea forming in the mind is the word of God or is that which the listener is waiting to hear.

As was pointed out at a Witney Monthly Meeting in June 1982 at Burford, when Quaker Universalism was being explained by John Linton:

`The Philosophy of Language in particular, has attempted to find out the meaning of words. Christian for example has many interpretations. What do we mean by Christian, it is a very personal view... Quakerism is wider than Christianity and should be open to new light which can come from other groups and Faiths...Christ said" I am the Way ", perhaps interpreted this could mean He was, showing, the way to Truth...' (minute 13)

Sometimes a Meeting for Worship can become too quietist when those gathered feelunworthy to speak, and when some only want silence anyway. This comes about when the point of Quaker worship is misunderstood when the space of the meeting room is thought to be there for `me' and `my needs'. It also comes about when the worshipper cannot imagine God as a voice through them. The following from Advices and Queries, Quaker Faith and Practice, is helpful:

Do not assume that vocal ministry is never to be your part. Faithfulness and sincerity in speaking, even very briefly, may open the way to fuller ministry from others. When prompted to speak wait patiently to know that the leading and the time are right, but do not let the sense of your on unworthiness hold you back. (1.02.13)

These Advices and Queries arise out of the early epistles that were delivered to Friends. They are not binding, but most friends read them frequently and refer to them often in meetings. Currently there are 42 of them. Some are very modern and only just included in the latest revision (1994). Others are the original and hardly changed since first written down. In 1682 *Yearly Meeting* decided to ask the representatives from each *Quarterly Meeting* to reply to three questions connected with factual information. *Who has died? Who imprisoned? How has the Truth prospered?* These questions expanded in the following century and as time went on they were less prescriptive and less evangelical.

In November 1993 at a Monthly Meeting at Swindon Alastair Heron spoke prophetically:

Children of What Light? Friends in What Truth? Our search for Quaker unity in a new situation. He explained that the origins of the phrase `children of light' was the presence of Christ within and his teaching as the source of our Faith by which, as Friends, we are led to the Truth that took the early Friends out of mainstream Christian tradition to discover primitive Christianity. He suggested that here lie our roots today. `Relying on the inward light is a risk operation and we need to test continually our individual understanding of the path of Truth within our Community of Faith. If we want the life of our meeting changed we must first be prepared to change our own lives. For this we will need the gift of Grace and the courage to live adventurously.'

Sometime after this an Oxford Friend, Emlyn Warren, felt called under concern to meet with Preparative Meetings and `be' with them. The Monthly Meeting was not certain at first in what way this was a leading from God, but felt that the Friend should be supported. Faringdon was one of the meetings that asked him to join them.

We had a special Meeting for Worship lasting two hours one Sunday evening in theMeeting House at Faringdon. It was well attended. There was a long period of silence and waiting and Emlyn ministered. Before he spoke it seemed as if indeed themeeting had centred down into deep silence and that 'the still small voice' could befelt in our midst. It seemed that Emlyn had by his example reminded us that weshould behave as early Quakers did and to use our silence aright. We were to patiently still ourselves and wait for meaning to occur, to trust in the system and let it enfold us. He reminded us of the power of the silent tradition by just experiencing it with him. We felt together in the stillness we knew a gathered-ness that was complete at that moment in time. We were held in the lap of God.

At a Monthly Meeting on Abingdon on 14th September 1997 Emlyn Warren reported back about these meetings:

He felt they were very special meetings and because there seemed much more time available than at Meeting for Worship on Sundays, he was able to give more extended ministry... He felt he was being led to take this concern to travel in the ministry more widely beyond our Monthly Meeting. Monthly Meeting agreed to support him physically and financially to do this.

Certainly receiving those travelling in ministry does help meetings, because when the same few gather weekly things can get rather inward looking and in fact a bit stale. Indeed from time to time Faringdon was very pleased to see a new face at meeting! Some Faringdon Friends also went visiting to worship in other meetings on some Sundays to `recharge their batteries'.

Once again the Faringdon Meeting House building needed repairs. The damp proofingneeded to be done and also the floor near the door end of the building was found to berotten. In 1993 a local builder was asked to look at the job and give a quotation.Meantime **Nigel Braithwaite**, the monthly meeting Trustee appointed to inspectMonthly Meeting Premises, had a good look at everything. He sent in a detailed reportand put forward various options. He also considered the proposals for there-development and wrote a lengthy letter to the PM Treasurer John Cottis. It said all sorts of things but the following is a summary:

It is always difficult to know how best to deal with the problems that face you.Unfortunately if you fail to grasp the nettle firmly enough and to take proper steps to eradicate the defects they will remain an ongoing problem and although in the short term there may be cost saving in the long term I suspect it will prove to be more expensive. To the extent that we are dealing with a listed building some of the options outlined above may not be permissible. (This letter is either in Oxfordshire Archives or with the PM Clerk)

Eventually it became clear that the overall cost was estimated to be over £10,000. The Grade Two listed status of the building had to be taken into account and the interior plain dado panelling with the ramped east end had to be preserved where possible and replaced where damaged. Finally the work was done by H.J. Knapp Constructions Ltd. of Stanford in the Vale. The Peter Cox Preservation did the damp course and timber treatment work. Whilst the work was being undertaken Friends met for worship on Sundays in the children's room. The work was finally completed in the Summer of 1995 and Friends were able to worship once again in the Meeting House itself. In the end the total cost of the building works and the special damp course treatment and timber treatment all came to £17,684.64. Fortunately the Society of Friends had got funds well organised for helping small meetings. Faringdon itself provided over £6,000 towards the costs which was a wonderful effort. The rest of the money came from old Quaker foundations that had set up Trusts for such work in the early part of this century. Those entrepreneurs that were so embarrassed by their riches were prudent. Some modern Quakers may sneer at the wealth made and dislike Trusts but they are there and very helpful too. The meeting was also helped by the Faringdon Joint Environmental Trust. A loan from Witney Monthly Meeting was arranged and, in the end, this was paid back within three years.

A very happy day was had when Attenders **Bronwen Evans** and **Peter Halford** got married after the manner of Friends on 2nd September 1995. The little Meeting House was packed. It was as full as it must have been in the very first days of its use.

In November the meeting held an Open Day and invited all who had helped with the recent building development to come. An exhibition of the Early Quakers was set up and refreshments served. It was also a chance to `put the newly renovated meeting on the map.' There were approximately 30 visitors and the general opinion was that it was good for the fellowship of the meeting too.

This was also the time when another **Manchester Conference** was being held, exactly a century after the very important one mentioned in chapter seven. This time three hundred Friends met, rather than the thousand who met in 1895. They again met in Manchester. Some from Witney Monthly Meeting and from Faringdon attended. This was a time for the Society to look at itself objectively and take stock of what we had that we should strengthen and build upon, what we had lost that needed to be recaptured, and where we could go in the future. **Jonathan Dale** insisted that as Quakers we had to rediscover our *Social Testimony*. This amongst other things required us to face uncomfortable facts about our own comfortable lifestyles. We must change ourselves and change the way we bought food and clothes, travelled, and lived in our environment. We realised that the time for selfish individualism was over: we needed to listen, worship and act as one - the gathered community. The words ofGeorge Fox rang with new meaning when **Harvey Gillman** uttered them:

`Then I heard a voice which said, "There is one, even Christ Jesus, that can speak to thy condition" and when I heard it my heart did leap for joy" QFP 19 .0*

For Vale Quakers this was a time to look back over the fifteen years of being a Meeting again and it was clear that this band of Quakers had done much. They had kept their Meeting going, they had renewed their building, theyhad been available to visitors who had worshipped with them. Always they had kept in touch with central and local Quaker work and outreach. They had continuously held discussion groups in each other's homes covering material from Friends House,Woodbrooke and various other spiritually enriching sources. They had paid their way, always giving generously to Central Funds and having monthly collections for `good causes'. This over the years amounted to thousands of pounds. They had especially given to Christian Aid, The Homeless, to Overseas needs such as Ulster, Madagascar, South Africa. Always they responded to crises and supported Peace work in the Gulf, in Romania, and Rwanda.

CONCLUSION

Thus a record of Quakers in the western parts of the Vale of White Horse over some three hundred and fifty years is completed. Hopefully new details will come to light and no doubt some of my interpretation of material may need amendment

If any good should come out of this little history of the Children of Light, at least, I hope anyone who thinks Quakers are special people, or too good to live up to people, will now see us as ordinary human beings very vulnerable to all human frailties and faults. I hope they will feel that the seeking after Spiritual Truth is an adventure that we all can share. Please can they be understanding of the silent path to God and see it as a valid interpretation of faith. They might like to come in to the midst of a Quaker meeting sometimes and help those waiting souls to reach the Truth. I ask that we Quakers should be open to those who need us, so that together we go forward into the next millennium with hope in our hearts and love in our actions. Especially, in this case, am I thinking of those in the Vale of White Horse, that you will be individually tuned to feel the spirit turning within you and be led to the places and conditions where you can nourish yourself and your community. We must never give up hope that we can build God's Peace on Earth.

While ye have the light, believe in the light, that ye may be the children of light.
John 12 36

NOTES

[1.] MARSDEN (Lorna*), letter in The Friend,Vol 143* (1985) p923, 26.51 Quaker Faithand Practice 1995. Lorna Marsden has been one of those who run a Quaker `Openletter movement', which has provided many with an opportunity to think more deeplyabout spiritual matters as regards themselves and the Society of Friends in general.

[2.]*Quaker Concern* Quaker Home Service 1988

[3.] FOX (George), taken from his *Journal of George Fox*, Revised John L.Nickalls1952 p.103

[4.]CREASEY (Maurice), *Prospect of Quakerism,* Study Fellowship 33, Friends HomeService 1973.

[5.] HERON (Alastair), *Caring Conviction and Commitment*, dilemmas of QuakerMembership, Quaker Home Service, 1991.

[6.] VIPONT (Elfrida), *address at Lancaster on August 15th 1952,* when celebratingthree hundred years of Quakerism.

[7.] FOX (George), this is an extract from a statement made in 1656 when he was in Launceston prison in Cornwall to Ministers. *Quaker Faith and Practice* 1995 19.32

[8.] Throughout this chapter extracts are taken from *Witney Monthly Meeting,Charney Meeting* and *Faringdon Preparative Meeting Minutes* etc. which are eitherlodged in the Oxfordshire archives or in the hands of the respective Clerks. (Thisparticular meeting was Witney MM at Oxford II .7.53)

[9.] Letter from Mrs Reeves, uncatalogued at Oxfordshire Archives

[10.] ISICHEI(Elizabeth), *Victorian Quakers,* Oxford University Press 1970.

[11.] HEATH (Douglas), *Peculiar Mission of a QuakeSchool ,*Pendle Hill pamphlet225,1979.

[12.] HERON (Alastair), *Quakers in Britain a century of change 1895-1995*, CurlewGraphics 1995

[13.] COMPTON (Dennis), unpublished *Thoughts on the Epistles Paul*, 1994/5

[14.] McGREGOR ROSS(Hugh), *The Gospel of Thomas presented by Hugh McGregor Ross*, Element Press, 1987. Logon. The Apostle Thomas probably started the Christian Church in India in AD 52. These texts are a direct Coptic version of the Greek version. These were hidden in the sands of Egypt since the fourth century until they were found in 1945. It is most probable that they were written into Greek from the oral Aramaic tradition and were the direct teachings of Jesus to his Disciples.

[15.]*Quaker Faith and Practice*,1995, Introduction p13

[16.]*Quaker Faith and Practice*, 1995 Chapter 9, Britain Yearly Meeting and theEcumenical movement 9.09

[17.]*Quaker Faith and Practice*, 1995 chapter 22, Close Relationships,22. 16

[18.]*Quaker Faith and Practice*, 1995 chapter 16, Quaker Marriage Procedure, George Fox, a collection of epistles No264 (1669) p281

[19.]*Quaker Faith and Practice*,1995, chapter 22 .35, Some fruits of solitude (1693)

[20.] *Quaker Faith and Practice*,1995, chapter 1 1, Membership, 11 .01

SOURCES

The following institutions have been very helpful in compiling this material:

Abingdon Library

Berkshire Archives, Reading: Minutes of Quarterly Meetings of Berkshire and Oxonand Berkshire, Papers and documents concerning the Reynolds family (B 0 D/EX F] -F17). Also a lot of material about those meetings that are still in Berkshire such asReading, Newbury and the early ones now gone. Earl of Radnor material.

Charney Manor Library

Centre for Oxfordshire Studies, Oxford Central Library

Faringdon Historical Society

Faringdon Public Library

Friends House Library, London

Haverford Library, Haverford, Pennsylvannia: The Quaker Collection

Ironbridge Museum Trust, Shropshire: Reynolds material both about RichardReynolds and also about the Faringdon family.

National Monuments Record Office

Office of National Statistics, Southport

Oxford Meeting House Library

Oxfordshire Archives, Oxford: These are well catalogued and all my extracts have been taken from the relevant Minute Books, membership lists, schedules and other materials, which are dated from 1668 to the present day. All the Vale and Witney Monthly Meeting Minutes (including Swindon) are housed here, as are the relevant Preparative Meeting Minutes that have surfaced. Most of the BOQM Berks Oxon Quarterly Meeting minutes are also housed here. Church Records Faringdon, Longworth and Charney and others.

The Oxfordshire Family Historian, Journal of Oxfordshire Family History VOL4 No7
Spring 1988

Reading Public Library

Uffington Museum

BIBLIOGRAPHY

BARBOUR (Hugh) The Quakers in Puritan England Yale 1964 Friends United Press 1985

BARCLAY(Robert) Barclay's Apology Edited by Dean Freiday 1967: SowersPrinting Company

BESSE Sufferings of Quakers' 1655 -1688 compiled 1753

BRAITHWAITE (W.C.) The Beginnings of Quakerism: Macmillan 1912Cambridge University press, 2nd edition 1955 prepared by Henry J. Cadbury,Sessions of York

BRAITHWAITE (W. C.) The Second Period of Quakerism: Macmilllan 1919.Cambridge University Press 2nd Edn. prep. Henry J. Cadbury, now Sessions of York

BOULDING (Kenneth) The meaning of the twentieth century Allen and Unwin 1965

CADBURY (Henry J.) Annual Catalogue of George Fox `rns' Papers': CambridgeMass, 1939

CORLEY (T.A.B.) Quaker Enterprise in Biscuits ' Huntley and Palmers' of ReadingHutchinson 1972

DALE (Jonathan) Beyond the Spirit of the Age. Quaker social responsibility at theend of the twentieth century 1996 Swarthmore Lecture given at the Residential YearlyMeeting at Aberwystwyth: Quaker Home Service 1996

ELLWOOD (Thomas) edited Journal of Oliver Sansom: 1 710 4th edn 1848

GOTT (Charles and Joan) The Book of Witnev Barracuda Books Ltd MCMCLXXXVI

GREG (Mrs Eustace) ed. Rathhone - Reynolds Diaries and letters 1753 -1839, /905

HAMMOND (Nigel) Rural life in the Vale of White Horse 1780 - 1914 : RectoryOrchard Books 1974

HERON (Alastair) Quakers in Britain -A century of change -1895 - /995: CurlewGraphics 1995

HILL (Christopher) The Century of Revolution 1603 - / 7/4 1961 second edition VanNostrand Reinhold 2nd edn 1962 (UK)

HODGSON (William)The Society Friends' in the nineteenth century Philadelphia,Pa: Smith, Elder and Co. 1875-76, 2 Vols

ISICHEI (Elizabeth) Victorian Quakers: Oxford University Press 1970

JONES(Rufus) The Quakers in the American Colonies' Macmillan 1911

MANNING (B) The English people and the English Revolution Penguin

MUNRO (Olive Fyfe ed.) George Fox 1624-1691 Our living Contemporarv

MILLAGAN (Edward H) George Fox: the seventeenth century background FarrendPress 1992

PENNY (Norman) ed.,Journal of George Fox 1911

PENNY (Norman) ed. The short Journal and itinerary Journals of George Fox Incommemoration of the tercentenary of his birth (1624-1924): Friends HistoricalAssociation 1925

NICKALLS (John L) ed The Journal of George Pox: Cambridge UniversityPress 1952, London Yearly Meeting rptd. 1975

QUAKER FAITH & PRACTICE, The book of Christian discipline of the ReligiousSociety of Friends (Quakers) in Britain Warwick Printing Company Limited 1995

PRYOR Hack (Mary) Richard Reynolds 1735-1816 Headley Bros 1896

PUNSHIOM (John) Portrait in Grey - A short History of the Quakers Quaker HomeService 1984

RAISTRICK (Arthur) Quakers in Science and Industry Bannisdale Press 1950. Davidand Charles 1968

RATHBONE (Hanna Maiy) Memoir of the life of Richard Reynolds 1852

REAY (Barry) The Quakers and the English Revolution St Martin's Press 1985

SCOTT (Janet) What Canst Thou Say - Towards a Quaker theology SwarthrmoreLecture; Quaker Home Service 1980

TAYLOR (Ernest E.) The Valiant Sixty Bannisdale Press London 1947

VICTORIA History Berkshire, Vol 111927

VIPONT (Elfrida) The Story of Quakerism 1652-1952 Bannisdale Press London1954

VICTORIAN History of Berkshire, VOL 11 43 1927 and VOL IV

Appendix 1

"Possible" Reynolds of Faringdon family trees

[The lists used for this compilation are in the brown envelope attached to the archives, Friends House.]

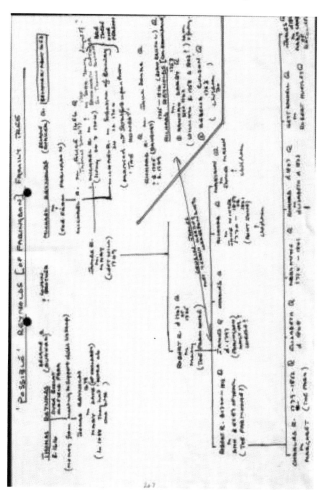

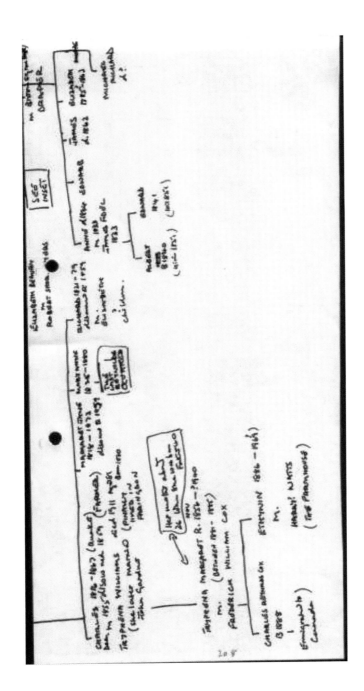

Appendix 2

Sufferings of Michael Reynolds 1678 extracts

Here followeth

A Brief RELATION

Of the late Sufferings of

Michael Reynolds

Of Farringdon, in the same County; because he could not for Conscience-sake, pay Tyths, to ROBERT PYE, Impropriator.

IN the 7th. month, 1678. *Michael Reynolds* was Arrested for Tyths, at the Suit of *Robert Pye*; and kept by the Bayliffs, Prisoner at an Inn one day; and one (unknown to *Michael*) who pretended himself an Attorney, promising to appear for him, he was let go: And *Robert Pye* prosecuted his Suit, (having no Defence made at all against him) and procured an Execution for sixty Pound.

And on the 19th. day of the 6th. month, 1679. there came *John Pullen* and *James Clark* of *Abingdon*, and *William Tombes* of *Farringdon*, (Bayliffs) with the said Execution, and seized on, and Drove away nine of *Michael Reynolds's* Cows, and a Colt of two years old, and likewise seized on a Barn full of Corn: and the same day also they arrested *Michael Reynolds* in the Suit of *Robert Pye*; and kept him Prisoner at an Inn most part of a day, and when they saw he could not imploy

imploy an Attorney (but was given up to endure Imprisonment) they set him go.

And the 22d. day of the same month, two of the fore-mentioned Bayliffs (viz.) *James Clarke* and *Willam Tombes*, took away a Mare from *Michael* upon the same Execution; and in a little time after, the same Bayliffs sent two men to thrash out *Michael's* Corn in the Barn (which they seized on before) whose Names were *William Farmer* and *Charles Bray* of *Farringdon*, and they thrasht and winnowed all the Corn in that Barn, which was carried away and fold.

Again, the 10th. day of the 8th. month following, the said Bayliffs came again to *Michael Reynolds's* House, and said they had not yet taken enough; and then they seized on the other Barn full of Corn, set the two Thrashers again to Work, and they thrasht out the Corn in that Barn also.

And the 25th. day of the 9th. month following, the two Thrashers (by the appointment of *John Fulline*) took Witness, and delivered up the Key and Lock of *Michael Reynolds's* Barn to him, and gave an account under their hands, that the Corn thrasht by them, and winnowed, which was carried away and fold, to answer the Execution before-mentioned: was in all, of Barly 56 *Quarters* and a half, and was by them judged worth, at the times when it was carried 17 s. a Quarter one with another, which came to ——————————— 49 l. — 8 s. — 9 d
Also of Beans and Pease 9 *Quarter*, at —————— 8 l. — 8 s. — 04
And the Cattle taken away, as before mentioned, were worth 46 l. — 0 s. — 04

Which amount to in all —— 97 l. — 16 s. — 9 d.

All this was taken away for one years Tyth from *Michael Reynolds*; and the whole Rent of the Land he holds is, but 55 l. a year, and of that there is in Medow, where they took the Tyth by Force, and in pasture, where *Robert Pye* claims none to the value of 20 l. a year; So that the whole Rent of that Land which he had any Colour of Law to sue for, will not amount to 40 l. a year: And it may be supposed that the Tyth cannot in all likelyhood exceed a 4th. part of the Rent, which at utmost cannot be above 10 l. a year.

And therefore it is evidently manifest, how cruelly and unjustly *Robert Pye* hath dealt in this Case with his Neighbour *Michael Reynolds* (although in other Cases we have not had much Cause to find Fault with him) who for the denial of scarce 10 l. demanded, hath caused to be taken away Cattle and Corn, the value of 97 l. 16 s. 9 d. which is near ten times much more. Oh horrible Injustice, that ever such Actions should be found

Epilogue

IN MEMORIAM

Janet Isabel [Forsey] Rothery

26th April 1935 to 1st May 2018

Janet was born to a Quaker Mother and Agnostic Father. Both women grew in faith in Northern England – within the Yorkshire General Meeting and elsewhere.

After an early education at the Kidstones School [Bishopdale, North Yorkshire], both parents being heavily involved in war work, Janet gained her secondary school education at The Mount School, York following her Mother and Aunts there. She trained as a junior school teacher at the Meltonia College [Doncaster] and then took on various posts including one at the Wennington School [near Wetherby, at the time in West Yorkshire].

She felt drawn to work overseas and her first posting was at a colonial preparatory school at Kaptagat [Western Kenya]. She then became Education and Arts Lecturer at a training college for African students in the American Quaker settlement at Kaimosi. Janet's six years of life and work in Kenya left her with permanent memories of its people, landscape and politics, her time there overlapping the independence of the country. On her returning to UK,she became Education Lecturer at what is now Nottingham Trent University. Her professional life was always balanced and enriched by her hobbies and enthusiasms, for example a long lasting involvement with Forest School Camps.

Her marriage to Alan [an Anglican] brought her to live in Yorkshire settling for many years with the Harrogate Friends Meeting House [FMH]. When the family moved to Oxfordshire she became clerk to the Charlbury FMH. This also meant becoming clerk of works since she was in charge of a complete re-design, extension, land purchase and financing thereof to update the original eighteenth century structure. Moving to Faringdon FMH she enjoyed researching the history of Quakers in the Vale of White Horse. Another move, to the Grimsby FMH, stimulated more research, into the history of Lincolnshire Quakers. At Grimsby she served on the Friends House Meeting for Sufferings and was a keen supporter of developing the social side of local Meetings.This interest continued with her final move to the Letchworth Garden City FMH [Howgills]. She relished the Howgills building, modelled as it was on the seventeenth century Brigflatts FMH in Cumbria where, as a teenager, she had taken her decision to become a Quaker.

Janet's Quaker faith was central to every aspect of her life and work.

Alan Rothery

Janet was a good friend and a lovely Quaker. She was much concerned about her religion including the place of Christian teaching in Quakerism. Some years ago an important Quaker pamphlet "To Lima with love" gave our response to a Churches conference on value of the Eucharist in Christian worship. Janet's knowledge was impressive and her contributions added much to the discussion. She had an international outlook on religious and social affairs. Was it 30 years ago that Janet was a representative at the Friends World Council of Churches held in Kenya? She re-established many connections and friendships from the time she taught there in her early career as a teacher. Janet was a valued Friend throughout her life giving a fine example of faithfulness to the Quaker testimonies of Truth, Simplicity, Equality and Peace. We will miss her greatly.

Perhaps unusually, I remember clearly both the first and last times I saw Janet. It was during the Letchworth Meeting centenary garden party at Howgills back in 2007 and I was temporarily looking after a stall at the back of the orchard. Janet came over with her granddaughter India. The event was very colourful and Janet struck me similarly.

I wasn't wrong. Janet was a member of Letchworth Meeting for a dozen years or so where she contributed in many and varied ways. She served as an Elder for a few years, was a frequent minister in Meeting for Worship and a regular representative at Area Meetings. However, Janet could equally well be found busy in the kitchen preparing food whenever the occasion arose. For Janet, being part of the wider Quaker community was important and she liked to attend Yearly Meeting sessions, sometimes along with her daughter Isabel. She was also a great initiator, organising several quiet days and very memorably getting another garden party off the ground in 2012 to commemorate the centenary of the gift of Howgills the building from Juliet Reckitt to the Society of Friends. I remember her and her husband Alan watching with great happiness as Friends and others did the hokey cokey and various folk dances in the orchard. There were also personal invitations to lunch at her and Alan's home.

Janet had a particular interest in the history of Letchworth Meeting. This resulted in, among other things, the research and subsequent production of a booklet on an early Letchworth Friend by the name of Edward Grubb. As Meeting Librarian, she took painstaking care of the collection of books which, I imagine, helped to feed her interest. A tremendous sense of energy was present around Janet.

She loved to talk, although I think it's fair to say that listening was not her strong point. She could hold strong views and could grumble, but these were indicators of how she cared – and her concerns could range from the life of the Meeting to trouble spots in the world at large. Janet was not afraid to speak her mind, but she did so in a loving spirit. I also think she showed considerable insight.

There has been a fairly recent scheme at Letchworth Meeting, all other things being equal, to hold a lunch when there are five Sundays in a month. Janet was keen to uphold this new-ish tradition and in April 2018 such a lunch took place. As usual she busied herself in the kitchen, was generous with her food donations, and there was much lively chat around the meal table. When the last of us left the building, and as a result of some thorny issue raised, Janet made the almost throwaway remark that hopefully God will take care of it for us all.

When just two days later Letchworth Friends learned of Janet's sudden passing, it was met with a palpable sense of shock and sadness. Without a doubt, she enriched the life of the Meeting and I hope she knew how much she was valued.

Sarah J Croton [March 2019]

Printed in Great Britain
by Amazon